Women Performing Music

Women Performing Music

THE EMERGENCE OF AMERICAN WOMEN AS CLASSICAL INSTRUMENTALISTS AND CONDUCTORS

by Beth Abelson Macleod

McFarland & Company, Inc., Publishers
Jefferson, North Carolina, and London

Library of Congress Cataloguing-in-Publication Data

Macleod, Beth Abelson, 1945–
    Women performing music : the emergence of American women
as classical instrumentalists and conductors / by Beth Abelson
MacLeod.
        p.   cm.
    Includes bibliographical references and index.
    ISBN 0-7864-0904-5 (softcover : 50# alkaline paper) ∞
    1. Women musicians — United States.   2. Instrumentalists.
3. Conductors (Music) — United States.   I. Title.
ML82.M24   2001
784'.082'0973 — dc21   00-64617

British Library cataloguing data are available

On the cover: Early publicity photo of Antonia Brico. (Colorado
Historical Society.)

Manufactured in the United States of America

McFarland & Company, Inc., Publishers
    Box 611, Jefferson, North Carolina 28640
    www.mcfarlandpub.com

For Evelyn Shuldiner, Margaret Macleod,
and Eleanor Sanderson, with love and gratitude

Acknowledgments

I thank the following for their generous help:

Central Michigan University and Dean Thomas Moore, who provided support in the form of a sabbatical leave and a semester-long research professorship.

My valued colleagues at the CMU Library, especially Julie Voelck for her friendship and support, and Bill Miles, David Ginsburg, Judy O'Dell, Rob Faleen, Dave Shirley, and Sandy Folsom, for assuming additional responsibilities while I was on leave.

The staff of the CMU Document Access department, particularly Ruth Helwig and Margaret Dodd, who patiently tracked down elusive materials.

Brandyn Edwards, who solved word-processing problems with admirable calm.

Carol Green, Susan Conner, Claudia Clark, and Larry Ward, for their provocative conversation and helpful suggestions.

The reference staffs of the New York Public Library for the Performing Arts, the American Jewish Archives in Cincinnati, and the Colorado Historical Society in Denver, for their expertise and assistance.

The *Journal of Social History* for allowing me to use material which originally appeared in their Winter 1993 issue.

James Lynch, piano teacher and former student of Ethel Leginska, who answered my *Los Angeles Times* query and, with Reinhold Schmidjell, presented me with a researcher's fantasy: unlimited time to peruse fascinating material in a lovely home adjacent to the beach, with occasional breaks for scenic drives and excellent food.

James Lynch, Marilyn Neeley and Lisa Sitjar, for sharing reminiscences of their teacher, Ethel Leginska.

Cecily Haeger, for her help and support along the way.

My two sons, Ian and Jamie, for providing welcome diversion, both musical and otherwise, from my labors.

And my husband David, whose help and encouragement were crucial at every stage.

Contents

Preface

I wrote this book for two reasons. First, my experience as a music student in the 1960s and 1970s made it clear that gender defined one's involvement and success as a musician. After a recital I was told that I had "played like a woman"; a respected male colleague sagely observed that women were physiologically incapable of being good organists; and my major professor in piano told me that he would never consider having a woman replace him during his sabbatical year. Although I did not always question such comments at the time, as they collected in memory I kept thinking about their implications. If people said these things in the United States in the late 1960s and early 1970s, what had they said a hundred years earlier, when women first began performing on the concert stage?

I began to investigate how certain musical instruments had historically come to seem more "appropriate" for women to play. As I examined reviews in late nineteenth and early twentieth-century American newspapers and music periodicals I found that the names of certain soloists and conductors recurred repeatedly. Several of these were women, and they were famous and beloved artists. But the names of Bloomfield-Zeisler and Leginska are hardly as familiar today as Paderewski and Rubinstein.

Which brings me to my second reason for writing this book: my frustration at being unable to find sufficient biographical information about most of the female artists — more than their dates of birth and death and the famous teachers with whom they studied. These women strove for professional distinction in an age when most female instrumentalists were consigned to the parlor; they were charting a new course. As feminist scholar Carolyn Heilbrun, in her work *Writing a Woman's Life*, has observed of notable women in many fields, "There were no models of the lives they wanted to live, no exemplars, no stories." Surely they deserved more than cursory coverage; surely their lives raised questions that called for answers.

How did a girl growing up in the Middle West in the 1800s become a concert artist hailed in New York, Paris and London? What compelled a person to spend her childhood practicing, her early teens studying in a foreign

1

country separated from her family, and her late teens trying to establish a career as a "serious musician" in a country where many had never attended a live concert and most were more accustomed to hearing "Yankee Doodle" or "Dixie" than the works of Mozart or Beethoven? How did these women present themselves to the public? How did they seek to develop images that reshaped gender to the needs of musical professionalism? How did audiences react to seeing a serious woman artist on the concert stage? What sorts of accommodations did these musicians make in their private lives in order to make their public lives possible?

I have examined the historical record for attitudes like those expressed to me as a student, and have sought to bring to greater prominence the lives of a number of women who deserve to be models, exemplars and stories for future generations of musicians.

Introduction

A central theme in nineteenth-century American women's history is the doctrine of separate spheres — the belief that men and women should move and dominate in different areas of life, with women predominating in the private or domestic sphere and men in the public world outside the home. At the turn of the century a gradual shift began, with women increasingly assuming more public roles. During this period a number of American women established prominent careers as instrumental musicians, shifting from playing exclusively in the family parlor to performing publicly on the concert stage. These women overcame many obstacles as they forged careers as professional musicians and, as with women in other professions, the nature of their success was shaped by issues of gender.

For most of the nineteenth and twentieth centuries women instrumentalists could succeed as public performers only on instruments that allowed them to look graceful when performing. Because they were expected to appear modest and unassuming, they also had difficulty being taken seriously as virtuosos and conductors. Because they were believed to possess less strength and stamina than their male counterparts, they were excluded from most symphony orchestras. Because they were considered emotionally fragile, any sign of stress was diagnosed as a nervous breakdown. And because appearances have played such an important role in the way women are perceived and judged, even those who became successful soloists and conductors have concerned themselves with presentation of self and the extent to which their manner of dress should emphasize or de-emphasize their gender. Many of the gender expectations that defined and limited women's musical participation at the end of the nineteenth century are still in place at the beginning of the twenty-first.

Building a career required successful image management for all soloists and conductors, but the problem was especially acute for women. Success depended in large part on how closely they represented an "ideal" — lovely, graceful, modest, expressive and yet restrained, competent but not overbearing in their mastery. The further they ventured from this image, the more difficult it became to achieve success.

The small group of American women who established careers as concert

artists in the late nineteenth and early twentieth centuries shared similar prepa-
ration. All were child prodigies who quickly outgrew the abilities of the local
music teacher. Most were from middle-class families — their fathers were typically teachers or tradesmen — who provided them with a musical education at
considerable personal and financial sacrifice. This sacrifice was particularly evident when the girl, still in her early teens, went to Europe to study. "Serious"
concert artists had to study in Europe before they could be respected in America, which meant spending anywhere from two to five years abroad. Since they
were too young to travel and live on their own, their mother or grandmother
generally accompanied them, thereby separating the family for an extended
period of time. Abroad, the young musician faced the challenges of total immer-
sion in a new language and the intensely competitive nature of conservatory
life. Then she returned to America to face new uncertainties as she attempted
to make the transition from student to professional musician.

This transition was all the more difficult because audiences were unpre-
pared for women soloists. The male instrumentalists who began touring North
America in the middle of the nineteenth century were flamboyant virtuosos
like violinist Ole Bull and pianists Louis Moreau Gottschalk and Ignace
Paderewski. These men combined entertainment and musicianship; they were
the country's first matinee idols. For audiences accustomed to such performances
the mere idea of a "woman virtuoso" was a ludicrous contradiction in terms.
It was also difficult for a novice of either gender to obtain performing engagements. Major piano manufacturers sponsored the tours of prominent pianists,
but such arrangements were relatively few and not given to unknown artists.
Finding a reputable agent was difficult, especially for a woman. Yet the aspiring musician and her guardian were not schooled in the business aspects of
establishing a musical career, a "business" that was still in its infancy.

The earliest women soloists joined small troupes of performers which
toured with a manager who handled transportation, lodging and other arrangements. Some of the best-known women also toured with major bands and
orchestras such as the Theodore Thomas Orchestra and John Philip Sousa's
band; the artist performed a concerto with the orchestra or a solo between selections by the band. American women were more sought after than American
men for such positions, since a woman contributed both an element of novelty and a colorful contrast to the stage full of soberly attired male musicians.
Traveling with an established ensemble allowed a woman to tour within a "protected" context, since it was unusual for women of the period to travel apart
from their families. When women eventually began touring as soloists in their
own right, many married the men who served as their managers; such an
arrangement provided them with a chaperon, a business partner, and an emotional mainstay while on the road.

The earliest soloists were judged by their image as much as their musicianship. Reviews evaluated their physical features, complexions, hair-dos and dress. They commented on the amount of motion expended and the emotion expressed in their performances. They evaluated their deportment both on and off the stage. They frequently reassured the public that the artist was not neglecting her home for her art.

Projecting an image of the ideal was difficult for the soloist, but it was virtually impossible for the conductor. Conductors directed the actions of men and this was "ideal" by practically no one's definition. Most women who managed to sustain conducting careers did so by forming orchestras made up primarily of women; by leading women and not men, they were less likely to offend. But women's orchestras were definitely outside the musical mainstream, resulting in the further marginalization of the woman conductor.

Chapters 5, 6 and 7 of this book explore these themes in the lives of three unusually prominent and talented musicians — pianist Fannie Bloomfield-Zeisler (1864–1927), pianist and conductor Ethel Leginska (1886–1970), and conductor Antonia Brico (1902–1989). Bloomfield-Zeisler and Leginska enjoyed national and international fame as pianists; both were frequently and favorably compared to the preeminent male virtuoso of their day, Ignace Paderewski. Although their careers overlapped, their lives evolved quite differently according to the choices they made. After many successful years as a concert pianist, Leginska shifted her attention to conducting, with sharply diminished acceptance. Her conducting career in turn overlapped with that of Brico, who led ensembles in the United States and Europe in the 1930s but never achieved, as a conductor, the acclaim enjoyed by Bloomfield-Zeisler and Leginska as instrumentalists.

Bloomfield-Zeisler manifested her aptitude for the piano at an early age. A frequently told anecdote describes her as a little girl surrounded by the devastation of the 1871 Chicago fire, playing her rescued piano amidst the rubble. Following several years of study in Vienna, she returned to the United States and in 1885 married Sigmund Zeisler, a Chicago lawyer and one of the defenders of the anarchists in the Haymarket riot of 1886. He appears to have been an enlightened and supportive husband. They had three sons and lived in comfort and affluence in Chicago.

She continued to perform both in the United States and in Europe, making arduous train tours all over the United States. She appears to have "had it all" in an era when a woman with an independent career, especially after motherhood, was highly unusual. Articles often emphasized the fact that she was a warm and loving mother in addition to being a successful pianist; her publicity stressed her image as a woman who did not neglect her family for her career. Both roles were important to her, and the effort to excel at both sometimes took its toll. Like almost every prominent woman instrumentalist of the period, she was forced on a number of occasions to stop performing for brief periods, usually termed "nervous breakdowns" by the press. In 1925 a large celebration commemorated the fiftieth anniversary of her first public performance; she played a strenuous program, once again dazzling the audience with her virtuosity. Much admired and publicly celebrated, she was a successful performer for most of her life.

Leginska was also a highly successful pianist for the first decades of her adulthood. Born in England, she met and married an American composer, Emerson Whithorne, when nineteen and studying in Vienna. Her American debut took place in her husband's native Cleveland, in a vaudeville show which also featured acrobats and elephants, but she quickly established a reputation as one of the most sought-after concert artists of the period. In 1917 she was involved in a highly publicized custody battle for her then eight-year-old son; her husband's lawyer implied that her public career was a reason she should not have the boy. She was outspoken about many "women's" issues and began to dress unconventionally, adopting plain black and white concert attire as the female equivalent to male concert dress. Paradoxically, she explained this manipulation of her public image as an attempt to draw attention to the music and not to herself.

In the 1920s she began studying conducting in Europe and tried to launch a conducting career in the United States. Reviews were generally positive, though guarded. Two weeks after her New York conducting debut, however, she failed to appear for a Carnegie Hall piano performance. The *New York Times* explained her disappearance by saying that she had "run away, just like a little girl." Like the few other women who tried to be taken seriously as conductors, she never found a permanent conducting position. She formed her own orchestra of men and women in Boston, and then a Boston Woman's Symphony, but was unable to survive financially. In 1939 she moved to Los Angeles, where she taught piano until her death in 1970.

Antonia Brico, who grew up in California, knew from childhood that she wanted to be a conductor. But not the single-minded pursuit of her goal, nor a conducting degree from an illustrious European conservatory, nor the endorsements of composer Jean Sibelius, pianist Artur Rubinstein, and conductor Bruno Walter could ensure her success. Lured to Denver in 1940 by what she hoped would be a permanent conducting position, she taught piano and led an amateur orchestra, the Denver Businessman's Orchestra (later the Brico Symphony), almost until her death in 1989.

When folksinger Judy Collins, who studied piano with Brico as a child, made a much-heralded documentary about her teacher in 1970, Brico's briefly resurrected career once again spotlighted her gender and not her musical accomplishments. Like Leginska, her abilities could not prevail over the issue of her gender. Both women also spent the last decades of their lives more traditionally, as piano teachers.

These lives and careers illustrate the premise that the further one ventured from a conventional image, the more remote the chances of success. Bloomfield-Zeisler, who remained within the confines of roles thought appropriate for women, enjoyed public acceptance and adulation through middle and old age. Leginska and Brico went beyond the bounds of what was appropriate by disengaging from domestic entanglements and attempting careers as conductors. Both were tolerated while relatively youthful novelties, but neither could sustain the long-term acceptance of the musical public.

Noted feminist historian Gerda Lerner once wrote in *The Majority Finds Its Past* that "only in the performing arts has individual female talent had the same opportunities as male talent." Although she immediately qualified her statement with the observation that women have been underrepresented in symphony orchestras, the reality is that gender has restricted women's musical involvement in ways more complex than just exclusion from traditionally male organizations.

Admittedly there have been changes. Women musicians in the early twenty-first century are not generally ridiculed for their strength and virtuosity; more are members of symphony orchestras, although the instruments they are most likely to play remain much the same; and the public does not need constant reassurance that a woman is not neglecting her husband and children for her career. But issues of image remain paramount.

One prominent conductor adopts the unisex dress devised by Leginska in order to minimize attention to her gender; another modifies her concert attire according to the perceived conservatism of her audience; a third employs flamboyant dress with the hope of generating a curiosity that will translate into increased ticket sales. Thus, even among women who are successful conductors, gender, image and presentation of self remain important concerns. And one has only to look at the covers of current CDs to see how sexuality is used to market women classical musicians. Whether the female musician personifies an image of late nineteenth-century propriety or early twenty-first-century sexuality, gender-based stereotypes continue to shape important elements of her performance and presentation of self.

"Whence Comes the Lady Tympanist?"

Gender and Musical Instruments

When the young ladies of Madison Female College gave a concert in 1853, John Dwight of *Dwight's Journal of Music* was there to document the novel event. He took pianists, guitarists and harpists in stride, but expressed shock at "13 young lady violinists (!), 1 young lady violist (!!), 4 violoncellists (!!!) and 1 young lady contrabassist (!!!!)."[1] As the rising chorus of exclamation marks shows, Dwight's tolerance was inversely proportional to the size of the instrument. His reaction was characteristic of the time. The fact that the young ladies were playing music was not the problem — his discomfort arose because these women went beyond the narrow range of what was considered their proper musical place by playing instruments that contemporary audiences were unaccustomed to seeing played by women.

There is irony in the restrictive views of Dwight and his contemporaries about women performing music, since many nineteenth-century writers endowed music with the same qualities as those imputed to women. In the words of one late nineteenth-century author and critic, music was the "interpreter and the language of the emotions.... It inspires, ... saddens, cheers, and soothes the soul ... and performs its loftiest homage as the handmaid of religion."[2] In much the same vein, the nineteenth-century woman was expected to be gentle and refined, "guardian of religion, inspiration to man, bestower of care and love."[3] The medical orthodoxy of the time enhanced this notion, asserting that in females the nervous system and emotions prevailed over rational faculties and that it was "inherent in their very being" to "display more affect than men."[4] Hence respectable opinion held that women had a special gift for music. But professional public performance of music required self-assertion, tight control of one's nerves, and pursuit of a career in a competitive milieu dominated by men — all qualities widely thought suspect in women. Countertenors notwithstanding, women were irreplaceable and therefore

9

widely accepted as vocal performers. Public instrumental performance, however, remained highly problematic and hedged about with restrictions.

At the time Dwight wrote, only certain musical instruments were considered socially acceptable for women, namely keyboard instruments, the guitar, the lute, and the harp. Their volume was relatively soft and delicate sounding, and the melody was in a high range, corresponding to the soprano voice.[5] The posture the lady assumed while playing was natural and graceful; she did not have to sit awkwardly or distort her features. She could usually remain seated while playing and perform adequately without much physical exertion. And since these instruments provided both a melody and a harmony line, she could pursue music as a solitary pastime, without the need for an accompanist. Critic Philip Hale in 1900 asserted that playing instruments plucked by the fingers "enhanced a woman's natural charms. They [the instruments] were held for the most part in her arms; they were fondled and caressed. She faced her hearer; and as he listened, he saw the whiteness of her hands, the soft curves of her arms; and, growing bolder, he looked into her melting eyes...." The "gentle notes" of the instrument "invited whispered confidences; they filled all lulls in conversation; they suggested hopes and favors...."[6]

When women played other instruments, they made themselves vulnerable to sarcasm and ridicule. As one critic noted in *Musical America* in 1906, "For the sake of the veneration in which all women should be held it is to be hoped that none of them will follow the suggestion of [Sidney] Lanier and take to playing the trombone, the French horn, or the gigantic Sousaphone for, as Byron once said: 'Seeing the woman you love at table is apt to dispel all romance.' And seeing a woman get red in the face blowing into a brass instrument is just as likely to prove an unpleasant shock...."[7] It was important that women always appear delicate and decorative; to appear otherwise by playing a massive or seemingly awkward instrument challenged accepted notions of what was appropriately female.

Not surprisingly, the piano was the first instrument to be seen on the concert stage with a woman soloist. The sight of a woman playing a keyboard instrument was hardly startling; reviewers, however, were unaccustomed to seeing a woman display the strength and mastery required of a soloist and invariably compared the style and tone of her performance to those of a man. Men of course were believed to be stronger and more vigorous than women; they had greater respiratory and greater muscular power. According to one source, they were better able to "discipline their strength," making their movements "more precise than those of women. Thus men make the best pianists."[8] An 1898 review of pianist Fannie Bloomfield-Zeisler, who received almost universally positive notices, stated: "The wonder of the little woman is that she can be both woman and man in the illustration of her art.... The marvel of her playing is that she commands so much virtuoso strength with such an abundance of feminine delicacy and subtlety of expression."[9] A 1906 review of a performance by pianist Minnie Coons remarked that "slight stages of virility in the fortissimo movement undoubtedly enhanced the refreshing delicacy of her pianissimo touch."[10] Pianist Olga Samaroff, who concertized extensively in Europe and America from 1905 to 1925, observed: "During all the years of my career as a woman pianist at least eighty percent of my press reviews either stated that I played like a man, or alluded to my playing like a woman. When the critic said I played like a woman, it meant that he did not like me at all."[11]

Another gender-based theme that emerges from contemporary reviews is the extent to which certain composers, such as Beethoven or Grieg, impressed critics as being particularly masculine, and therefore more difficult for a woman to interpret. At the turn of the century the concept of "manliness" was being challenged both at home and in the workplace, and men — as well as women — felt threatened by proposed reforms.[12] In this context the idea of a woman musician interpreting the work of a male composer was a particular concern, especially when the music of the composer expressed massiveness and strength. A 1900 observer was typical: "Last Saturday's performance of the [Grieg] Concerto by Mrs. Bloomfield-Zeisler was indeed a wonder! Strange too, in one way, for Grieg was one of the most ... masculine of men, and Mrs. Bloomfield-Zeisler pushes femininity of conception and feeling to extremes; she is not only a woman all through, but seems tacitly to acknowledge and glory in it; she never attempts to ape virility. But herein lay the rare perfection of the situation; in the singular capacity of the very feminine woman of Southern blood for doing full justice to the work of the entirely masculine Northern man...."[13] Music by other composers, most notably Chopin, was commonly said to be more delicate sounding and thus considered to express more feminine emotions; reviewers did not comment in a similar way, however, when a man performed a piece by Chopin.

The other solo instrument that gradually became acceptable for women to perform with publicly was the violin. In addition to its physical virtues — it was light in weight, had a high range, and did not require distortion of facial features — two other factors contributed to its emergence. First, several young violin prodigies began performing in America and paved the way for female soloists. The most publicized was Camilla Urso, who toured parts of North America in 1853 when she was 11 years old. Reviews of her performances were uniformly positive, and her visibility did much to establish the appropriateness of the violin as an instrument for females.[14] Maud Powell, a noted American violinist who concertized in the early 1900s, said that she knew she wanted to be a violinist after she saw Camilla Urso play.[15] A second source of support for female violinists was the enlightened attitude of Julius Eichberg, the violinist and teacher who founded the Boston Conservatory of Music in 1867. The conservatory allowed both sexes to study violin, and sources of that era frequently comment on successful performances by female violinists who studied there.[16]

The visibility of prodigies such as Urso and of the Boston Conservatory students who then became performers and teachers made it possible for the public to see violin performances by females. Even so, some early reviews of female violinists questioned the appropriateness of the instrument. An 1878 reviewer, for example, complained: "A violin seems an awkward instrument for a woman, whose well-formed chin was designed by nature for other purposes than to pinch down this instrument into position."[17] As with accounts of piano recitals, reviewers almost invariably used gender-related stereotypes to describe the performances, assuming strength, energy and dignity to be masculine virtues and expressing surprise to find them in a woman performer. Maud Powell's style was "full of masculine power and of superb spirit; ... her entire handling of the movement was devoid of anything tentative or timid."[18] Florence Austin's "most marked characteristic is a certain reserve force, a strength and dignity that are masculine rather than feminine. Nevertheless she possesses all the grace and delicacy that are so distinctly a part of the successful woman violinist, but she combines with these a dignity and repose that could never mistake hysteria for temperament or an emotional spasm for abandon...."[19] An early twentieth-century publicity poster for violinist Maud Powell announces: "The arm of a man; the heart of a woman; the head of an artist."[20] The successful woman performer was one who could play like a man ... but not appear unfeminine.

As new professions opened to women, fresh theories appeared as to why the feminine mind and nature were innately suited to the tasks. Teaching allowed women to nurture children; social work and nursing gave women opportunities to express their inborn capacity for sympathy and compassion.[21] So it was with violin playing—as women violinists became more common, reviewers began to describe playing the instrument as not only an acceptable but even an appropriate and noble pursuit for women. Critics emphasized the emotive qualities of the violin, with the implication that females, as emotional creatures, might be among its finest interpreters: "The instrument [is] justly considered to be most preeminently suited to woman because [of] its lightness, its form, the natural grace required in its treatment, but, above all, because of the deep poetry of its tones, its emotional qualities and its sympathetic appeals."[22]

Once the violin became acceptable, the door was open for other stringed instruments as well. At the turn of the century the cello was just beginning to evolve as a solo instrument in its own right and no longer merely the bass line for other melodic instruments. Composers such as David Popper and George Goltermann wrote showy pieces for the cello; and new performers, most notably Pablo Casals, who made his first tour of North America in 1901–02, demonstrated

Publicity poster of Maud Powell, designed by her husband and manager Godfrey Turner. (Maud Powell Society, Arlington, Virginia.)

its technical and emotional capabilities. The obvious impediment to its acceptance for women was physical: anything held between the legs — whether horse, bicycle, or cello — engendered discussion as to its suitability for women. Before the mid-1800s, viols and cellos were held steady between the knees or calves. Around 1860, however, the end-pin (a sharp, pointed rod extending from the bottom of the instrument) became standard equipment on the cello. While this did not occur in response to women's concerns, the result made the cello more acceptable for women, since anchoring it to the floor enabled a woman to play side-saddle. One cello methods book, published in 1898, describes the side-saddle position in great detail. Yet even this restriction faded fairly quickly as more active pastimes became acceptable for women, and new styles of dress evolved which allowed more freedom of movement.[23] The third edition of the same book, published in 1915, states that by then almost all women were placing the instrument between their knees because that position "brings the instrument under more complete control. The other methods, which were considered more graceful, have become almost obsolete on account of the obvious disadvantages."[24]

Since the cello did not have a long history as a man's solo instrument, public acceptance of women soloists was almost immediate. Turn-of-the-century music periodicals describe the solo performances of a number of young women cellists. Leontine Gaertner, Elsa Reugger, A. Laura Tolman, and others performed regularly for an appreciative public. There were occasional derisive references, such as a 1902 *Boston Eagle* review which described Reugger as "a winsome lass" who played with an artistic expression and grace "not often commanded by women who have to hold a baritone violin with their knees,"[25] but such comments were definitely the exception.

Largely because of the absence of facial contortion, for a long time the flute was the only blown instrument considered socially acceptable for women. The flute embouchure (the way the lips make contact with the mouthpiece) allows the player to form a pout and blow much as one would make a sound by blowing into the mouth of a soft-drink bottle. This is very different from the process of forcing air through the thin reed of the clarinet, oboe or bassoon, which results in tightly pursed lips and possibly a flushed face. It also differs significantly from blowing into the mouthpiece of a brass instrument, which necessitates pressing the cup-like mouthpiece directly against the partially open mouth. As a reviewer in the *American Art Journal* commented approvingly in 1880, "The unusual sight of a lady playing such an instrument did not strike people as strange as we thought it would be. She ... avoids the ugly contortions of the lips.... Thus managed, the flute is decidedly not an unfeminine instrument."[26] As with the violin, once women began to perform publicly on the flute, some observers found reasons to declare female superiority on the instrument. "On the flute," the American poet and musician Sidney Lanier wrote in 1898, "a certain combination of delicacy with the flexibility in the lips is absolutely necessary to bring fully out that passionate yet velvety tone ... and many male players ... will be forever debarred from attaining it by reason of the intractable, rough lips, which will give nothing but a correspondingly intractable, rough tone."[27]

If a woman somehow achieved prominence on another wind instrument, problems remained. Saxophonist Elisa Hall (also known as Mrs. Richard J. Hall) studied at the Paris Conservatory and was the first amateur to play with the Boston Symphony. Hall commissioned Debussy to write a piece for her; but even though she had already paid him, he postponed writing it. According to one account, "He thought it ridiculous when he had seen her in a pink frock playing such an ungainly instrument, and he was not at all anxious that his work should provide a similar spectacle."[28] In a more contemporary context, Matt Groening, creator of the popular television show *The Simpsons*, says that he chose to have Lisa Simpson play the saxophone because he thought it would be more amusing to have an eight-year-old girl play such an incongruous instrument.[29]

Relatively few musicians, male or female, could have careers as instrumental soloists; ensemble playing was the obvious performing option. But few women could join ensembles, both because men resisted admitting women into all-male groups and because attitudes persisted regarding the appropriateness of particular instruments on the basis of gender. Sexual segregation already prevailed within most work settings. The issue of morality was a frequently cited concern. "Wherever the sexes work indiscriminately together," argued the Bureau of Labor Statistics in 1911, "great laxity obtains." Intermingling of the sexes was "thought to threaten the virtue of even the most well-intentioned young women." "There is such an obvious impropriety in the mixing of the sexes within the walls of a public office," declared Robert McClelland, President Pierce's Secretary of the Interior, "that I am determined to arrest the practice."[30] Wives supposedly feared that career women could lead their husbands astray, while husbands might feel threatened if their wives competed in the workplace.[31] One observer expressed concern that the mere presence of women in orchestras would distract the men: "You shouldn't expect a man to keep his eyes divided between the music on his stand and the stick of his conductor when his sweetheart is a member of the organization, and is seated somewhere across the room."[32] Tour managers were also reluctant to deal with the complications of sharing accommodations, a difficult task "when womanhood must be protected."[33]

Invariably in discussions of women's ability to function as orchestral musicians the issue of stamina arose. An article in an 1895 issue of *Scientific American* stated unequivocally that a woman did not have the stamina to be an orchestral musician: "Her physical incapacity to endure the strain of four or five hours a day rehearsal, followed by the prolonged tax of public performances, will bar her against possible competition with male performers."[34] In a 1908 U.S. Supreme Court case involving the number of hours allowed in a woman's workday, the authors of the winning brief stated that "women are fundamentally weaker than men in all that makes for endurance: in muscular strength, in nervous energy, in the powers of persistent attention and application"[35]: certainly all qualities necessary for an orchestral musician.

The idea of women in orchestras had occasional supporters, but their opinions did not change hiring patterns. Sidney Lanier wrote in 1898 that woman's "patience, fervor and fidelity, combined with deftness of hand and quick intuitiveness of soul" were desirable qualities in a perfect orchestral player. And Leopold Stokowski, in 1916, described the exclusion of women from symphony orchestras as an "incomprehensible blunder."[36] It was a blunder he did not and possibly could not correct: Stokowski conducted the Philadelphia Orchestra from 1912 to 1935, yet in the 1934–35 season the orchestra included only three women — two harpists and one cellist.[37]

When critics and observers commented on the occasional woman member of a predominantly male ensemble, they were unable to suppress their snideness and innuendo. A 1935 editorial in the *New York Sun* responded to a reader who expressed "astonishment" that the reviewer of a Philadelphia Orchestra performance had not noted that "a woman was seen operating a cello at the last desk, which she faced in solitary devotion." The music reviewer generously observed that he saw no good reason why women should not be employed in orchestras. "Are there female performers on all kinds of instruments? Certainly." But he proceeded to question the "soul" of the woman who takes up the timpani. "What is the outlook for the female bassoonist?" he continued.

"Does anyone wish to see a woman playing a bass drum or an E flat tuba? ... And a forgiving heaven has often looked down on the puffings of the lady cornet soloist."[38]

Women responded to exclusion from orchestras by forming their own.[39] The existence of early all-women's orchestras has been described by Judith Tick and Carol Neuls-Bates.[40] While Tick believes that the reason for women's exclusion was primarily economic (if a woman got the job, a man was denied one), gender stereotypes also played major roles in fostering and shaping these all-women's groups, affecting both their early instrumentation and the public perception of them as oddities and novelties.[41]

Because women were less likely to have learned larger instruments or winds and brasses, many early women's orchestras had gaps in instrumentation. The Vienna Lady Orchestra, which performed in New York in 1871, lacked horns, trumpets, trombones, clarinets, oboes, and bassoons.[42] The Women's Philharmonic Society of New York, performing in 1899, had a double bass, several flutes, clarinets and cornets, but no "heavy brass." The same was true of a women's orchestra which performed in Salt Lake City in 1915.[43] Reviewers sometimes expressed surprise: "The orchestra turns out to be only half an orchestra," declared an indignant reviewer of the Vienna group in the *New York Sun*.[44] There were two solutions to this problem. Some early groups supplied the missing parts on other instruments considered more suitably female. The missing brass parts in the Women's Philharmonic Society orchestra were played on the piano; the missing wind parts in the Salt Lake City orchestra were played on an organ.[45] When such substitutions were made in public performances, however, reviewers frequently complained about the thin sound of the group as a whole and the inappropriateness of the substitute instruments as permanent fixtures in the orchestra.[46]

As women's orchestras sought recognition as serious groups on par with their male counterparts, they tried a second solution: if a suitable woman could not be found to play a particular instrument, they used a man instead. An account of a performance by the Chicago Woman's Symphony in 1927 indicates that male players filled in to play oboe, French horn, bassoon, tuba, and double bass, "because it is impossible to secure women players of these instruments in Chicago."[47] Three years later the orchestra's conductor, Ebba Sundstrom, still expressed concern over the lack of women players of oboe, French horn, and double bass: "It has been one of our greatest troubles, for we want the personnel to be 100 per cent feminine."[48]

It is difficult to gauge audience response, since most reviewers comment on the audience only if its response is highly unusual. Audiences appear for the most part to have received performances by women's orchestras favorably. Reviewers, however, were simply not ready to accept without qualification a first-class performance by an orchestra of women. A description of Ethel Leginska's New York conducting debut with the National Women's Symphony Orchestra in 1932 declares, "Where Miss Leginska found them all can only be conjectured.... [She] had eight double basses, all women, and evidently no novices. Only one of them used an Italian bow; the other seven went at it full-fisted.... Where, when and why do women take up horn? ... [Where] do you get a female tuba player? And whence comes the lady tympanist? No matter. There they all were...."[49]

One of the principal reasons for the popularity of some early women's orchestras *was* their oddity, an oddity derived from the perceived incongruity of women playing instruments usually reserved for men.[50] Much of the heyday of the women's orchestras, from about 1880 to 1930, was also the height of the vaudeville era, and some early women's ensembles sought acceptance by embracing features of vaudeville — notably the effort of performers to appear unusual or otherwise distinctive.

An early example of women in masculine musical roles was the popular vaudeville troupe known as the British Blondes, which toured the U.S. in 1868. "The assumption of masculinity permeated their performances; ... they did clog dances and played banjos and trumpets."[51] Douglas Gilbert lists many vaudeville acts prominent from 1880 to 1930. It is not possible to determine the sex of many performers, since acts were frequently known by their last names, such as Adams and LeRoy. But many were novelty items that featured women in stereotypically masculine roles — lady cornetists, trombonists, and baritones are listed alongside the lady fencers, boxers, and strongwomen.[52] Caroline Nichols' Fadettes Orchestra, which was formed in 1888 and performed regularly throughout the country until 1918, used a more sophisticated version of this strategy of playing upon mixed gender roles. The women musicians wore shimmery feminine gowns while playing the whole range of musical instruments.[53] This juxtaposition provided the kind of incongruity that vaudeville audiences found entertaining.

Publicity for smaller instrumental ensembles of women playing nontraditional instruments particularly stressed entertainment rather than artistic distinction. One group of four women, a saxophone quartet called the Saxonians, pose on an advertising flyer from 1918. Billed as "Four Young Women Who Entertain Delightfully," they stand in a row wearing frilly dresses, smiling flirtatiously, and holding their saxophones.[54]

While performance remained problematic, it might be assumed that public-school teaching — generally conceded to be a female domain — would have been one area in which women could excel as teachers of instrumental music. This was not the case. Before 1900, when music in the public schools was exclusively vocal, songs were taught and led by the classroom teacher, who was usually female. With the introduction of instrumental music around 1900, the job of music instruction in the public schools grew larger. School officials now wanted a "music supervisor" — someone who could organize the program, teach the various instruments, and then conduct the school band and orchestra. Joseph Maddy, a noted music educator and author of the standard book on how to begin an instrumental music program in the public schools, wrote in 1926, "The development of the instrumental side of school music demands training for a new and difficult profession. Musicians there are in plenty who know one or two instruments, but to be supremely successful in this work one must know them all."[55] This expectation that the music supervisor have some ability to play the whole range of band instruments effectively barred women from the job.

In an era when leading educators often lamented the purported feminization of the schools,[56] writers also expressed concern that music not be stigmatized as a sissified activity. One way to combat this perception was to have men teach the new subject in the public schools. "Might it not have a wholesome influence if at this most impressionable age the boys could receive their first associations with music through a man — and a real man at that, one who could show them in the only way an average boy can understand, i.e., by illustration, that music is as much a man's job as a woman's...."[57] Ironically, despite the association of artistic appreciation with women and the prominence of women in elementary and even secondary teaching, the teaching of instrumental music became a predominantly male specialty.[58]

In a broader context, this phenomenon is consistent with what has been termed "the ascendancy of the male expert," the most notable example being the replacement of the birth attendant or midwife of the late nineteenth century with the male gynecologist.[59] Similar patterns have been noted in the professions of social work, teaching, and librarianship, where control was "removed from the hands of largely female practitioners to become the nearly exclusive preserve of male bureaucrats."[60]

The expectation that the music supervisor would conduct the band and orchestra was a significant factor in women's exclusion. Of all the areas in music, the one in which it has been most difficult for women to gain acceptance has been conducting, for the obvious reason that it connotes the ultimate in forcefulness, leadership, and control. Early twentieth-century women conductors met the same scorn and derision as players of "unusual" instruments. A 1925 review of a Boston concert conducted by Ethel Leginska, one of very few women who tried to succeed in this endeavor, acknowledged that the public was "handicapped by an unexplainable distaste for women as orchestral leaders."[61] A 1932 review of one of her New York performances referred to "the reluctance of the superior male in the command of a slip of a woman."[62]

Public-school music educators professed commitment to providing boys and girls equal opportunities in their study of music. Adam Lesinsky, an Indiana music educator, observed: "Now that instrumental music in the public schools is recognized by all progressive educators as a part of the regular curriculum ... there should be no discrimination made between boys and girls."[63] But even within the relatively egalitarian public-school context, there were different standards for boy and girl instrumentalists. When 147 Chicago schoolboys competed in a solo competition for band instruments in 1929, girls were excluded. Instead, 59 girls were allowed to compete in a separate contest. An observer commented merely that "the girls do not compete against the boys, not that they aren't willing to — or able, but because it isn't believed to be the thing to do." When the awards were given out, the boys received eleven gold medals, twenty-one silver, and thirteen bronze. But instead of gold medals, the twelve first-place girls received only bronze ones.[64]

Though girls did play a variety of instruments in school bands and orchestras, the extent of their participation in the band aroused male concern. One reason for continuing gender distinctions was the desire of school band directors to recruit boys. Early literature describing the formation of a school band invariably drifted to discussions of the needs of preadolescent boys and the adult desire to control them. Writers touted band membership as an antidote to juvenile delinquency and gang membership. They claimed that the exercise of playing wind and brass instruments would change the frail boy into a "deep-chested, sturdy youth." Such writers were consequently eager to make bands appear masculine, believing that boys would be attracted through their desire for uniforms and their "inherent love for the military."[65]

It was the marching band in particular that made directors especially anxious about girls' participation. Adam Lesinsky listed the reasons his colleagues gave for the exclusion of girls. One said he simply couldn't be bothered; another said girls would ruin the appearance of the band; a third said girls could not learn wind instruments as well as boys; and a fourth expressed doubts that girls would be interested in playing the larger instruments. There was also the usual speculation that girls lacked the necessary stamina.[66] Band directors in the 1930s and 1940s solved the perceived dilemma of girls in the marching band by forming separate all-girl bands, especially in high schools large enough to support two groups. One educator observed that such an arrangement would be comparable to what is done in "athletics, glee clubs and industrial subjects." "The main reason for having a girls' band in Benton Harbor, Michigan, is merely to segregate boys and girls," explained one director.[67]

Another way in which band directors dealt with their discomfort over girls in the marching band was to develop other ways for girls to perform on the playing field. Joe Berryman, director of the school band in Fort Stockton, Texas, extolled the virtues of the "Bugle-Lyra," a set of bells especially designed for marching which would substitute for the bugles normally used. This would counter any objections that the bugle would "alter the shape of the girls' lips.... The Bugle-Lyra are easily played and a group of girls can be taught several 'bell-tunes' in even so short a time as a week.... This new instrument is not heavy, has a very attractive appearance, and in every way fills a long-felt need."[68] More common substitutes abandoned musical performance altogether in favor of decorative display. During the 1930s and 1940s baton-twirling grew increasingly popular, and "pretty girls with flashing batons" decorated the playing fields. Flag-waving — the swinging of decorative flags to music — was another alternative. To accompany the girls, the boys in the band usually played a familiar waltz, "the ideal type of music for flag twirling. The combination is most effective and beautiful."[69] Activities such as baton-twirling and flag-waving flourished because of the discomfort music educators felt with girls playing and marching with brass and wind instruments.

Even those who got to play a band instrument won approval as much for appearance as for performance. In school music magazines, captions on photographs of female instrumentalists almost invariably commented on physical attractiveness as well as performing ability. According to the caption writer, the Brownsville, Tennessee, high-school drum corps was "widely known for the beautiful girls ... not, of course that pulchritude is particularly essential to the success of your drum corps." A line of female tuba players from Lawton, Oklahoma, won praise as "a background pretty enough for any band."[70] A high-school director advised his colleagues who conducted all-girl bands: "Buy the members of such a band pretty uniforms and their appearance will even surpass that of the boys." Most telling of all were photographs of the winners of a national solo contest in 1934. The boys' photo was labeled "Lads of the Third Division" while the page of girl winners bore the heading "Beauty Plus."[71]

Thus twentieth-century public education, while professedly egalitarian, was less so in practice. In orchestras, meanwhile, although official rhetoric declared that opportunities for women were increasing, unofficial restrictions regarding women's choice of instruments remained unchanged. In 1952 Raymond Paige, music director of the Radio City Music Hall orchestra, assured readers of *Etude Magazine*, the foremost publication for music teachers, that the girl who desired a position in a symphony orchestra would be judged on "musicianship and character and not at all the fact of her being a girl." While he urged teachers to tell the girls to play whatever instrument they liked best, he also noted that "instruments requiring physical force are a dubious choice, partly because women lack the strength for them, partly because the spectacle of a girl engaging in such physical exertions is not attractive. There are women who play the heavier brasses, the contrabass, the big drum, but their employment chances are slimmer. The orchestral manager, thinking in terms of full audience enjoyment, is reluctant to hire a player whose appearance at her instrument gives off a feeling of forcing or incongruity. In general, women who want orchestral work do better to avoid anything heavier than the cello, the clarinet and the French horn. On the other hand, their natural delicacy gives them an advantage with the violin, the viola, the flute and the oboe."[72] In other words, any instrument was all right, but appearance would ultimately determine success.

Gender-based perceptions of musical instruments created a paradox for middle- and upper-class white women. On the one hand they were expected to be proficient in music, the "language of emotions"; on the other hand this proficiency was unquestioningly accepted only when women stayed within the bounds of what was traditionally female. A woman could play an instrument, but only if she looked attractive; she could play in an orchestra or conduct, but it was best if the organization consisted only of women; she could be an educator, but rarely hold a supervisory position; she could march on the playing field, but preferably as a decorative object rather than as a musical performer. The "debilitating aspects of gender stereotyping"[73] altered or stunted women's musical growth, forcing some to develop their talents in different ways and others to abandon music altogether.

2

"He Is Himself a Grand Piano"

The Virtuoso and the Conductor

Just as gender expectations influenced the instruments women were likely to play, so too they influenced women's style of playing. During the nineteenth century, charisma and pyrotechnics emerged as expected features of solo performance. While music of the Baroque and Classical periods was characterized by its symmetry of melody, rhythm, and form, music of the Romantic period was more expansive, with longer melodic lines and greater rhythmic flexibility. As a result, an artist presenting a composition by Bach or Mozart could appear to exercise restraint, whereas a soloist performing a composition by Chopin or Liszt was generally required to exhibit more physicality and extroverted emotionalism. The traditional modesty and restraint expected of a woman performing in the parlor was the antithesis of the physical freedom and appearance of emotional abandon required of the virtuoso performing Romantic music in the concert hall.

Another hindrance to women's acceptance was the convention that a soloist would perform his own compositions. Although there were fine women composer/performers — Clara Schumann, Cécile Chaminade, Fanny Hensel, and Amy Beach are among the better known examples–the compositional potential of these and other women was not nurtured with the same seriousness as their playing ability. Females were encouraged to perform and not to create. Women also labored under the historical assumption that they simply lacked the innate ability to compose music.[1] Clara Schumann, for example, who wrote that she was filled with ideas for compositions, confided to her diary, "I once thought that I possessed creative talent, but I have given up this idea; a woman must not desire to compose — not one has been able to do it, and why should I expect to? It would be arrogance."[2]

Contemporary writers reinforced the notion that women were inherently incapable of musical composition. Prominent critic George Upton, for example, the first of many essayists to puzzle over why there had been no great women composers, wrote that because women were dominated by emotions, they could only "absorb and interpret" music; whereas men, with their superior abilities to control their emotions and to think mathematically, were able to create it.[3] Sometimes writers used the word "productive" to describe men's creative ability and "reproductive" to describe women's.[4]

Pianist Franz Liszt and violinist Niccolò Paganini were the most celebrated European virtuosos of the nineteenth century; their dramatic performances of their own compositions electrified audiences. Liszt, who was the first musician to give solo recitals, possessed a physical presence as striking as the music he played. His chiseled features and shoulder-length hair, combined with an air of elegance and sophistication, caused women to swoon and men to call him the Don Juan of music.[5] American music student Amy Fay described him as "the most interesting and striking-looking man imaginable.... He made me think of an old-time magician more than anything, and I felt that with a touch of his wand he could transform us all."[6] Paganini was equally arresting, a dark, lean figure whose dazzling feats of technical facility had such a mesmerizing effect on his audiences that many thought his powers superhuman.

Most performances by nineteenth-century virtuosos were characterized by an extravagance of physical gesture. Louis Moreau Gottschalk described a performance by Liszt: "The movement of his head, his arms, the contraction of his enormous fingers, made him seem like a fakir in the throes of an ecstatic convulsion, ever leaning backwards, eyes closed, the mouth tense, shaking his immense locks, ever hurling himself upon the keyboard like a wild beast over its prey, flooding it with the surge of his hair, which, tangled with his fingers on the suffering keys, seemed to be struggling like the ancient python in the embrace of an invisible god."[7]

The earliest virtuosos performed their own compositions exclusively, but gradually some began to include the music of others on their programs. Violinist Joseph Joachim, for example, performed what he described as the "best" music, even if it was composed by someone other than himself; he presented the solo sonatas of Bach and Brahms as well as chamber works by Mozart and Beethoven. Liszt, Anton Rubinstein, and Ignace Paderewski also performed music by Bach, Beethoven, Saint-Saëns, and Chopin. The inclusion on a program of works by a variety of composers marked an important precondition for the ascendance of women to the concert stage.

Neither Liszt nor Paganini toured North America, but several European virtuosos did cross the Atlantic in the mid-nineteenth century, lured primarily by the large sums a well-known virtuoso could earn in a relatively short time. Norwegian violinist Ole Bull toured in 1843, followed by Austrian pianists Leopold de Meyer in 1845, Henri Herz in 1846, and Swiss-born Sigismund Thalberg in 1856. Louis Moreau Gottschalk, born in New Orleans but European in background and education, toured during the Civil War.[8]

The early virtuosos combined showmanship and musicianship, often with more emphasis on the former than the latter. Outside large cities like Boston, New York, and Philadelphia, Americans had few opportunities to hear performances by professional musicians, and audio-duplication technology was a thing of the future. On the occasions when people could attend a performance they expected to be entertained, and the touring virtuoso cultivated eccentricity and flamboyance in an attempt to fulfill this expectation.[9] Leopold de Meyer, for example, sometimes played the piano with his fists and his elbows, and occasionally his cane. "He made the piano ring bells, he invented thunderclaps in the base [sic], he waved at the ladies with his right hand while his left executed roulades."[10] Virtuosos added such flourishes both to their own compositions and to elaborately ornamented versions of popular melodies like "Home Sweet Home" and "Yankee Doodle."

Not all virtuosos were as theatrical as de Meyer; critics praised Sigismund Thalberg for his "serious and simple stage manner." The *Newark Daily Advertiser* noted approvingly in 1856 that Thalberg "never once got his feet upon the keys, nor even his elbows; nor did his hands toss over each other, showering colored lights from diamond fingers." Indeed, during all his performances there was no more movement of his head and shoulders "than would be observed in a Wall Street banker passing over his golden notes from one side to the other, as if there were almost too many to inspect within bank hours."[11] Performances like those of de Meyer and Thalberg illustrate the gradual evolution of the touring musician from flamboyant showman to "serious" artist.

The first serious artist to tour North America playing an equally serious repertoire was Anton Rubinstein in 1872–73. Like his predecessors, Rubinstein had a compelling stage presence; one critic described him as "the most fiery, most fabulous, and most hypnotic of living pianists."[12] Rubinstein was followed by Hans von Bülow in 1875, Rafael Joseffy in 1879, and von Bülow again in 1889. By the time Ignace Paderewski embarked on his enormously successful American tour in 1891–92, promoters were ready; newspaper headlines touted the arrival of the "King of Pianists" and "The Wizard of the Keys."[13] There was Paderewski soap, Paderewski candy, and even a toy replica of a little man with a black frock coat, a white bow tie and a huge head of flame-colored hair, sitting at the piano; when a screw was turned, the little man's hands rushed up and down the keyboard and his head shook violently.[14]

Contemporary reviewers effused over performances by virtuosos, whose most admirable qualities of strength, endurance, force, and assertive power were stereotypically masculine traits. John Sullivan Dwight, the usually quite restrained editor of *Dwight's Journal of Music*, marveled at the sheer girth of pianist de Meyer: "His *physique* is extraordinary; he is himself a Grand Piano, and can stand any amount of violent vibration without any symptom of exhaustion."[15] George Upton described Rubinstein as "athletic in mould, his head was large, and his hair luxuriantly abundant and carelessly worn. His features were rugged, reminding one of some of the portraits of Beethoven.... He was at his best, it seemed to me, in concertos. By his titanic power and impulsive force he not only made his piano take its proper place in the sea of sound, but he fairly led the orchestra in an authoritative manner."[16] James Huneker quoted George Bernard Shaw's description of Paderewski as "an immensely spirited, young, harmonious blacksmith, who puts a concerto on the piano as upon an anvil and hammers it out with an exuberant enjoyment of the swing and strength of the proceedings."[17]

Nineteenth-century virtuosos were the first matinee idols, and as such, American women helped perpetuate their cult status. One reviewer estimated in 1898 that women formed about four-fifths of every afternoon and three-fifths of every evening audience, and that women were "unquestionably more impressed" by male than female performers.[18] Charles Allis of Boston, pianist Olga Samaroff's agent from 1906 to 1911, noted that most people who were interested in piano playing were women and that women were more likely to prefer performances by men. Women reputedly paid violinist Ole Bull's valet for vials of his bath water; they stormed the stage hoping to snatch a piece of Gottschalk's white gloves; and they strained for a glimpse of Paderewski as his train went by. The *New York Herald* reported that Paderewski "bears about the same relation to the women of New York as a cookie jar does to an orphan asylum."[19]

Even in a parlor performance a woman who dared to exhibit a virtuosic performing style or a serious commitment to music could face male mockery and alarm. Critic Philip Hale described with concern the frustration of a young man whose beloved exhibited signs of virtuosity at the keyboard. The youth observed with dismay that her eyes were on the keys instead of his face; he worried that constant practice would make her fingers "thick and bony" and he wondered whether she could possibly care for a house or minister to his "petty but necessary wants" given that she obviously spent a great deal of time practicing the piano. "Love," Hale lamented, "is driven from his heart by her very fingers."[20] Hale concurred with John Sullivan Dwight, who had pronounced fifty years earlier that even though almost every "cultivated" maiden is "musical," she should stick to what is "simple" and "not try to be a virtuosa."[21]

The first woman musician to achieve widespread popularity in the United States — indeed the only one from the nineteenth century whose name and reputation have survived in the public imagination — was not an instrumentalist but a singer, Jenny Lind, whose enormously successful American tour, masterminded by P. T. Barnum, took place in 1850. Much has been written about Lind and the sensation she created; the public was gripped by what was variously called Jenny Lind Mania, the Jenny Fever, and Lindomania.[22] Critic George Upton recalled the evening of her October 7, 1850, Boston debut: "The usually staid city was in a state of delirium ... the crowds, the enthusiasm, the great audience inside, the vastly greater crowd outside wishing it were inside.... Her voice ... was full of volume and extraordinary range.... Her high notes were as clear as a lark's, and her full voice was rich and sonorous."[23]

No matter how exceptional her singing voice was, however, an underlying reason for her unqualified popularity was her ability to project on stage the qualities considered appropriate in the perfect woman — beauty, grace, generosity, modesty and humility. Unlike the male virtuoso who strode onto the stage and instantly asserted his authority, Lind was escorted from the wings by her handsome and dignified conductor/accompanist Jules Benedict, whose "protective attitude ... enhanced her own air of youthfulness and of being something rarely precious." When Jenny Lind came on stage to sing, Benedict walked with her to the center of the stage, bowed to her and solemnly handed her the sheets of music. Sometimes she made her appearance on his arm; sometimes he led her forward by the hand.[24] Nathaniel Parker Willis of the *Home Journal* marveled at the seeming contradiction between Lind's ladylike perfection and her masterful artistry: "To give away more money in charity than any other mortal — and still be first of the prima donnas! To be an irreproachably modest girl — and still be first of the prima donnas! To be humble, simple, genial and unassuming — and still be the first of the prima donnas! ... It is the combination of superiorities that makes one wonder."[25]

It was that very "combination of superiorities" that proved the undoing of many women musicians — the necessity that one's image on stage conform to an idealized notion of perfect womanhood. What was possible for Jenny Lind, who sang like a nightingale and gave vocal expression to her innermost feelings through song, would prove less so for women performing on musical instruments, who would find it difficult to simultaneously perform and project an image of female perfection.

Musicologist Lucy Green has discussed audience perception of women singers and instrumentalists within the context of feminist theory, observing that the body of the woman singer is more on display because the body is the instrument being played. In the case of the instrumentalist, however, an instrument, or "piece of technology," mediates between the performer and her audience. As Green states, "The display she [the instrumentalist] enacts, rather than that of a playful or alluring singing bird, is that of a more controlled or rational being who appears capable of using technology to take over a situation."[26]

The first women to achieve renown as instrumental soloists in the United States were violinist Camilla Urso and pianist Teresa Carreño. Urso was born in Nantes, France, in 1842 and Carreño in Caracas, Venezuela, in 1853. Both made their American debut performances as child prodigies — Urso at the age of ten and Carreño at the age of nine. Critical response to both performers was enthusiastic and their acceptance was clearly helped by their prodigy status.[27]

Some observers found it easier to accept female soloists if they were children; the emotions they expressed were safe. Contemporary reviews of girl child prodigies contrast "mature passion" with the childlike innocence expressed in their performances. "Such music has not the stuff of manhood or womanhood in it," remarked an observer of an 1852 performance by Urso. "It has not actual passion, either of love or ambition.... It is fantastic, fairy-like, belonging to other wondering instincts of childhood geniuses."[28] Nineteenth- and early twentieth-century audiences more read-

Violinist Camilla Urso (1842–1902), who toured the United States in the 1850s. (From *The Great Instrumentalists in Historic Photographs*, p. 137, edited by James Camner. New York: Dover, 1980.)

ily accepted expressions of passion and mastery from a child than from a grown woman.

Unlike early male soloists who depended on various stage antics to keep the audience entertained, early female soloists presented themselves as straightforward, serious performers, the mere fact of their gender providing the necessary element of novelty. There were only a handful of prominent women performers at the turn of the century, and managers assumed that there was room for only one per instrument at a time. Camilla Urso was the reigning

Child prodigy Teresa Carreño (1853–1917), Venezuelan pianist who gave a recital at New York's Irving Hall at the age of 8. (From *The Great Instrumentalists in Historic Photographs*, p. 20, edited by James Camner. New York: Dover, 1980.)

woman violinist of the middle to late nineteenth century; as her career came to an end, Maud Powell's was on the ascendant. Pianist Teresa Carreño paved the way for Julie Rivé-King, who was "replaced" by Fannie Bloomfield-Zeisler, who in turn was succeeded by Olga Samaroff and Ethel Leginska. New York manager Henry Wolfsohn clearly believed that the market for women performers was limited when he speculated in 1904 on Samaroff's chances for success. As she later related, he had had a "hunch" she could succeed. "There was room for a woman pianist at the moment. Carreño was getting on and Fannie Bloomfield-Zeisler was devoting much of her time to her teaching and her family. The important thing was to have all the conditions right."[29]

As women virtuosos began performing in public, reviewers struggled to reconcile their perception of the virtuoso as a strong and masterful male with the reality that the virtuoso they had just seen was a strong and masterful female. They constantly invoked qualities assumed to be inherently male and expressed disbelief that such qualities could be found in a female who still appeared to be feminine. Typical were the comments about Teresa Carreño by a *Musical Courier* critic who stated that although her playing showed "mastery," he hesitated to use that word because it implied "some taint of masculinity," and Madame Carreño was the finest type of "eternal feminine."[30] A reviewer for the *Boston Post* praised pianist Julie Rivé-King's playing, but hastened to reassure readers that her stage presence was "modest and unassuming"; a Portland reviewer in 1882 noted approvingly that Rivé-King's position at the keyboard was "dignified, reposeful and utterly devoid of mannerisms" and that the impression she made on her audience was "a very pleasant one indeed."[31]

Women instrumentalists challenged the expectations of audiences in ways that women singers had not. In contrast to Jenny Lind, Fannie Bloomfield-Zeisler took charge when she made her entrance, signaling to the conductor when she was ready to begin playing. She walked onstage "as a queen would approach the throne," sat down, arranged herself at the piano, looked out at the audience, smiled at the orchestra, and nodded to the conductor when she was ready to begin. One reviewer observed that the audience might easily have assumed that Hans von Bülow, "that most masculine of all virtuosos," was about to perform, had they not seen Bloomfield-Zeisler's "graceful feminine appearance" approach the piano.[32]

Reviewers expressed discomfort when women used what they considered too much body movement in their performances. Julie Rivé-King pleased most commentators because she remained quite still as she played. As one Boston critic noted approvingly, "Once seated at the piano, she does not move, not even to toss her head or her hands!" A San Francisco critic warned: "He who directs his steps to Platt's Hall in the expectation of seeing Madame Rivé-King swoop upon the keys, rave musically, or work herself into any sort of a melodic frenzy will be wholly disappointed. She is of a prudent type, guarded, cautious, and beautifully calm."[33] Fannie Bloomfield-Zeisler performed with more physical movement, which disturbed some reviewers. Bostonian Philip Hale criticized what he termed her "superficial and annoying manifestations.... There were tossings of arms aloft; there was facial italicizing of deep-seated emotions." All this, he felt, was unnecessary. "The volcano that sweeps away a village does not cry out to the dismayed inhabitants, 'come here and feel my pulse. Is this hot enough for you?'"[34]

Reviewers were not the only ones who were startled by what seemed an excess of movement. Adeline Graham, a young woman from rural Michigan, described a performance by Teresa Carreño in her diary: "Her playing was grand, but I couldn't see much beauty in it. I always thought a musician should sit as quiet as possible and should not move her arms from the shoulder at all. But she went through all sorts of motions and reminded me of our dog when he [charges] for chipmunks."[35]

Women soloists were also judged by their physical beauty, and early reviews invariably included descriptions of physical appearance. Russian pianist Anna Essipoff possessed "dark hair, dark eyes, a graceful figure, and a fine complexion."[36] Reviews also described the artist's gown with an attention to detail generally reserved for bridal gowns on today's society pages. For a recital in St. Louis in 1883, Julie Rivé-King wore a "train of cherry satin over a flame and white petticoat, corsage square filled with Duchesse lace, diamond ornaments, lace sleeves, [and] cherry satin Marie Antoinette shoes."[37] For an appearance in Bridgeport, Connecticut, in 1903, Fannie Bloomfield-Zeisler wore "a gown of pink satin with a lace flounce at the bottom and following the outline of the train. Angel sleeves of lace over accordion pleated chiffon were very stylish. A lace yoke was outlined at the corsage with a decoration of chenille, and about her throat was a collar of six strands of pearls. A diamond sunburst fastened the large velvet bow to the corsage."[38]

The fashionable woman of the period was encumbered by clothing that could both hinder her movement and damage her health. The principal villain was the corset, which was believed necessary to support the muscles and desirable to cinch in the waist. Girls as young as three or four were laced into juvenile versions of the device, and stays were lengthened, stiffened, and tightened as the girl grew older; by late adolescence a girl commonly wore a "cage" of heavy canvas reinforced with whalebone or steel.[39] Not surprisingly the corset restricted breathing and freedom of movement, arousing concern that wearing one could adversely affect one's musical performance. As late as 1914, a letter to the editor of *Musician* magazine asked, "Should a woman singer wear a corset? My teacher claims it hinders my breathing, but my mother says that a well-dressed woman must wear a corset."[40] Singing teacher J. C. Wilcox responded that he was "constantly handicapped" in his efforts to teach his female students how to acquire adequate breath control because of their "miserable muscle-killing corsets." Dr. Arthur de Guichard agreed: "Can you imagine a sprinter or a marathoner, or a bicycle rider, or a race horse wearing a belt, or a corset, or anything that will embarrass the action of the lungs?" Voice teacher Herbert Wilbur Greene contended, however, that corsets were a necessity in women's dress: "Those who do not wear them are not well dressed.... Most women aim to make an attractive appearance and the corset is necessary to that end."[41]

Victorian women also commonly wore multiple layers of fabric, often including three or more petticoats, that could weigh anywhere from ten to thirty pounds.[42] Violinist Maud Powell recalled a "bright red plush skirt, quite full, over which was draped a much-shirred yellow silk 'drop' with a square collar, an imitation décolletage neck, and bits of lace in every imaginable spot," which she was convinced had contributed to one of the worst performances of her career.[43] She experimented with ways to make her concert gowns allow more freedom of movement and devised, for example, a set of "cleverly hidden weights and heavy cords" that attached a train to her gown. Powell went to such lengths because she believed that fashionable gowns were essential to maintain the "dignity and beauty expected of a female concert artist."[44] Most women soloists of the period agreed with Powell and wore fashionable clothes when performing. Others, however, began experimenting with more comfortable dress. The most notable was pianist Ethel Leginska who, as early as 1908, began modifying her performing garb in order to allow herself more freedom of movement and keep her warm enough in drafty concert halls.[45]

With caution and some inconvenience, a female virtuoso could craft a publicly acceptable image. No such image management, however, would avail a woman who aspired to conduct. The very idea of a female conductor seemed ludicrous to the few nineteenth-century commentators who gave it notice. A worried female music teacher wrote *Etude Magazine* in 1887 asking whether it would be appropriate for her to stand before her chorus of eighteen women and "direct them with a baton, in a public recital." American musicologist John Comfort Fillmore replied by urging her to try her utmost to secure the desired musical results by directing from the piano instead; the thought of her conducting with a baton seemed to him as incongruous as the idea of her smoking a cigar. "I know of no earthly reason why it is less proper for my wife to smoke a good cigar than for me," he mused, "but I confess I should be very sorry to see her do it, while I have no scruple whatever in doing it myself."[46]

The performing demands of the conductor in the nineteenth century evolved in much the same way as those of the instrumental soloist — Romantic music required a more expansive style of performance. In Bach's time, no one stood in front of the musicians and conducted; small instrumental groups depended on the keyboard player to keep the performers together. The "conductor" would direct from the harpsichord or organ and remove his hands from the keyboard to direct when necessary. Later in the eighteenth century, however, much responsibility for direction shifted from the keyboard player to the first violinist; in the time of Haydn and Mozart, leadership of the orchestra was divided between these two instrumentalists, with the person at the keyboard serving as "time beater" and the violinist indicating when the music should be loud or soft and generally coordinating interpretation. By the nineteenth century, direction passed to a single individual who stood in front of the group. The longer melodic lines of nineteenth-century Romantic music, and the rubato, or "give and take" allowable in its performance, contributed to the need for a conductor who could combine the functions of time beater and interpreter.[47]

By the late nineteenth century the conductor had achieved almost mythic status and become the dominating figure of the orchestra.[48] This phenomenon was particularly evident in the United States in the early decades of the twentieth century; European conductors were imported to conduct American

THE MAD RUSH AFTER THE THIRD ENCORE

Depicting the Worship of Genius as Demonstrated at the Concert of a Great Violin
Virtuoso—From the "Illustrated London News"

The adulation of the male virtuoso. (From the *Illustrated London News*; published in *Musical America*, November 12, 1910, p. 25.)

orchestras, and audiences and critics were awed by their "foreign" charisma. Gustav Mahler observed in 1908 that the conductor in the United States had "unlimited sovereign power" over the musicians and "a social standing such as the musician cannot attain in Europe."[49] By the 1920s there were many prominent European conductors based in the United States, including Leopold Stokowski in Philadelphia, Serge Koussevitsky in Boston and Fritz Reiner in Cincinnati. Wilhelm Furtwängler and Otto Klemperer made regular appearances in New York and Arturo Toscanini served as guest conductor of the New York Philharmonic during the 1926–27 season, becoming its permanent conductor in 1928. By then conductors had become such prominent personalities that audiences who had previously flocked to concerts to see famous soloists now crowded the auditoriums to see famous conductors. By the early 1930s, the concerto featuring an instrumental soloist had virtually disappeared from the programs of symphony orchestras in New York, Boston, and Philadelphia.[50] Even more striking, the players in the orchestra had become almost incidental participants as well. One critic intoned that under Wilhelm Furtwängler, "the opening pages of the symphony ... were unforgettably read." The music was not being *played* by the musicians, it was being *read* by the conductor.[51]

Contemporary reviews document the ways audiences and critics perceived these musical giants. Otto Klemperer was one of the most imposing because of his 6'4" height: "The new leader loomed above his players in a manner that seemed to dwarf the ensemble and to bring it, almost visually, into the commodious hollow of his hand." Critic James Huneker described Anton Seidl's expression as "eminently ecclesiastical.... His Gothic head I've seen in medieval triptychs."[52] Critics frequently invoked military imagery to describe the orchestra and its leader: "The conductor's entrance is like that of a commander before his troops, for he is, in truth, a commander upon whom the whole responsibility of from sixty to one hundred men must fall. It is he who maps out the campaign like a strategist ... and who gathers his men for a concerted attack.... His little army is ready to obey his will." Sometimes a headline said it all. "Stokowski's Men Invade Baltimore," announced a typical 1920 headline.[53] The editor of *Musical America* summarized the characteristics of the ideal conductor: "He must be a man who has a big mental and emotional conception of the greatest in music, that is, a true appreciation of music, one who has a 'personality' of sufficient command, and, finally, one who has had the opportunity for practical experience, and who has thus gained technical proficiency in conducting."[54] It is no wonder that the 1925 reviewer of a Boston concert conducted by Ethel Leginska acknowledged that the public was "handicapped by an unexplainable distaste for women as orchestral leaders," and that a 1932 review of one of her New York performances referred to "the reluctance of the superior male in the command of a slip of a woman."[55]

As with instrumental soloists, the expectations and attitudes of women in the audience contributed to the reception of conductors. American music student Amy Fay described her reaction to a performance conducted by Alicia Hurd in 1871: "All the men were highly disgusted because she was allowed to conduct the orchestra herself. I didn't think myself that it was a very *becoming* position, though I had no prejudice against it. Somehow, a woman doesn't look well with a baton in her hand directing a body of men."[56] Almost 60 years later, in 1928, Hungarian pianist Yolanda Merö, on tour in North America, confessed to a reporter that she had a "secret ambition" to be a conductor, which the reporter pronounced "delightful." "You see," Merö explained, conducting was the "biggest, most magnificent thing a musician can do, but I shall never do it, because I think a woman in front of an orchestra looks ridiculous as a rule. Why it shouldn't be done, however, if the woman is really capable of it, I can't see. Women can accomplish anything nowadays."[57]

Appearances clearly determined the nature of the successes possible for women virtuosos and conductors. Audiences and critics were uncomfortable when women exhibited the strength and abandon of the virtuoso, and they were even more so when women demonstrated the assertiveness and leadership of the conductor.

3

"Spoiled for Domesticity"

American Students Abroad

Male and female virtuosos of the period shared many common experiences. Almost all began as child prodigies, studied in Europe with one or more noted teachers, and embarked on extensive concert tours of Europe and North America. Many struggled with performance anxiety at some time in their careers, and all had to strike a balance between personal and professional demands. Women, however, faced many situations in which issues of gender exacerbated their difficulties.

Musicians had to study in Europe before they could be taken seriously in America. Americans generally viewed Europe as a Mecca of serious culture; most virtuosos who had toured the United States in the nineteenth century were European, as were the majority of professional musicians in early American bands and orchestras. Even as the number of native-born American musicians increased, a reverence for European musicians persisted; it was generally assumed that American musical training and standards were by definition inferior to their European counterparts. In order to be respected as a serious musician, one had to study for several years with an acknowledged European master, perform successfully in European cultural centers like Berlin and Vienna, and return to America with a sheaf of laudatory reviews that could be used for publicity. As Henry Wolfsohn, a leading New York concert manager, told young Olga Samaroff in 1904, "It isn't what I think of your playing, but what Europe thinks of it that counts."[1]

Between the Civil War and the turn of the century, many upper- and upper-middle-class American families sent their daughters abroad for a year or so after they had attended boarding or finishing schools. The trip was intended to broaden their education and administer a dose of European culture.[2] This dose usually included a smattering of music and art. A correspondent for the *New York Sun* noted in 1888 that hundreds of American "ladies" were "working at music" in Berlin. And in 1891 the *Musical Courier* estimated that most of the city's 2,000 American residents were there to study music — the majority were women.[3]

The much smaller number of young American women who went abroad to study music with the intention of becoming professional musicians differed substantially from those who traveled for finish. Almost all had been gifted child prodigies whose skills quickly eclipsed those of the local music teacher. Most were quite young when they left for Europe — they were typically in their early teens as compared with late teens and early twenties. And they stayed longer, usually from two to five years. By the time they went abroad, these students had already invested years of their young lives mastering their discipline. They were for the most part *not* from the upper class, but instead from middle-class families who were educating their daughters at considerable personal and financial sacrifice. Since the girl was obviously too young to travel by herself and live on her own, a female relative — usually a mother or grandmother — served as traveling companion and remained with her for the several years she spent abroad.

The course of study at a German music conservatory generally lasted three years, although a gifted student could complete it in less time, and some students chose to stay longer. The academic year had two semesters and classes met Monday through Saturday. Studies at the Leipzig Conservatory covered, in addition to the student's major instrument or vocal concentration, courses in harmony, counterpoint and fugue, form and analysis, composition, instrumentation, playing from the score, and conducting. There were also courses in history, aesthetics, and acoustics.[4]

The experience of these music students differed considerably from that of the first generations of women to attend college between 1870 and 1920. Unlike the typical college woman, who studied a variety of subjects with a group of peers, the conservatory student concentrated almost exclusively on music and spent many hours practicing alone. Barbara Solomon's history of women and college education in America includes a late-nineteenth-century photograph of students working together in a chemistry lab at Wellesley College. They crowd around a table, leaning toward each other clearly excited by what they are learning and eager to share their experience.[5] The conservatory experience for a solo performer was very different — not only did she work alone, but there was always an awareness, even if distant, that each of her classmates was a potential competitor. College women also shared a variety of activities outside the classroom — in addition to dormitory life, they participated in athletic programs, theater groups, political and religious organizations, and a variety of clubs. All of these provided opportunities to work and play together and to form lasting friendships. The younger music student still lived with her parent or chaperon. Even though she attended some classes with fellow students, her educational experience was, by comparison, more solitary.

The leading cities of Germany were the favored destinations of many American music students. The classified pages of the *Musical Courier* for this period carried regular advertisements for music conservatories in Leipzig, Dresden, Hamburg, Weimar, and Sonderhausen. Fifteen-year-old pianist Julie Rivé left Cincinnati for Leipzig in 1874 to study with Carl Reinecke and then with Franz Lizst. Fifteen-year-old Fannie Blumenfeld (later Bloomfield), accompanied by her mother and grandmother, traveled from Chicago to Vienna in 1878 to study with Theodor Leschetizky: she was gone for five years. Thirteen-year-old violinist Maud Powell, along with her mother and younger brother, departed Aurora, Illinois, for Leipzig (and later Paris and London) in 1881: she also stayed for five years. Fourteen-year-old Lucie Hickenlooper (later renamed Olga Samaroff), left Galveston, Texas, for Paris (and later Berlin) in 1891 accompanied by her grandmother: she was gone for four years. Samaroff did not see her father for the entire time and only saw her mother once. The fathers of both Maud Powell and Fannie Blumenfeld sold the family home in order to finance the sojourn in Europe.[6]

The mothers and grandmothers of these young virtuosos were frequently strong-willed women whose own career ambitions had been thwarted. This pattern is consistent with that of the supportive mothers who helped the first generation of women to attend college. Willa Cather's mother, for example, was the one who insisted that her talented daughter enter the University of Nebraska in 1891. Similarly, in the 1880s and 1890s the mothers of Virginia Gildersleeve (Barnard dean), Vida Scudder (Wellesley professor), Hilda Smith (Bryn Mawr dean), Mary Austin (writer), and Elizabeth Wallace (Chicago professor of English) all encouraged their initially hesitant daughters to continue their education.[7]

Some of the music students' mothers and grandmothers had been musicians themselves. Julie Rivé's mother, for example, was a singer who had studied at the Paris Conservatory with Jenny Lind. Olga Samaroff's grandmother was an accomplished pianist who had performed with the French Opera Orchestra in New Orleans in 1856.[8] She stopped performing publicly when presented with a decent marriage proposal (the common pattern) and became a teacher.[9] Although Fannie Blumenfeld's mother was not a musician, she was a confident and assertive woman who contributed much drive and organizational skill to the family business. "I owe a great deal to my mother," Bloomfield-Zeisler reminisced years later, "[and] to my father, too, only in less degree. He was ambitious for me in a worldly sense, but my mother was most in sympathy with me, as mothers usually are."[10] Maud Powell's mother had wanted to be a musician, but since this was unthinkable at the time, she resolved that her first son should be a violinist — the fact that her first child was a girl did not deter her. Mrs. Powell was clearly ambitious for her daughter. As family and friends gathered to say good-bye before they sailed for Europe, Powell's father smiled and said, "When Maud returns, we expect her to be a fine violinist." Her mother quickly interjected, "She must be better than a 'fine violinist'; she will be a second Camilla Urso."[11]

These mothers bear a close resemblance to the "ballet mothers" described by Suzanne Gordon in her 1983 study of young ballerinas; ambition for their daughters was not their only motivation. "They were often trapped in conventional lives themselves, creative women who had married and had children and were now seeking fulfillment through their daughters' activities."[12] For the mothers of the musicians, the European experience was an outlet for their own thwarted ambitions.

Conservatories provided neither housing nor practice facilities, so the first order of business for the music student and her guardian was finding lodging and renting a piano. Some boardinghouses catered to music students. Maud Powell and her mother, for example, boarded with eight other American musicians who were studying at the Leipzig Conservatory. Such residences commonly allowed students to practice during many hours of the day and night. One such house in Leipzig in 1901 permitted practice from seven in the morning to 10 at night. In other parts of the city, practice could not begin until eight in the morning, with an hour or two of mandated quiet at midday and a rule that practice must cease after eight in the evening.[13] The cost of such accommodations, which also included food, was generally not prohibitive. In Berlin, for example, one could get a small comfortable room with meals and snacks for about $50 a month.[14]

Mothers and grandmothers handled the practical aspects of the girls' lives while the girls concentrated on their studies. The older women also served as chaperons and advocates as their daughters competed with one another for the musical attention of the likes of Leschetizky, Joachim, and Liszt. They served as emotional mainstays as well, walking the fine line between supportive parent and stage mother. Maud Powell once remarked that she sympathized with any mother of a talented daughter. "If I think about Leipzig, I can still see three mothers accompanying their daughters to their music lessons. My mother was one of them, a Mrs. Carpenter, another one. Here we were, sometimes the three of us sitting next to each other, afraid that one of us could be set back or might not get as much attention because she was a foreigner. If there was a concert in which the daughter was a participant, the mother had to worry about everything — the dress, the fitting, and the fear ... as if she were playing herself." Powell reported that the experience caused one of the mothers they knew to spend five months in a psychiatric institution.[15] In spite of the stresses involved, however, these competent and energetic women were in many ways on their own while in Europe, where they enjoyed more freedom than they had experienced in the United States. Mrs. Powell noted approvingly that "ladies are allowed to go anywhere alone here [in Leipzig], even to the opera," and every night were provided the opportunity to attend first-rate concerts at affordable prices.[16]

Most of these music students flourished in Europe. "When I went abroad," recalled Maud Powell, "I fell right into the foreign way, loving the new impressions and sensing the artistic atmosphere at once." Although she knew there were fine teachers in America, she felt that one should go abroad to be with other talented and ambitious students and hear so many excellent concerts and recitals.[17] Fannie Bloomfield-Zeisler similarly appreciated European musical life and culture, in contrast to the dearth of concerts in America: "We [in America] have to lay in music like the camel does food and then live on it for weeks, while in Germany, we may have the pleasure and benefit of listening to all of the greatest artists in the same season."[18]

The young women could, however, rarely forget the sacrifices being made on their behalf. Fannie Blumenfeld was loath to tell her father she was not getting the highest grades at the conservatory, knowing how he had sacrificed to send her there. Maud Powell wrote in 1908 that her family was "broken up" when she was taken abroad, leaving her father temporarily "homeless, wifeless and childless" while he worked to send the monthly checks that paid for the lessons, concerts, clothing, rent, and food. Olga Samaroff recalled that she had agonized over her decision to study abroad. She knew that to go would mean not seeing her parents for years and require her grandmother, who was to be her companion, to suspend the teaching career which furnished her only source of income.[19]

One of the few contemporary published accounts documenting the experience of the American music student in Europe was by Amy Fay, a New Englander who studied in Germany from 1869 to 1875.[20] Although Fay was a serious student, in many ways she more closely resembled the young women who went abroad to enhance their education. She was twenty-five years old when she went, considerably older than the average music student, and she also came from a prominent, well-connected New England family, which enabled her to move about easily in interesting social circles and to meet prominent musicians. Fay wrote home to her sister Melusina who, with the encouragement of Henry Wadsworth Longfellow, compiled, edited, and published the letters in 1881 as *Music Study in Germany*. The book proved immensely popular, remaining in print continuously until 1922. It was frequently presented as a prize for proficiency in finishing schools and female academies and influenced many Americans to study music both in America and abroad.[21] A keen observer, Fay wrote animated and evocative letters in the breathless style of many nineteenth-century American travel writers. Her descriptions of cities and famous musicians — particularly Liszt, with whom she studied for a time — conveyed her excitement and enthusiasm.

Fay described her fellow students in Berlin as accomplished and self-assured. "Many of the girls played magnificently and I was amazed at the technique that they had, and at the artistic manner in which even very young girls rendered the most difficult music, and all without notes [memorized]. It gave me a severe nervous headache just to hear them. But it was delightful to see them go at it. None of them had the least fear, and they laughed and chattered between the pieces, and when their turn came they marched up to the piano, sat down as bold as lions, and banged away splendidly."[22]

Fay then described a master class in which these "bold" and "fearless" girls encountered the autocratic style of the German music master. In a master class, students perform for an audience of their peers and for their teacher, who is often a prominent musician. The teacher, or master, critiques each performance and gives suggestions for improvement. It is like having a music lesson with an audience. Fay observed that some of the girls were "mortally afraid" of their teacher, Carl Tausig, who frequently lost his temper and hurled insults like, "You play like a rhinoceros!"

She described the experience of a young Russian, "Fräulein Timinoff," who Fay judged to be a "little genius" and who arrived at her lesson very well prepared. She began to play a Schubert sonata, "in her usual nimble style, having practiced it evidently every minute of the time when she was not asleep, since the last lesson…. He kept stopping her every moment, in the most tantalizing and exasperating manner. If it had been I, I should have cried, but Timinoff is well broken, and only flushed deeply to the very tips of her small ears…. Tausig grew more and more savage, and made her skip whole pages in his impatience. 'Play here!' he would say, in the most imperative tone, pointing to a half or whole page farther on. 'This I cannot hear!— Go no farther!— It is too bad to be listened to!'" Tausig finally threw up his hands in despair, and cried, "Child, there is no soul in the piece. Don't you know there's a *soul* in it?" Fay wisely observed that Timinoff was too young to exhibit much "soul" and was "not sufficiently experienced to counterfeit one."[23]

On another occasion Tausig became so exasperated with a student that he snatched her music from the piano, shouting that he had heard enough. The girl returned to her seat and began to cry. "But she is too proud to let the other girls see her wipe her eyes," Fay continued, "and so she sits up straight, and tries to look unconcerned, but the tears trickle down her cheeks one after the other, and drop off her chin all the rest of the hour." Fay concluded, "It is his principal [sic] to rough you and snub you as much as he can, even when there is no occasion for it, and you can think yourself fortunate if he does not hold you up to the ridicule of the whole class."[24]

Theodor Leschetizky, who taught Fannie Bloomfield, Ethel Leginska, Ignace Paderewski, Artur Schnabel, and many other noted virtuosos, often exhibited behavior similar to that of Carl Tausig. A complex figure who inspired both fear and devotion in his students, Leschetizky was dedicated and generous, but he could also be brutally frank, and students of both sexes were sometimes traumatized by their weekly encounters. Clara Clemens, pianist and daughter of Mark Twain, who studied briefly with Leschetizky, remembered his "terrifying classes" and her "dread" of performing in them.[25] Leschetizky's sister-in-law described his verbal assaults as "often of too personal and stinging a nature to amuse the victims, but always to the point and full of wit." She referred to the "exciting little drama enacted in the studio — the lightning-flashes, the often hasty retreat of the unfortunate pupil, the thundering rage of the old man, who was so quickly soothed, and so prompt to regret his harshness, which he often expiated by a sleepless night of remorse."[26]

Leschetizky appears to have possessed a keen sense of timing, which he used to keep students emotionally off-balance. He would build someone up, tear them down, and then gently reach out to them again. English pianist Katharine Goodson recalled a two-hour lesson, after which she "came away brimful of wonderful ideas.... I pondered carefully on what he had told me, made notes ... practiced with the utmost delight. I looked forward eagerly to my next lesson. To my complete mortification, however, I never received severer punishment from the master than at that lesson. Nothing seemed to go right and he did not spare my feelings. I stood it bravely for a time but presently tears ran down my face and on my new gown. 'Now come, my dear child,' said Leschetizky in a softer tone, 'don't be foolish. You must not spoil your new dress.'"[27]

"Leschetizky loves his pupils as if they were his own children," another student recalled, "but, as a good father, he considers his duty better done through the aid of discipline than of sympathy." Yet another student remembered him fondly as a person who taught "with passion and with care," recalling that he frequently took late-night walks in student neighborhoods, stopping to listen beneath the windows of his pupils, to make sure they were practicing correctly. On one such occasion a girl emerged from her room only to find him sitting in a rocking chair on the landing of her boardinghouse. "I have been here two hours," he calmly announced. "You will never play those triplets unless you take them more slowly."[28] The easy authority with which he entered her boardinghouse and listened without her knowledge reveals the extent to which he presumed the dual roles of teacher and father.

Leschetizky further revealed his inclination to blend these roles when he dispensed personal advice. He told pianist Katharine Goodson, for example, that he was "deeply grieved" to learn that she was engaged to be married, "for he did not wish me or most of his other pupils, for that matter, to marry. Marriage, it seemed to him, would put an end to or otherwise mar my musical career and he was always pleased with me because it had never been my intention to marry at all."[29] Leschetizky's attitude was at the very least hypocritical. He was married four times, and all his wives were former students.[30]

Swiss psychologist Alice Miller has described the German concept of "Erziehung," which involves training the child for "absolute obedience, willing subordination, and conformity," observing that it has existed for centuries in German styles of parenting and pedagogy. As early as possible, the parent trains the child to suppress his or her own will; an independent sense of self or will is viewed as a negative attribute which must be crushed. Miller maintains that parents (especially fathers) are encouraged to use either physical punishment or mental cruelty to accomplish this end. She cites child-rearing manuals that endorse techniques like ridicule, mockery, scorn, and manipulation in order to achieve the desired submissiveness, and other guides that teach parents how to rid their children of spontaneity. (An 1896 manual bears the title *On the Character Fault of Exuberance in Children.*)[31] Miller theorizes that patterns of authority and submission pervade many aspects of German culture, and that the patterns between parent and child are replicated in other settings, particularly schools. She cites nineteenth-century books on techniques for breaking a child's will, a system which Miller labels "poisonous pedagogy." Amy Fay's descriptions of master classes in which confident and talented young students are reduced to rage and tears resemble the techniques described by Miller.

Miller does not distinguish between boys and girls in her work, and evidence shows that boys as well as girls suffered a master's verbal assaults. Paderewski once stated that he would rather play before a large audience in Paris, New York, or London than perform in one of Leschetizky's master classes.[32] Austrian-born pianist Artur Schnabel studied with the teacher in 1891, when Schnabel was only nine years old. As the pianist's biographer recounted: "Many stories are told by fellow-pupils of the pathetic little youngster who had to undergo humiliating tongue-lashings by the irascible master. Once, because he left out a few notes in a Beethoven sonata, he was told that he was a thief, since stealing from Beethoven was as reprehensible as taking money out of someone's pockets. Artur took it silently, sat immovable on his chair against the wall, his feet dangling and tears running down his face."[33] Pianist and critic Samuel Lipman similarly described the psychological bullying he endured from his teacher, Lev Shorr. "It was not so much that he raved and ranted; most teachers who take seriously what they teach rave and rant from time to time. It was rather that his onslaught was so personal, so directed toward the center of my pride and self-respect. My every flaw was for him a moral flaw."[34]

Of course there is no reason to believe that either Schnabel or Lipman was less affected by these experiences than the young girls who endured similar verbal and psychological assaults. Miller argues, however, that the effects of "poisonous pedagogy" are potentially more damaging to girls, because boys who experience shame or humiliation will eventually inherit paternal authority and social prestige as they grow older, whereas in girls' lives such negative early experiences are more likely to be replicated and reinforced with age.[35] It is interesting to note, however, that both male and female students participated equally in Leschetizky's master classes, unlike Tausig's Berlin studio, where students were taught in segregated groups.[36]

Older, more mature students could presumably handle Leschetizky's behavior with more objectivity and detachment. American music student Clarence Bird observed that "learning to *take* a lesson [with Leschetizky] was as important as playing well. If the student were excessively silent or retiring, woe to him or her! ... He wanted [students] to talk, to ask, to be animated — above all to be intelligent and impersonal. Not to take to heart some of the difficult sayings and criticism was a thing one had to learn for self-sustainment and equilibrium. With that accomplished, the sky completely cleared for me."[37]

Leschetizky's many positive qualities should not be underestimated. He apparently encouraged each student to develop an independent musical personality. As Bloomfield-Zeisler once described, "He studied the individuality of each pupil and taught them according to that individuality. He often escorted students to concerts and plays, invited them to dinner, and engaged them in stimulating conversations about art and culture."[38]

Many of Leschetizky's most successful students maintained a friendship with him into adulthood. Fannie Bloomfield-Zeisler and her family visited him in Europe whenever possible, and when he died she devoted much time and energy to the creation and dedication of a memorial statue in his honor, in Vienna. When the statue was unveiled in an elaborate ceremony she and many other former students spoke movingly about his importance in their lives.[39] The success of so many of Leschetizky's students provides evidence that they learned from him, either because of or in spite of the methods he employed.

American students endured the additional burden of the European musician's anti–American bias. Amy Fay reported that her teacher Theodor Kullak had a "deep-rooted prejudice against Americans" and never lost an opportunity to make a cutting remark. Although he acknowledged that some of his American students were "remarkably gifted," he also maintained that Americans had "no real talent." One of Tausig's most fearsome epithets was, "Why Fräulein, you play exactly as if you came from America." Olga Samaroff similarly reported that her teacher Eugène Delaborde greeted her at her first lesson at the Paris Conservatory with the taunt, "You are an American, are you? Why do you try to play the piano? Americans are not meant to be musicians!"[40]

Some of this antipathy could have been exacerbated by a language barrier. In Leschetizky's classes, for instance, German was the official language of instruction, but few American students would have mastered it.[41] Fannie Blumenfeld spoke German fluently but she was unlike most American students in that regard. Amy Fay advised a friend to continue his German-conversation lessons before coming abroad. "Even the few I took prove of immense assistance to me, as I can understand almost everything that is said to me, though I cannot answer back," she wrote in an early letter home.[42] On another occasion she reported that Liszt disliked teaching in German and often spoke to her in French. It obviously helped if a student was multilingual, and many American students were not.[43]

The culmination of the European experience was a public performance attended by local critics, whose reviews would appear in newspapers. These comments, when favorable, were taken back to America for use as promotional publicity. Some concerned individuals argued that such public performances put students under too much pressure and distracted them from their daily studies. Noted German musicologist and teacher Hugo Riemann suggested that newspaper reviews of student performances be banned entirely in order to alleviate what he termed "this circus atmosphere."[44] Nonetheless, even a less-than-favorable review was salvageable by replacing an uncomplimentary word or two with a strategically placed ellipsis.

As in the United States, gender clearly influenced some critics. Amy Fay recalled a young woman who was panned by the critics in Hamburg, even though Fay felt that she had "played magnificently." Fay believed that the "whole secret of Frau Rappoldi's want of success was that she did not *look* pretty. She was so dowdily dressed, and her hair looked like a Feejee [sic] Islander's. People laughed at her before she began."[45]

By the early 1900s prominent American music periodicals began to include articles challenging the advisability of American girls subjecting themselves to these ordeals by studying abroad. Authors questioned the necessity for Americans to leave their own country, especially considering that the United States now had several excellent music conservatories. The Oberlin, Peabody, Boston, and Cincinnati Conservatories and the Institute of Musical Art (later the Juilliard School) were all founded between 1865 and 1905, and some public colleges and universities had begun to allow girls to study instrumental music as well.[46] The critical issue in these articles, however, was neither patriotism nor the quality of American music education, but rather the risk that American girls would be compromised by going abroad to study.[47]

John Freund, editor of the widely circulated weekly *Musical America*, addressed the subject in 1908 when he published a reply to a hypothetical letter from a young music student asking whether she should study in Europe. Freund framed his answer tellingly: "Shall I tell you to abandon your ambition, become the gentle, loving wife of some good American, and the mother of children, and so fulfill woman's noblest destiny, or shall I tell you to persevere [with your musical career], and to the end?" Freund discouraged the girl from going to Europe and advised her to study in America instead, pointing out, sensibly enough, that the life of a prima donna demands genius, hard work, and self-sacrifice, and warning her not to glamorize it. His advice evoked a more sustained response than almost any other issue discussed in the magazine. For years, readers requested copies of both the original letter and Freund's answer until over 50,000 copies had been sent out; both were reprinted eight years later in the October 14, 1916, issue.[48]

Exploiting the contemporary panic over "white slavery," Freund lectured all across the country on the evils that could befall the American girl in Europe, transposing the standard narrative of decline and fall from New York and Chicago to Paris and Berlin. One of his stories told of a singer who was "only a farmer's daughter" who had "inherited wonderful health and a splendid form from a long line of hard-working, clean-living peasant ancestors." After studying voice for several years she took all her savings and went alone to study in Paris. She quickly learned that it was difficult to support herself and was "pursued by every human creature that wore pants, both old as well as young," especially music teachers. When her savings were exhausted she found work in a department store and then in a small theater. Finally, "the inevitable" happened after a supper at which she was induced to drink a little too much wine, "and from that the descent became easy.... step-by-step she went down — till one gray morning her body was found on the banks of the Seine, and was saved from being buried in an unknown grave by some of the chorus girls in the theater where she had last appeared."[49] Freund's speeches were covered by prominent newspapers in Baltimore, Chicago, Detroit, Cincinnati, and other American cities. At one point the United States ambassador to Germany was interviewed regarding the safety of American girls in Berlin.[50]

The problems were not confined to singers — instrumentalists too were warned that they were vulnerable to the teacher who would rob them of their money or their innocence. In an article, aimed at parents, entitled "The Truth About Music Student Life in Vienna Revealed by a Viennese Virtuoso," Franz Wilczek warned that it was unwise and impractical to send a daughter abroad and subject her to "all sorts of temptations" just so she could come home and play the "$5,000 tune" she had learned in Europe.[51] In 1918 foreign correspondent Lenora Raines warned readers of *Musical America* that even those girls who realized the error of their ways and returned to America might already have been irreparably damaged — "spoiled for domesticity, for the appetite for the glamor, irregularity and unconventionality of pension or restaurant life has got into their blood; and it is difficult to resume old habits of routine work once they have been given up."[52]

The advisability of a young woman pursuing music seriously was also an issue in the fiction of the period. Novels generally urged caution and idealized the life of the girl who stayed home, or at least returned there to do her domestic duty. Typical was *The Charlatans*, published in 1906.[53] It tells the story of Hope Winston, a farmer's daughter from the town of Stillwater, who longs for a more exciting life. Her musical talent leads her to the Colossus Conservatory of Music, where she encounters, among others, its director Dr. Erdmann, who is obviously attracted to her beauty as much as her talent. She also meets

Cartoon from a 1914 issue of *Musical America.* Caption read, "The American Woman in Berlin — Oh, Professor, don't play so languishingly, or I'll write to the musical paper that my morals are jeopardized." ("How Berlin Views the Propaganda." *Musical America*, March 28, 1914, p. 9.)

Mr. Gray, a music critic with the profile of a Greek god. One evening she attends a recital of the world-famous pianist Madame Friedenthal, a character modeled after Fannie Bloomfield-Zeisler.[54] Friedenthal derives no pleasure from her music. "She is always working, always thinking ... striving to produce this and that effect. It is pathetic."[55] Overwhelmed by Madame Friedenthal's artistry and filled with self-doubt, Hope asks the artist's advice regarding her own chances for success. When Madame is encouraging, Hope rededicates her life to music. But then something terrible happens. A fellow conservatory student drowns herself just before her debut recital. The newspaper describes the incident as "the self-destruction of a pretty music student whose reason had been unsettled by excess of study."[56] Hope, dressed in black, performs in her place. She then returns to Stillwater, pursued by Mr. Gray. They pledge undying love. She says that she always wanted him more than she wanted music. And they live happily ever after. The plot of this novel underscores several of the themes which dominated the popular literature for girls: big cities were dangerous places where girls could lose both money and virtue; the best life was at home with a husband and family; and too much work and thought were dangerous to female health. (This last argument was also used to discourage young women of the period from attending college.)

Both Fannie Bloomfield-Zeisler and Maud Powell, previously ardent supporters of study abroad and certainly not advocates of women trading their ambitions for domesticity, changed their positions and advised young women to study music in the United States. Bloomfield-Zeisler went so far as to state she would rather see her daughter "in her grave" than embarking for Europe to prepare for a musical career. On another occasion she stated that she was not "against Europe, but for America," calling on artist colleagues, orchestras, managers, publishers and musical societies "to educate the public up to an impartial attitude toward our native talent."[57] Maud Powell advised that a girl should not go abroad alone because the temptations were more numerous, and her "bold and unselfconscious American ways" could be easily misinterpreted. Even Amy Fay's effusive book contained a disclaimer at the end, as Melusina wrote, "My sister hopes that no American girl who reads this book will be influenced by it to rashly attempt what she herself undertook ... to be trained in Europe from an amateur into an artist. Its pages have afforded glimpses only, of the trials and difficulties with which a girl may meet when studying art alone in a foreign land, but they should not therefore be underrated. Piano teaching has developed immensely in America since the date of the first of the foregoing letters.... American teachers best understand the American temperament, and therefore are by far the best for American pupils until they have got beyond the pupil stage."[58]

It is difficult to distinguish between moral concern and growing pride in American autonomy from Europe, particularly in the comments of Powell and

Cartoon which appeared in a 1914 issue of the *Ohio State Journal,* portraying the innocent American music student entering the sinister world of "study in Europe." The bag of money she holds reads, "Eight Million Dollars Annually." (*Ohio State Journal,* January 21, 1914, p. 3.)

Bloomfield-Zeisler. Both women believed strongly in the potential of the United States and felt that America was making great strides in its musical development. But other commentators such as Freund played upon fears about the moral vulnerability of young American women, invariably advising them to stay home and chart a less precarious course.

For those musicians who did study in Europe, the period immediately following their return to the United States was one of stress and uncertainty. Most were not yet twenty years old. While in Europe they had been immersed in music and art; when they returned, they frequently found themselves isolated, both geographically and culturally, with no role models to guide them. In addition, they had returned to a country where the market for their services remained underdeveloped because Americans had few opportunities to hear fine playing; where artist management was still in its infancy; and where there were no established recital circuits and relatively few sponsoring organizations with which to negotiate contracts and launch a career. Trained in music, not in business, these young people generally had no clue as to how to begin. Most settled temporarily in a large city — usually New York — with their parent or guardian. While they immersed themselves in practicing, their mother, former teacher, or other advocate tried to find a way for them to break into the performance market. Maud Powell remembered this as the unhappiest time in her life. "I missed the student life, the sound of music all about me, the talk of music and comparing of ideas with fellow-students. I missed the architecture, the parks, the organized life of well-governed cities. In fact I was miserably homesick. I felt lost and was like a rudderless ship.... Many were the times when I longed to seek advice in both a musical and a business way, but I was morbidly shy and foolishly proud, so I pegged away alone, often wondering if I were on the right track." Powell said she felt this way for most of six or eight years. "Despair was in my heart, and I wondered constantly if I was a fool to keep on. I doubted my talent (at times), I doubted my strength and endurance, I doubted the ultimate reward of my labors. Yet I kept on, simply because of the 'something' within that drove me on."[59]

John Freund recalled the time when young Fannie Bloomfield was "struggling, in despair, to gain a hearing in New York. I recall those tearful scenes when imperious talent could not understand why it did not receive instant recognition."[60] Olga Samaroff told how she and her mother shared a "dismal little room on a dark court at the St. Hubert Hotel near Carnegie Hall.... New York, vast, stony and indifferent, chilled us both as we aimlessly walked the streets discussing the visit to [manager] Wolfsohn and the next move. Mother was in favor of going at once to St. Louis where she had already made new friends. She believed I could earn my living there as a teacher, but I was haunted by the thought of all the sacrifices my family had made for my education. It seemed out of the question to renounce all possibility of a concert career without making a more determined effort to justify what had been done for me." Samaroff remembered this as a "period of agonizing uncertainty," and said that only her mother's spirits and ingenious handling of their meager funds allowed her to persevere.[61]

Fortunate timing was vital when launching a career because managers assumed that the market for women soloists was limited, and they were unwilling to take one on as a client unless the token position at the top was vacant.[62] The key to launching a successful career was meeting and impressing an influential musician, manager, or wealthy patron who would back or promote the new talent. Gaining such support usually required a degree of courage, or at least temporary boldness, on the musician's part. Maud Powell, for example, gained the support of conductor Theodore Thomas after she returned from Europe in 1885, but not until she took the initiative. Powell's violin teacher from Aurora, Illinois, knew Thomas and wrote him several times, requesting a hearing for the young artist. When they received no reply (Thomas was on tour and apparently did not receive the letters until later), eighteen-year-old

Powell took things into her own hands. She and her mother went to New York's Steinway Hall, where Thomas was rehearsing his orchestra. When the rehearsal ended, Powell approached Thomas: "My heart was in my throat, but I managed to say pretty bravely, 'Mr. Thomas, I am Maud Powell, and I want you to give me a chance to play for you.'" With Thomas conducting the orchestra, she played the Bruch violin concerto (which she had performed with the Berlin Philharmonic earlier that year). Thomas immediately engaged her for his next concert and several thereafter.[63]

In the case of Olga Samaroff, several years had elapsed between her study in Europe and her desire to launch a career because she had been briefly married and then divorced. Manager Henry Wolfsohn advised her to return to Europe and perform in order to get more recent European press notices. But she and her mother were almost completely out of money, so another trip to Europe was out of the question. Wolfsohn then suggested that they rent Carnegie Hall and hire an orchestra — he would see to it that the hall was filled by giving away the tickets. They scraped together the money to finance the concert and the performance resulted in enough positive press to launch Samaroff's successful career.

Since success depended upon public image as much as musical ability, an artist's name formed an important part of the package. Managers believed that a European surname — especially if it sounded Russian or Slavic — could contribute significantly to one's credibility, since most virtuosos in America had been Europeans with Russian or other Slavic names. The public should think they were hearing an exotic European and not an ordinary American. Thus, in an ironic reversal of the usual pattern in which a European name was anglicized to allow an immigrant to assimilate more easily, artists with American-sounding surnames often changed them the other way. Hence Lucie Hickenlooper became Olga Samaroff and Ethel Liggins became Ethel Leginska. As Hickenlooper/Samaroff observed, "It is no reflection upon Mr. Paderewski's art to wonder if his box office success would have been quite as great if, while playing the piano just as wonderfully, he had been a Mr. John Doe from Emporia, Kansas."[64] Thus equipped with a European education, European press notices, and a European-sounding surname, the American musician was ready to embark on a career in the United States.

"An Able Musician and Delightful to Look At"

Touring North America

The emergence of the United States as an economic power in the mid–nineteenth century set the stage for growth in many areas including the arts. Thousands of miles of new railroad track tied distant locations together; during the 1850s and 1860s alone, total mileage increased from 9,000 to 30,000. Prosperity and urban growth encouraged the founding of new musical institutions: the New York Philharmonic Society in 1842, the New York Symphony in 1878, the Boston Symphony in 1881, the Chicago Orchestra (later the Chicago Symphony) in 1891, the Cincinnati Orchestra in 1894, and the Philadelphia Orchestra in 1900. The American Opera Company began performances in New York in 1886 and the Castle Square Opera Company in Boston in 1897. In 1889, *Harper's Weekly* estimated that there were more than 10,000 military bands active in the United States, and professional bands such as those led by Patrick S. Gilmore and John Philip Sousa enjoyed great popularity.[1]

The spread of cultural events was not restricted to large cities. The "secularization of leisure"[2] was evident across the country as towns of all sizes from Utica, New York, to Red Cloud, Nebraska, built concert halls, opera houses, and assembly halls. Since only the largest cities could support resident performing groups, local managers sought outside talent to attract audiences. Drawn by the new markets and aided in their mobility by the recent proliferation of steamboat and railroad routes, touring groups took to the road. These itinerants represented a broad spectrum of "highbrow" and "lowbrow" genres — acrobats, minstrel shows, and trained animal acts went on tour, as well as theater and opera companies, bands and orchestras, and smaller performing ensembles.[3] It was not an easy life: distances were enormous; travel was slow and connections awkward; weather conditions often interfered with plans; hotels were not guaranteed to be clean or comfortable; and the food could be

51

unspeakable. Success required nerves, patience, endurance, and flexibility as much as it did performing ability.

The first European piano virtuoso to tour America was Leopold de Meyer in 1845. Usually traveling alone, de Meyer made all the necessary arrangements when he arrived at his destination. He came several days before a performance, found and rented a hall, placed ads in newspapers, posted playbills, and distributed tickets that were sold in bookstores, music stores, and hotels. He often hired other artists to share the program, since soloists in this period did not perform whole concerts by themselves. Sometimes he arranged to play between the acts in the local playhouse. Once in New York, for example, he performed during the intermissions between three light comedies, *The Green-Eyed Monster*, *The Bengal Tiger*, and *My Neighbor's Wife*.[4]

As engagements multiplied and arrangements grew more complex, it became impossible for the performer to do it all. Both the size of the country and the constantly changing nature of the touring circuits rendered a manager or impresario indispensable to make publicity, transportation, and theater arrangements. By the late 1840s a small group of New York–based, European-born impresarios appeared on the scene to plan the tours. The three most prominent were Maurice Strakosch, Bernard Ullmann, and Max Maretzek. Motivated by economics, managers planned tours which packed the largest number of concerts into the shortest possible time or distance.[5]

Touring imposed intense and unrelenting demands on the artist. For eight months in 1856 Sigismund Thalberg performed almost every night of the week except Sunday. Sometimes he played two or three times a day — a concert for schoolchildren in the morning, a matinee in the afternoon, and another recital in the evening. In 1862 Louis Moreau Gottschalk gave 109 concerts in 120 days. On his 1872-73 tour, Anton Rubinstein performed 215 concerts in 239 days.[6]

Traveling by steamboat and railroad in the nineteenth century was not always easy or pleasant. One performer taking a steamboat down the Mississippi to New Orleans around 1860 reported that the boat got stuck on sand bars three times — once for 36 hours. At another point on the same trip the boat appeared to be sinking, and half the cargo had to be thrown overboard before help arrived.[7] Railroad schedules took no account of the rhythms of a performer's life — trains commonly left the station at daybreak, allowing no time to relax or unwind if there had been a performance the previous night. Emilie Cowell, traveling with her actor husband in 1860–61, described their twelve-and-a-half-hour trip from Louisville, Kentucky, to Nashville, Tennessee — a distance of 175 miles. They got up at 5 a.m. to catch the 6:30 train and arrived in Nashville at seven in the evening, traveling at an average speed of 14 miles an hour.[8] Louis Moreau Gottschalk once said he spent so much time on the railroad that his home was "somewhere between the baggage car and the last car on the train."[9]

The train trip itself was often hot, dirty and uncomfortable, plagued by overheated cars and uneven railbeds. Emilie Cowell endured "ceaseless jolting, the stifling fumes from the stove, and the nauseating hawking and spitting and 'greasy sweat'" that pervaded the cars, while bumpy tracks often caused the cars to sway. Cowell recorded feeling ill when she and her husband boarded the hot and crowded train, "especially as the outside was so keen and frosty." Passengers frequently opened windows in the overheated cars, allowing so much soot and dust to enter that "one could watch one's clothes change color." The Lackawanna Railroad advertised in 1905 that it had solved the dirt problem when it switched to anthracite coal. It ran a series of ads showing "Miss Phoebe Snow," always spotless in her white clothing. One caption read, "Miss Phoebe Snow/ About to go/ Upon a trip to Buffalo/ My gown stays white/ From morn to night/ Upon the road of Anthracite."[10]

Another problem was the necessity of changing trains, sometimes in the middle of the night. Since the rail system included many short, independent lines, it was not unusual to have to transfer. Sometimes it was possible to switch a sleeping car from one train to another without the passengers having to disembark, but even then it was difficult to sleep through the noise of the switch. The standard inconveniences of train travel were especially stressful for performers — if they had to change trains and missed a connection, or if a train was late, they could arrive too late for a performance.[11]

The average speed of trains in 1888 was 25 miles per hour, due in part to frequent stops. The schedule for an acting company on tour in 1887–88 indicates that the fastest run among the 66 towns on the tour was a 354-mile stretch from Pittsburgh to Philadelphia which took nine and one-half hours racing along at an average clip of 37 miles an hour. The slowest was a 102-mile jog from Dubuque to Davenport, Iowa, which consumed 11 hours and 20 minutes at an average speed of about nine miles an hour.[12]

Touring pianists had the additional problem of transporting a piano. The earliest European virtuosos brought their own instruments with them, since no American piano had yet achieved an international reputation and grand pianos were scarce in the 1840s, and even if an instrument were available in a given location, its condition would be questionable. Hence the performer normally transported his piano with him on the train. On one particularly crowded and noisy ride in New York State, Louis Moreau Gottschalk escaped to the baggage car for a quiet cigar, only to realize that he sat resting between the crate containing his Chickering piano and two coffins.[13] Sometimes the piano was shipped independently of the performer, occasionally with startling results. When pianist Henri Herz began his recital in a coastal California town in 1845, his instrument could only produce variously tuned gurgling sounds. Apparently the movers had found the "box" too heavy to carry and had "floated" it part of the way from San Francisco.[14] Leopold de Meyer, Sigismund Thalberg, and Hans von Bülow compounded their problems by traveling with not one, but *two* pianos, which were placed on the stage facing each other. By playing half the program on one piano and half on the other, the virtuoso enabled the audience on each side of the hall to see his face and fingers for at least half of the concert.[15]

By the 1860s and 1870s several established American piano companies sponsored the tours of the most prominent virtuosos. Chickering, Steinway, Decker Brothers, and others provided the artist with a piano to take on tour in exchange for the unsurpassed publicity of having him perform all over the country on their instrument. The manufacturer's name was generally displayed prominently on the side of the piano facing the audience.[16]

One of the most successful examples of piano sponsorship was the relationship between the Steinway Piano Company and Paderewski. Steinway sponsored Paderewski's first tour of America in 1891, a tour so profitable that the firm was willing to promise him almost anything if he would undertake another. Since the pianist had been particularly upset by the travel conditions on his first tour, Steinway offered him his own Pullman car fitted with all the comforts of home — a bedroom, a bathroom, a dining room, and a sitting room with piano. He was also given the means to travel with the largest entourage of any artist on the road. At one time there were 13 in his party including a secretary, a treasurer, a baggage master, his wife and her maid, a chef, two porters and another traveling companion. "The prepared [train] timetables read like military operations, with minute instructions as to which train the carriage was to be coupled to at what time, which siding it was to be left on, and when it would have to be shunted up to a platform so Paderewski could emerge to go and give his concert, but he remained detached from all this and could relax in its comfort, keeping his own hours."[17]

Most virtuosos were less fortunate. Italian-German pianist Ferruccio Busoni articulated his ambivalence about life on the road in a letter to his wife in 1910. After traveling by train from New York to Columbus, Ohio, to Pittsburgh and back to New York in a three-day period with two concerts in between, he wrote, "From the standpoint of a touring artist, the concert yesterday was very satisfactory — full house, a feeling of excitement and enthusiastic criticisms ... a beautiful piano, good acoustics, and the feeling of great expectation in the hall hypnotized me for the two hours I was on the platform. From the standpoint of the thinking artist, no longer young, it was an unforgivable waste of strength, time and thought, which can never be recovered, in order to make a momentary impression on a small number of insignificant people."[18]

A woman contemplating a performer's life faced additional obstacles. Not until the early decades of the nineteenth century did women begin to travel independently of their families. The more than seventy new etiquette books published between 1830 and 1870 provide evidence of the need for rules to guide women as they left the confines of the home to navigate dangerous public spaces. By the time of the Civil War one such book allowed that an unmarried young woman in the North could take the train by herself, although she was advised to travel with a male companion, avoid contact with strangers whenever possible, dress modestly, and wear a veil.[19]

The woman traveling alone was sailing uncharted waters. Louisa May Alcott described her experience as a Civil War nurse going by train from Boston to Washington, D.C. When she boldly took the initiative and spoke to a husband traveling with his wife, the gentleman answered "very civilly" but was unaccustomed to being addressed by "strange women in public conveyances." Alcott reported that his wife "fixed her green eyes upon me, as if she thought me a forward huzzy, or whatever is good English for a presuming young woman."[20] By the later decades of the century it grew more common for unmarried professional women to travel, so that by 1907 *Mary Sherwood's Rules of Etiquette for Spinsters* stated that in the United States it was socially acceptable to travel alone if you were a "woman of talent," such as a physician, artist, or musician.[21]

One of the only published accounts of a woman musician traveling unescorted is that of violinist Camilla Urso's train journey from New York to Boston in January of 1867 for a concert with the Harvard Musical Association. As the story was told by a contemporary biographer, she set out two days before the performance but the train took 36 hours to get from Worcester to Boston because of a snowstorm. Snow again blocked the train when it arrived in Boston an hour before the concert. A gentleman and fellow passenger, carrying Urso's violin, set out with her to walk the rest of the way, but her hands got uncomfortably cold and she began to feel faint. The man carried her to the signal house to get warm, and when she had sufficiently recovered (supposedly restoring the warmth to her hands by rubbing them in the signalman's shaggy hair), they took a sleigh to the hall.[22]

Most early women musicians in effect traveled with escorts since they usually performed as members of small concert companies — mixed groups of five or six singers and instrumentalists who traveled together on tours lasting anywhere from several weeks to several months. A typical group, organized by Max Strakosch in 1873, consisted of three singers — a soprano, a contralto, and a tenor, violinist Émile Sauret, pianist Teresa Carreño, a conductor, and an accompanist. Before embarking on their tour the troupe gave a debut performance at Steinway Hall in New York in September of 1872. According to the *New York Tribune* the next day, "Fashionable society was fairly well represented, and a multitude of people from the world of art was there also ... including pianist Anton Rubinstein and violinist Henryk Wieniawski." The group was on the road from September 1872 to May

1873, performing in east-coast cities, the South as far as Galveston, the West as far as Chicago, and parts of Canada.[23]

Such troupes usually presented a variety of short selections, generally alternating serious music with lighter fare in order to provide something for every taste. Often one of the performers would provide comic relief, frequently the tenor who would sing a humorous song from a comic opera. On this particular tour, Teresa Carreño and Émile Sauret performed violin and piano sonatas from the standard classical repertoire, the most popular being the Kreutzer sonata by Beethoven.[24]

Audiences were for the most part less sophisticated outside the large cities, and serious musicians sometimes found this disheartening. A singer on tour with Camilla Urso's company in 1875 concluded regretfully that it was not the music itself that aroused people's interest, but instead the things which seemed astonishing in some way, such as an especially high or soft note that reminded them of something else or a sustained tone held for what seemed an impossibly long time. In one small town the singer impulsively substituted a song about a little bird for the opera aria listed on the printed program; she "represented the feathered songster in a long, drawn-out high note." It was clear from the newspaper account the next day that neither the reviewer nor the audience had noticed the substitution.[25] Sometimes the astonishing element or "stunt" was featured in the advertising, which also distressed some musicians. Teresa Carreño sardonically observed that P. T. Barnum advertised Jenny Lind in the same way he advertised a great elephant: "Those who were interested in animals went to see the elephant, and those who were interested in music went to see Jenny Lind." One of Carreño's friends urged her to give up performing in America altogether and return to Germany, where people understood and appreciated "music in all its dignity."[26]

Concert troupes were often hastily assembled, sometimes teaming a well-known performer with a group of lesser-knowns — as one contemporary account described it, "a fading stellar magnitude giving its name to a group of lesser satellites." It was especially difficult to tour together for months at a time when performers barely knew one another or had little in common. The most successful tours combined artists who enjoyed each other's company. Edward Marzo, the accompanist on the 1873 Strakosch tour, noted that there was "much good fellowship" in this particular company. But, he added, that they did spend time apart, "for at the hotels where we stopped we separated in little coteries." He also reported that during this tour Carreño and Sauret became "very much attached" to each other and married soon after.[27]

The most prominent women musicians toured as featured soloists with leading bands and orchestras. American women were more sought-after than American men for these solo positions, partly in the belief that a woman's presence would lend a decorative element to a stage full of soberly clad men, but also out of concern that a featured virtuoso should be somewhat exotic. Since American audiences pictured male virtuosos as dashing Europeans like Rubinstein or Paderewski, American men simply did not measure up in the public imagination. Although several American men *were* prominent instrumental soloists in the late nineteenth and early twentieth centuries, they appeared ordinary compared to their European counterparts. According to music historian Arthur Loesser, even outstanding performers such as John Pattison, Charles Jarvis, and William Sherwood seemed to audiences more like "house agents or soap salesmen" than exciting virtuosos — a phenomenon which opened the door for a few exceptional women.[28]

Bandmasters like Patrick Gilmore and John Philip Sousa commonly employed the finest women soloists to perform between selections by the band. Both Camilla Urso and Maud Powell toured with Gilmore's band, and Powell traveled with Sousa's as well. Sousa, who toured regularly from 1892 to 1932, chose vocalists (always sopranos), violinists, or harpists for this purpose. Gilmore also regularly hired women vocalists and violinists. Amy Leslie, critic for the *Chicago News*, reported that every "girl" who sang or played with the Sousa band was "an able musician and delightful to look at."[29]

Sousa saw these soloists as women first and musicians second, obviously viewing their careers as temporary interludes. In his autobiography he included a copy of a note that he wrote to a singer whose pitch was consistently high: "Dear Madam: Please raise your petticoat two inches and lower your voice one inch." He also cheerily reported that almost all of the "splendid group of American girls" who accompanied his band on tour eventually "married and led happy, successful lives…. The band got the reputation of being a sort of matrimonial bureau … [and] even if the girl was disinclined toward matrimony, the moment she sang with our band marriage came her way." He then listed the soloists who had toured with him and the names of the men they married.[30]

Sousa was very protective of his women soloists, requiring them to room together and avoid unnecessary association with the bandsmen. Violinist Powell and soprano Estelle Liebling, for example, were treated to first-class hotels that were different from the men's. Sousa also expected the young women to dine, travel, and go sightseeing with him and Mrs. Sousa. Occasionally a soloist would rebel at being "penned up like a hot-house flower." If Sousa ever learned that a band member made a derogatory remark about a female soloist, he reputedly "promptly and physically thrashed the individual and personally removed him from the train at the next stop."[31]

In addition to touring with the prominent professional bands of the period, women instrumental soloists traveled with several of the orchestras that began touring North America in the late decades of the nineteenth century. Usually the featured soloist performed a concerto with the orchestra; occasionally she played a solo between orchestral selections. The most famous touring orchestra of the period was the Theodore Thomas Orchestra. Thomas, who eventually founded the Chicago Symphony, traveled with his orchestra along a railroad route which formed a core itinerary of 28 cities in twelve states that became known as the "Thomas Highway." The group played in the east from Maine to Georgia, the south as far as New Orleans, the midwestern states, and the far West through to California. The orchestra also presented concert series — often as many as 12 or 14 programs annually — in cities like Boston and Chicago, until these cities established their own resident orchestras.[32]

Touring orchestras performed in out-of-the-way locations where many in the audience were attending their first professional musical performance. One story that made the rounds among members of the Thomas Orchestra concerned a person in the audience who was greatly disappointed because the bass drum was given "only one smash" during the entire performance, even though "they toted it all the way from Chicago." Townspeople were often startled to see men with musical instruments disembarking from the train — occasionally someone asked a musician when the parade was going to start.[33]

Thomas did not hire a soloist for his first tour in 1869 because he could not afford the extra expense. Instead he called upon members of the orchestra to play the solo parts. For his second tour in 1870, however, he felt he could afford to hire a soloist of reputation and chose the "pretty and energetic" twenty-one-year-old German pianist Anna Mehlig. Mehlig sometimes performed solo pieces between selections by the orchestra but primarily performed piano concertos. She had a large repertoire that included concertos by Beethoven, Chopin, Liszt, Weber, Gade, and Schumann. Not only were these pieces large and demanding, the pace of the trip was relentless as well. The tour began in Boston with concerts on seven consecutive evenings plus a Saturday matinee, and Mehlig played in all but one of the concerts.[34] When Thomas took his orchestra on its first transcontinental tour in 1883 he chose pianist Julie Rivé-King as featured soloist. She often performed six or seven times a week and sometimes twice in one day, playing one concerto for an afternoon matinee and another the same evening.[35] During the first season of the Chicago Symphony, 1891–92, three of the seven soloists scheduled by Thomas were women — Adele aus der Ohe, Julie Rivé-King, and Fannie Bloomfield-Zeisler.[36]

Conductors sometimes exhibited a paternalistic attitude toward women soloists. When Rivé-King toured with the New York Philharmonic in 1875, conductor Carl Bergmann was "dreadfully anxious" about her performance of the Liszt piano concerto because she intended to perform "without notes" (by memory), as was her usual practice. "My dear little girl," Bergmann asked her at a rehearsal, "what if you should happen to forget?" Rivé-King, then twenty-one years old, confidently replied, "I shall *not* forget; I know not only my own part of this concerto, but every note of the orchestra parts, also."[37]

As with smaller performing troupes, train schedules often required orchestras to arrive on the day of the performance and leave immediately afterwards, necessitating many all-night train rides. When the Theodore Thomas Orchestra toured in 1883, a Kansas City newspaper reported that the musicians arrived in the morning after an all-night ride from St. Louis, where they had just completed a series of three concerts. After the morning rehearsal, the group "did not feel much like sight-seeing," and soloist Julie Rivé-King felt so bad that she remained in the hotel until the evening performance.[38]

Sometimes, of course, trains were dangerous as well as inconvenient. Derailments and collisions were fairly common. During the 1873 tour of the Strakosch concert troupe, the passengers traveling from Atlanta to Macon, Georgia, were abruptly awakened in the middle of the night when their train collided with another. Some passengers were hurt and since the musicians occupied the only sleeping car, they gave it up to the injured. After the troupe had camped in the woods from four o'clock in the morning until four the following afternoon, a rescue train picked them up. For most of this time it rained, and they had nothing to eat.[39] A 1908 review reported that cellist May Muckle gave a fine performance with the Theodore Thomas Orchestra despite the fact that she had been "seriously shaken up" in a railroad accident. A 1917 review similarly reported that pianist Ethel Leginska gave a "brilliant program" with the New York Symphony, even though she had been struck by a falling partition the previous night when her train collided with another.[40]

Some concerts took place in structures originally intended for other purposes. Musicians frequently performed in hotel ballrooms or dining rooms, especially in small resort cities like Niagara Falls or Newport, Rhode Island. Occasionally they played in churches.[41] Julie Rivé-King once appeared with Theodore Thomas in two concerts in Chicago's Exposition Building and in 1883 performed with the Thomas Orchestra in a cavernous building in Memphis which usually served as an exhibition hall for products manufactured in that city.[42] Such spaces were often inadequately heated. It was so cold in the theater in Elmira, New York, that the Strakosch troupe performed wearing furs and overcoats. One reporter described a performance in Grand Rapids, Michigan, as having taken place in a hall that would "make a good training school for a polar expedition."[43]

Hotels ranged from excellent to dismal. Olga Samaroff divided pre–World War I American hotels into three categories: "very good, fair to middling, and the kind that had ropes beside the windows by means of which one was supposed to lower oneself to the ground in case of fire."[44] Theodore Thomas's letters to his wife during the orchestra's 1900 tour included frequent complaints about overheated rooms and occasional references to bedbugs. Pianist Ferruccio Busoni wrote his wife on a particularly bleak winter afternoon in Chicago in 1910: "My window faces the sea, and I overlook an endless flatness of shining ice and snow. A white desert! Boundless and hopeless, and behind me lies the town, just as black as this is white. I sit the whole day in the hotel; my most serious occupation is regulating the central heating."[45] Pianist Yolanda Merö started to fill the bathtub in her Cincinnati hotel in 1911 only to learn that the murky water flowing from the tap came directly from the Ohio River.[46]

Food on the road was erratic as well. Even though trains arrived at all hours of the day and night, hotels served meals only at set times, and musicians frequently survived on apples, stale bread, or frozen eggs. Pianist Katharine Goodson and her husband subsisted on a cereal concoction called "cream of rye" for several days in Minneapolis in 1913, while pianist Mark Hambourg claimed to have eaten nothing but bread and milk for three days on tour in the West.[47]

The informal camaraderie that was possible for women members of a small concert troupe was almost nonexistent for those touring with a band or orchestra. Being a soloist and not a member of the ensemble set one apart from members of the orchestra, who had been friends and colleagues before the tour and would remain so afterwards. In addition, since almost everyone else on the tour was male, the informal activities between concerts were naturally male oriented, usually involving sports, smoking, and cards. A 1911 photograph in *Musical America* shows the local baseball management offering the members of an orchestra the use of their playing field before the concert. Another photograph from the same period pictures the men enjoying a game of impromptu volleyball near the train. Orchestra manager Frank Edwards reported in 1911 that between concerts the members of his orchestra got as much fun out of a trip as possible, "just as any crowd of men would. On the train they talk, read, smoke, play skat, and break the monotony with any diversion which suggests itself." He added that on one tour the Cincinnati Orchestra played softball at every opportunity.[48]

When women began touring on their own as solo recitalists they generally traveled with at least one friend or family member. Well-known pianists also included in their entourage a piano tuner/manager provided by the manufacturer to maintain the instrument and help the artist with the practical details of the trip. This arrangement eased the way for pianists of both sexes, but for women in particular it guaranteed that at least one member of her party served as a manager/escort. Fannie Bloomfield-Zeisler toured the Pacific Coast in 1894 and again in 1896 accompanied by her tuner, a secretary, and her brother. Pianist Olga Samaroff toured seven American cities with singer Geraldine Farrar in 1909 taking along two tuners, two maids, and their two mothers. During violinist Maud Powell's first years of touring, she was always accompanied by her mother.[49] Since a violinist was not subsidized by a manufacturer, and thus could not depend on the services of a tuner/manager, for most of her long career Powell toured with her husband and manager, W. Godfrey Turner.

Many of the most successful women musicians were married to their managers, including Camilla Urso, Julie Rivé-King, Maud Powell, and, briefly, Ethel Leginska. This arrangement was mutually beneficial in many ways, since it provided the women with emotional support and companionship, protected them from "predatory" males, gave them a respectability that unmarried female performers did not necessarily have, and kept the proceeds of the tour in the family.[50]

One of the earliest examples of a successful instrumentalist who was married to her manager was violinist Camilla Urso, who wed Frederic Luer in Paris in 1862. Luer arranged tours that took his wife's concert troupe all over the United States and Europe, and as far afield as Australia in 1879 and 1894, and South Africa in 1895. He expertly handled all the innumerable details. As one satisfied member of the troupe reported, "Mr. Luer never failed to telegraph ahead both for rooms for our party and for a closed carriage to take us to the hall." He also provided emotional support in stressful situations. In one dramatic example the troupe had to cross the frozen Missouri River in an omnibus in order to make a train connection in Nebraska. Urso was frightened that the ice would break. "With every rasp and creak of the wheels she took to shrieking hysterically with fright. We all of us did our best to quiet and reassure her, and her husband, who was always very patient with her in her outbursts, tried to soothe her as one might a child. I shall never forget that crossing of the Missouri."[51]

Teresa Carreño was another prominent instrumentalist who was married to her manager, at least for the latter part of her career. After three tempestuous marriages to musicians, her marriage to nonmusician Arturo Tagliapietra proved successful. Tagliapietra combined the duties of secretary, companion, and maid. "Arturo knew by intuition when to be silent [and] when to disappear.... In a thousand little ways Arturo knew how to make himself useful; ... he tirelessly made order in the business files; ... he got along with her children — he soothed her nerves."[52]

Both Julie Rivé and Maud Powell married experienced concert managers. Frank King, who had worked at various times as a music critic and a representative of the large American piano firm Decker Brothers, managed the Theodore Thomas Orchestra during its most extensive American tour in 1883. The editor of *Musical America* described King as "a character. He was a big man, weighing 300 pounds, genial in nature, a good musician. The combination of her playing and his advertising ability proved a worthy collaboration."[53] Frank King's sister observed that he "never let the public get at her; ... he made friends for both and did everything for her, keeping her as sacred as a queen." Rivé-King relied heavily on her husband's advice and had great difficulty making career-related decisions when he died. Faced with the choice of continuing to concertize or accepting a teaching position, she wrote, "O, for my angel Frank to help me think." During the same period, when she tried to arrange performance engagements without his help, she expressed frustration at having to correspond with male managers, saying she found it easier to make arrangements through women's music clubs because women were less intimidating to deal with. She felt that as a single woman she was treated unfairly in business dealings, and many of her friends and business associates urged her to remarry. Although she apparently received several offers, she chose to remain single. "I am not easy to please in that respect," she said. "I look at life very differently without Frank."[54]

Godfrey Turner was likewise a well-respected concert manager when he met Maud Powell while serving as manager of the Sousa band during Powell's tour with them as soloist. A genial man with a mischievous sense of humor, he took obvious pride in his wife's accomplishments. His skillful advertising created the striking silhouette of Powell standing in profile holding her violin, an image which became immediately recognizable to readers of contemporary music periodicals.[55]

Ethel Leginska was also married for a time to the man who served as her manager. For the first two years of her marriage to writer and composer Emerson Whithorne, from 1907 to 1909, Whithorne added managing her career to his list of musical responsibilities. Theirs was initially a mutually beneficial professional partnership — she promoted his compositions by performing them in recitals, and they sometimes performed two-piano works together. Before long, however, their strong wills clashed. Although they did not legally divorce until 1917, they separated around 1910 and pursued their individual careers.

Starting in 1921 Leginska was aided substantially by the energies of her friend and former student Lucille Oliver. While there is no evidence of a physical relationship between the two, the younger woman took over all the practical aspects of Leginska's life from that year until they died within months of each other in 1970. Oliver's friendship with Leginska appears to resemble that of Willa Cather and Edith Lewis. For 39 years Lewis "fended away callers, helped correct the galleys, and did everything that 'literary wives' are supposed to do."[56] Oliver explained in 1932: "Leginska has time for her art. She never sewed on a button, nor bothered about cooking, nor thought about anything connected with the housework.... She simply doesn't bother about any of the petty daily duties that are expected of most women, and which can so easily take twenty-four hours of the day. Most women can't stop bothering about these things and, therefore, they never become real artists."[57] Oliver served Leginska in a musical capacity as well, teaching some of Leginska's students until they were advanced enough to study with her. Oliver's versatility was challenged still further when she served for a time as tympanist in Leginska's National Women's Symphony.[58]

On tour, female virtuosos emphasized their devotion to high art, eschewing overly facile showmanship and programming predominantly from the classical repertoire for their recitals. Julie Rivé-King, for example, typically performed pieces by Bach, Handel, and Beethoven, followed by those of Romantic composers such as Chopin, Schumann, and Liszt. A Carreño program usually consisted of works by Chopin, Schumann, Liszt, and American composer Edward MacDowell. Fannie Bloomfield-Zeisler frequently programmed sets of shorter pieces by Chopin, Schumann, or Mendelssohn. These women employed none of the "stunts" used by the early male performers, lest they cross the fine line between artist and entertainer. The closest they came was performance of "program music" which expressed an emotion, conveyed an image, or told a story — this shifted the element of "entertainment" from the performer to the music itself. Julie Rivé-King frequently performed her popular composition "Bubbling Spring," in which the sound of the piano imitated the sound of rippling water. One of Fannie Bloomfield-Zeisler's most frequently requested pieces was a piano arrangement of Schubert's song "Erlkönig," which tells the story of a dying child.

Audiences accustomed to performances which included a mixture of types of entertainment were sometimes startled by whole programs consisting exclusively of "serious" music. On one occasion in the South, someone in the audience called out a request to Fannie Bloomfield-Zeisler that she play "Dixie." On another in 1888 the reviewer of a Bloomfield-Zeisler recital, a small-town reporter who usually covered sports, observed that the program was made up of "a series of unpronounceable names which developed into the most delightful music.... It was strictly classical however — rigidly and exclusively so. If a few numbers of popular music had been interspersed it would have been a pleasant change."[59]

However purist her programming, the successful touring musician had to be flexible enough to adapt to varied performance settings. On one occasion in 1907 when Olga Samaroff was scheduled to give a recital at a girls' school in the Middle West, the piano failed to show up, her trunk went astray, and she and her mother arrived after dark at a train station where there was no cab or carriage to take them to town. The railroad agent found a "stray boy" to help carry their baggage through the rain to the school, which was a half mile away. When they finally arrived cold, tired, and wet, Samaroff assumed that the recital would be postponed, but the disappointed students had been waiting and begged her to play. They brought her dry clothes and she performed on an old upright piano. By the end of the program all were in such good spirits that the floor was cleared and everyone danced.[60] For a Seattle recital in 1907, violinist Maud Powell performed in the huge Dreamland Rink, since the city had no large concert hall and so many people wanted to attend. "Mattresses were placed against the windows to keep out the noise of the trolleys, and the evening was one of the most successful of the whole tour."[61] As with appearances of touring bands and orchestras, performances by internationally known soloists were major events in many of the towns along the route. A grateful listener told Maud Powell after a recital in Ogden, Utah, in 1907, "Miss Powell, this is not the best concert we have ever had; it is the first."[62]

Most women performed fewer concerts per season than the earliest virtuosos like de Meyer, Gottschalk and Rubinstein, but they still kept up a strenuous pace.[63] Camilla Urso's concert company performed more than 200 concerts in 15 states, two territories, and Canada during the 1878–79 season. The Rivé-King Concert Company gave at least 136 concerts during the 1880–81 season. During a six-month period in the 1886–87 concert season, Rivé-King performed in approximately 126 concerts in 14 northeastern and midwestern states and two Canadian provinces. Teresa Carreño's management estimated in 1888 that she had performed an average of 150 concerts a year for the past 11 years. Olga Samaroff gave 70 performances between October 1906 and May 1907. In 1911, Maud Powell played 27 concerts from October to the Christmas holidays, after which she began an extensive tour of the South. In the single month of March 1917, Ethel Leginska played 14 recitals in 14 different American cities including Duluth, Chicago, Baltimore, New York, Boston, Charleston, and Forsyth, Georgia.[64]

It is difficult to compare the concert fees paid to male and female virtuosos since most contracts have not been saved or were verbal agreements between the performer and his or her management. Even when a fee appears in a printed source it is often uncertain whether the figure quoted refers to an entire season or a smaller number of performances. Not surprisingly, however, Olga Samaroff observed that in the music industry, male and female pianists were as separate "as the congregation of a Quaker meeting," and that women invariably received lower fees than men although they had the same degree of success and reputation.[65] In 1872–73 Anton Rubinstein's contract for his American tour called for 200 concerts at $200 a concert. A few years later he refused to undertake a second American tour, even though the fees offered were reputedly in the range of $500,000. In 1875 Hans von Bülow received $20,000 for a concert tour of the United States lasting four or five months. His 1889 contract gave him $12,000 for a five-week period. Paderewski netted $95,000 on his first American tour in 1891, $160,000 for 63 concerts in 1892 (or $2,539 per concert), and $280,000 for 92 concerts in 1895 (or $3,043 per concert.)[66] Women earned less. Julie Rivé-King was paid $200 per concert for forty performances when she toured with the Thomas Orchestra in 1883, with the stipulation that she would play no more than four times a week. In reality she played in 61 concerts, sometimes appearing in two performances a day and always performing more than four times a week. The Casino Concert Company offered Teresa Carreño $400 per concert for forty concerts in 1897. In 1898 Fannie Bloomfield-Zeisler's standard fee was $300 per recital. By 1910 it

Violinist Maude Powell traveling with a trio of musicians in 1909. Pictured are, left to right, Anne Muckle Ford, an unidentified woman, Maud Powell, and cellist May Muckle. (Maud Powell Society, Arlington, Virginia.)

was $500, but this was sometimes reduced for an appearance that could be sandwiched between two other geographically distant performances. In 1905 Olga Samaroff's manager arranged about 30 engagements all within a radius of 200 miles of New York — $300 was the highest fee on the list and $150 was the fee in some small towns. Samaroff reported that the highest fee a woman pianist could earn around 1906 was $500 to $600 per concert.[67]

European virtuosos toured America because they knew they could make a great deal of money relatively quickly. This does not mean that they were not fine musicians, but their reason for choosing America over Europe was financial. Many American musicians, however, notably Theodore Thomas, Julie Rivé-King, Maud Powell, and Fannie Bloomfield-Zeisler, espoused a "higher" calling, believing that bringing great music to the people of the United States was the musical equivalent of spreading the gospel in a new land. Imbued with the conviction that aesthetic and religious truths were of a higher order, they were convinced that music served not merely for entertainment and pleasure but also had a nobler purpose, and that by performing the best music all over the country they could lift people to a new level of beauty and understanding.[68] Theodore Thomas spoke of great music as a "character-building force" and an "uplifting influence" and called concerts "sermons in tones." When Maud Powell's friend commended her for playing at so many schools

all over the country, she replied, "I must carry a message as long as I am able." Powell's husband and manager Godfrey Turner explained that she wanted "to carry inspiration to the people who do not ordinarily hear artists of her rank. It is a sacred trust with her, and she will continue to do it as long as she can." Sigmund Zeisler observed that his wife was "not only possessed by ambition but considered it her duty to carry her message of beauty wherever people were enterprising enough to invite her."[69]

For female performers, living under this recurrent pressure at such an elevated pitch could

An early publicity photo of violinist Maud Powell. (Maud Powell Society, Arlington, Virginia.)

prove debilitating. All musicians, of course, deal with a variety of stresses generated by the demands of the profession rather than the gender of the performer. Performance anxiety or stage fright, constant travel, frequent changes of hotels and food, the stress of repeated performance, and the public nature of a performer's life — any or all of these can temporarily erode the physical or mental health of the hardiest individual, whether male or female. Nonetheless, articles in late nineteenth- and early twentieth-century periodicals allude with surprising frequency to a woman musician's temporary absence from the concert stage — an absence invariably said to have been caused by neurasthenia or a nervous breakdown: "Teresa Carreño in Stage of Collapse: Great

Pianiste Breaks Down Physically"; "Fannie Bloomfield-Zeisler in a State of Collapse Due to Acute Nervous Trouble"; "Mme. Olga Samaroff ... Found in New York Hospital After Nervous Breakdown"; "Leginska Ordered to Take Year's Rest: Buffalo Physicians Find Pianist Suffering from a Severe Nervous Breakdown."[70] Similar articles do not appear about men. Does this mean that women were less able to withstand the rigors of a performer's life?

Physician George M. Beard first coined the word "neurasthenia" in 1869 to describe a condition he viewed as increasingly prevalent among middle-class urban Americans. Beard, a forerunner of Freud and a pioneer in psychological medicine,

AT THE MENDELSSOHN CONCERT.

I AM ASKED TO SAY THAT HER OTHER CLOTHES WERE DETAINED ON THE RAILWAY

Mrs. Fannie Bloomfield-Zeisler.

Cartoon of Fannie Bloomfield-Zeisler. The stage manager is announcing to the audience, "I am asked to say that her clothes were detained on the railway." (Unidentified newspaper clipping, American Jewish Archives, Cincinnati.)

hypothesized that both men and women suffered from this "malady of modern culture" as a result of the difficulties they experienced adapting to the fast pace of industrialized society.[71] Nineteenth-century physicians attributed neurasthenia in men to their increasingly demanding role in society, while neurasthenia in women supposedly resulted from their inadequate brain capacity for dealing with complex thought and roles outside the home.[72] Physicians began increasingly to assign the labels of neurasthenia, hysteria, or nervous breakdown to women's disorders that appeared to have no physical cause. This diagnosis was usually restricted to women of the upper and middle classes — Virginia Woolf was called neurasthenic whereas a lower-class woman with similar symptoms would have been labeled insane.[73]

Given the prevalent belief that a woman's procreative function governed her life's work and that the human body contained only a limited amount of energy, it naturally followed that a woman should spend her finite energy supply on motherhood and other domestic activities. Many physicians opposed education for girls after puberty because it would "divert precious energy from ovary to brain." In addition, since the reproductive and nervous systems were believed to be inextricably intertwined, any disturbance in one could inevitably lead to malfunction in the other. All of this created a proverbial double-bind — women were either ill because they were women, or they became ill if they tried to do anything outside their traditional female role.[74]

Prominent male virtuosos also experienced anxiety and exhaustion. Louis Moreau Gottschalk wrote in 1863 of the "distressing monotony" of his touring schedule. He described feeling that he was "swirling in space" and had reached a point where the very sight of the piano gave him nausea. Hans von Bülow wrote after his long and arduous 1875 American tour, "My condition is exceptional and can only be called nervous prostration.... My brain is so weak that I have difficulty expressing myself coherently." Ignace Paderewski wrote in 1906, "Something was happening to my nerves that made me completely *hate* the piano.... I no longer wanted to play. No matter what I played, I did not feel in touch with the instrument. It was a kind of torture." Pauline Ornstein, wife of early twentieth-century pianist and futurist composer Leo Ornstein, described her husband's nervousness before every performance as "not just the usual stage fright. It was a monumental inner panic and only a will of steel could ever have gotten him out on the stage. His blood must have almost stopped flowing for he would become ghostly white, and for hours after a performance there were painful nervous reactions, the result of the overdose of tension."[75] More recently Vladimir Horowitz, Glenn Gould, and Van Cliburn among others have dealt with the stresses of public performance by withdrawing entirely for prolonged periods.

In male performers, however, such conditions have generally been viewed as situational rather than pathological. As a result, men were more likely to alter aspects of their professional lives in order to accommodate their physical and emotional limitations. Paderewski negotiated with Steinway to provide him the amenities he lacked on his first tour; Leo Ornstein stopped performing in public and devoted his time exclusively to teaching and composition. And since most men revealed their distress only within the privacy of letters, diaries, and private conversation, it did not become fodder for speculation in newspapers.

Many women musicians, on the other hand, seemed either unable or unwilling to recognize or acknowledge their own breaking points and pushed themselves until unbearable stress manifested itself in public behavior such as failure to appear for a performance or collapse after a recital. Perhaps men were socialized to take control of themselves whereas women understood that it was permissible for them to break down. Or women may have been reluctant, albeit unconsciously, to acknowledge their limits because that was tantamount to admitting to themselves and to society that they were not up to the task. At any rate, the inevitable newspaper publicity that resulted from such public displays provided evidence for those who believed that women were unfit for public life.

When a female performer became ill with a nervous disorder, the explanation was generally overwork and the cure prescribed was rest. Rest, however, could take a variety of forms: for mild cases it simply meant a temporary cessation from work, as when doctors told Teresa Carreño to stop performing for a time and go on holiday in Europe. (More specifically, doctors told her that she could die within six months if she did not rest, but that if she did rest she could resume touring in three months.)[76] For more serious cases, however, rest took a dramatic form, as when Fannie Bloomfield-Zeisler was confined to a darkened room for several months and deprived of almost all intellectual stimulation.[77]

Carroll Smith-Rosenberg has observed that the causes of neurasthenia could frequently be traced to a specific situation in the person's life, such as a death in the family, a miscarriage, or a financial setback.[78] In cases for which it is possible to reconstruct events in the private lives of the women musicians who suffered reported breakdowns, we see that this was, indeed, the case. We find, for example, that Fannie Bloomfield-Zeisler's weeks-long depression in 1906 was not caused by overwork, as was reported, but instead by the psychological aftereffects of a miscarriage. Olga Samaroff's reported breakdown in 1910 did not result from "nervous strain coincident with the pianist's long struggle for success," but instead from a difficult recovery after an appendectomy. Samaroff's disappearance in 1917 coincided with press speculation that her husband, conductor Leopold Stokowski, was guilty of infidelity. Ethel Leginska's failure to appear for one of a series of demanding recitals occurred a few months after the birth of her son. And the Carnegie Hall recital before which Leginska disappeared was scheduled less than two weeks after her conducting debut on the same stage had been greeted with ridicule by some in the audience. Thus many "breakdowns" were neither mysterious maladies of unknown origin nor the results of overwork, but more prosaic, though extreme, reactions to the stress of difficult personal circumstances.[79]

An episode of amnesia or psychological withdrawal frequently followed a musician's failure to appear for a performance or appointment. Descriptions of these episodes bear an almost uncanny resemblance to each other: "Pianist Returns from Unaccountable Absence; Her Memory a Blank," announced a 1915 headline when Chicago pianist Grace Stewart Potter returned home after nine days with no memory of what had happened during that time. "Mme. Olga Samaroff a Victim of Amnesia," proclaimed *Musical America* in February

1917 when the pianist failed to meet her husband for dinner at a Philadelphia restaurant and was found the next day at Roosevelt Hospital after having taken the train to New York. Fannie Bloomfield-Zeisler returned to her home after an unexplained absence of seven hours, saying she had no memory of what had happened.[80] In each case the woman "disappeared" or wandered away without telling anyone where she was going. When she returned after an absence lasting anywhere from several hours to several days, she could not remember what had happened or how much time had passed. Psychiatrists term such an episode a "fugue," derived from the Latin "fugere," meaning to run away. There are several types of fugue, but the one that most closely resembles the experiences of women performers generally occurs as a direct or symbolic result of a conflict or stressful event. The person suddenly becomes mentally disconnected from his or her situation and wanders apparently aimlessly for a period of time. Sometimes he or she travels to another town or spends the night in a hotel or unfamiliar place. Although the causes of such behavior remain unclear, some researchers believe it to be a fairly common phenomenon.[81]

Ethel Leginska offered her account of what happened when she "disappeared" before her Carnegie Hall recital in January 1925. "I left my apartment ... the night of the concert to look for a taxicab. If I had found one right away I probably would have gone there automatically. But, as I slipped through one dark west side street after another, the world grew hazy and unsubstantial. I must have walked for about two hours like this. I have no recollection of becoming unconscious, if I did, and I have no idea where I went. It was like being intensely preoccupied and then coming to with a start without being able to recall what you were preoccupied about. The thing which brought me up with a start was the sudden realization that the concert must be over." She went to the home of nearby friends, where she remained for a week, informing the press that she was safe, but not revealing her location.[82] The inevitable news stories that chronicled these disappearances perpetuated the image of the female artist as an hysterical woman unable to handle the stresses of public life.

That gender influenced the careers of women musicians is incontestable. But the influence itself, of course, had no simple formula. In subtle and complex ways, prescriptive yet changing gender roles — and the artists' individual responses to gender-related restrictions and opportunities — shaped both the public images of musicians and their private lives. In order to understand the effects of gender on the lives and careers of women performers, let us examine more closely the experiences of three of the most prominent: Fannie Bloomfield-Zeisler, Ethel Leginska, and Antonia Brico.

"A Paderewski in Petticoats"

Fannie Bloomfield-Zeisler

Fannie Bloomfield-Zeisler was one of the most remarkable and success-ful of the early women musicians. She enjoyed national and international fame, and received almost uniformly positive reviews.[1] Perhaps the measure of her acceptance as a pianist is the fact that she was frequently and favorably com-pared to two male virtuosos: Ignace Paderewski and Anton Rubinstein. Frail and sickly as a child, she insisted on pursuing a career as a pianist even when parents, doctors, and teachers expressed serious doubts about her chances for success. Married to a prominent Chicago lawyer who valued her career as much or more than his own, she performed in North America and Europe for more than half a century, successfully combining the roles of wife, mother, and vir-tuoso. An examination of Bloomfield-Zeisler's life both documents the career of a remarkable woman and illustrates the ways in which a successful career woman confronted her choices, particularly with regard to marriage, mother-hood, and health.

Fannie Blumenfeld was born in 1863 in Bielitz, Silesia, which is now part of Poland. (She changed her name to Bloomfield at age 20.) Her father Salomon Blumenfeld, a retail merchant, was less interested in business than in Hebrew philology and literature. He viewed commerce as a way to make a modest liv-ing for his family and provide a good education for his children. Her mother, like the mothers of many successful professional women of the period, was a strong personality. Bertha Jaeger was a practical, energetic woman who chafed under the strict tenets of the orthodox Judaism practiced by her parents. As a young woman she read "profane" literature, studied French grammar, sang songs, gave her beautiful hair an extra brushing before the mirror, and talked with men other than her brother and father—all officially forbidden activi-ties. Even as she prepared for an arranged marriage to the learned and thus presumably superior Salomon Blumenfeld, Bertha refused to let the barber shave her hair before the ceremony, as was the orthodox Jewish custom, and bribed him to merely shorten it. Married life proved difficult for the couple;

their temperaments clashed and they had little money. The early years of marriage were especially difficult for Bertha, who had three sons in rapid succession, one of whom died in infancy. Fannie was their fourth child. She was a serious little girl who rarely smiled and hardly ever laughed. Lacking the companionship of other children except her brothers, she was very close to her grandmother, who doted on her, playing games with her and telling her stories.

In 1866 Fannie's Uncle Abraham, her mother's brother, became one of the many Jews who sought to improve his lot by migrating to America. Like many of these immigrants, he found a mercantile niche, starting a modest dry-goods business in the small, pleasant town of Appleton, Wisconsin. He prospered there and soon urged the rest of the family to join him. In 1867 Fannie, her mother, father, grandmother and two brothers embarked on the stormy fifteen-day ocean voyage, the women staying in a second-class cabin while the father and two boys traveled steerage. After arriving in New York, they took the train to Appleton.

Abraham had acquired a small cottage for the family and made Fannie's father an equal partner in his business, with the understanding that Bertha would help out in the store. Fannie flourished in her new environment. Her health improved and she lost some of her shyness. In 1869 the family moved to Milwaukee and in 1870 to Chicago, where Fannie's father started his own dry-goods store with his older son Sigmund as his assistant. Bertha's sound judgment proved a major contributing factor in the success of the business.

When their younger son, Moriz, began to study the piano, seven-year-old Fannie was fascinated. Her brother taught her the notes and some simple pieces, and soon she began taking lessons from her brother's teacher, Bernhard Ziehn. With Ziehn she studied etudes by Czerny and learned to play sonatas by Clementi, Haydn, and Mozart.

After the great Chicago fire wreaked havoc on the city on October 8, 1871, the child gained notoriety when a passing newspaperman observed her playing her rescued piano amidst the rubble. The story circulated widely and understandably became an oft-repeated anecdote of her musical life. In spite of the devastation of the fire, the family was able to rebuild the business. Fannie continued to study piano, switching in 1874 to the noted teacher Karl Wolfsohn, who taught her more pieces from the classical piano repertoire, especially the music of Beethoven. One of Wolfsohn's most notable accomplishments in Chicago was founding the Beethoven Musical Society, an organization of musicians which regularly presented concerts featuring choral works, chamber music, and solo performances. For many years the group provided the only concerts of "serious" music in the city. It was at one of these Musical Society concerts in 1874 that Fannie Blumenfeld, at age 11, made her first public appearance. "How highly they complimented me," she recalled in an interview 21 years later. "I can even now recall with a deep sense of pleasure how happy I felt."[2]

In 1876 Fannie graduated from public grammar school and entered the Dearborn Seminary in Chicago, a fashionable private school for girls. She attended for two years but was not happy there. She was the only Jewish girl in the school, her plain dresses stood out in stark contrast to the elegant ones of her classmates, and she was snubbed for her academic excellence. Things were difficult at home too, as differences in temperament caused visible strain between her mother and father. Conflicts also arose between her parents and grandmother as both generations struggled to acculturate.

In 1878, noted Russian pianist and pedagogue Anna Essipoff toured North America and performed in Chicago. Essipoff had concertized widely in Europe and America and later taught many famous pianists and composers, including Prokofiev.[3] Fannie was asked to play for her, and the artist was so taken with the child's ability that she advised that Fannie study in Vienna with her teacher (and future husband), Theodor Leschetizky. Leschetizky and Liszt were arguably the most famous piano teachers of all time. Leschetizky taught many noted virtuosos and possessed an incomparable musical lineage: he had studied with Carl Czerny, and Czerny had studied with Beethoven.

Fannie, then 14 years old, wanted desperately to study in Vienna at the end of the school year. Her parents opposed the idea: she was too young and weak; they could not afford it; her mother would have to go too and yet could not be spared from the business. It was the first of a series of confrontations in which Fannie defied authority in pursuit of her goal. She "clenched her fists and set her jaw, and with blazing eyes declared over and over again that she was going, and that if her parents did not consent, she would run away." They relented when Karl Wolfsohn enlisted the help of a wealthy family friend to help finance the venture. Even so, Salomon Blumenfeld was forced to sell the family's home to raise enough money. He and his oldest son moved into a boardinghouse and continued to run the business while Fannie, accompanied by her mother and grandmother, embarked for Europe.

In 1878 they sailed for 12 days aboard the *Main*, a 300-foot-long, 50-foot-wide steamer. The ship hardly qualified as a luxury liner, but the ecstatic Fannie wrote home rapturously, "My darling Brother: you can have no conception of my joy when I again felt German soil under my feet and realized that my inexpressibly passionate longing to breathe again the air of Europe had been satisfied." When the family arrived in Germany, Fannie and her mother went over the border to Franzensbad, a Czech spa known for its treatment of anemia, where Fannie took the "cure" for four weeks. They then traveled to Bielitz, where they spent a few weeks at the home of the Zeislers, who were both friends and distant relatives.

Fannie experienced both happiness and anxiety during her time with the Zeislers. There were two sisters and two brothers in the family, and she enjoyed the companionship of young people her own age. One of the brothers was eighteen-year-old Sigmund, who later became her husband. As Sigmund described their early relationship, their conversations were not at first dialogues between equals. "She considered herself a quite ignorant girl, although she was far from that, and looked upon me as a 'walking encyclopaedia.' She was most eager to fill up any gap which she discovered in her mental equipment, but no more eager than I was to exhibit what, in the conceit characteristic of my youth, I considered my cornucopia of learning." He described her behavior during their early courtship as being somewhat worshipful: "Our conversations, if they can be called such — I fear they were mostly monologues — were on serious subjects. Fannie would ask me some question and I would reply by a lecture."

A visit by Sigmund's cousin Moriz Rosenthal, however, caused her much anguish. Rosenthal was the same age as Fannie but had already studied piano with well-known virtuoso Rafael Joseffy and held successful concerts as a prodigy in many European capitals. As Sigmund recalled, "his [Rosenthal's] conversation was brilliant and witty, but his conceit was colossal and his tongue was biting.... His criticism of her playing — and there was a good deal of it — was never kindly, but always sharp and sarcastic."

When Fannie and her mother finally traveled to Vienna, they learned that Leschetizky had changed his plans and would not arrive for another full year. They sought out Julius Epstein, another noted piano pedagogue at the Vienna Conservatory, on the assumption that he could teach her until Leschetizky arrived. Much to their dismay, however, when Epstein heard Fannie play, he declared that she possessed neither the musical talent nor the physical strength to justify the sacrifices necessary to make her a concert pianist. Her mother felt that they should return to Chicago but Fannie insisted on applying for admission to the conservatory regardless. She passed the required examination and was temporarily assigned another teacher, Professor Rabeneau. Although Rabeneau was apparently a good technician, he was unemotional and unimaginative in his teaching methods, and his manner was particularly unsuited to her temperament. He gave her poor grades and although these were later rescinded when the Examining Board of the conservatory judged them to be unfair, she was upset to have to report poor marks to her father when he was sacrificing so much for her musical education.

When Leschetizky arrived the next year, he too expressed doubts about her physical strength. She pleaded so persuasively, however, that he accepted her as a student. She proved to be one of his most gifted pupils and was clearly one of his favorites. He affectionately referred to her as his "electric wonder" in an attempt to describe the unique clarity and "aliveness" that were hallmarks of her playing.

During their time in Vienna, Mrs. Blumenfeld sought medical advice about her daughter's curvature of the spine — a condition that had been previously noticed but had remained untreated. She took Fannie to many doctors, each of whom recommended a different course of treatment. Eventually, Fannie was fitted with an "iron corset" that she was forced to wear both day and night, causing great pain and discomfort. When her condition showed no improvement after several months of this treatment, Mrs. Blumenfeld took her to another physician, Theodor Billroth, who was also an excellent amateur pianist. Billroth naturally took an interest and asked her to play for him. Although greatly impressed with her talent, he "gravely shook his head" when he learned of her artistic aspirations, saying that the curvature of the spine had caused "considerable dislocation of various internal organs," which would be aggravated by sitting at the piano for several hours a day. This, combined with her other ailments, caused him to state categorically that Fannie should give up the idea of being a pianist and stop playing immediately or she would not live to be 20. Fannie responded to this ultimatum with her characteristic determination: she declared that she would not stop playing, "not if I knew I were to die in a year."

Throughout her youth Fannie Blumenfeld was diagnosed with a variety of ailments that historically have been more frequently identified in females than in males. As a young child she was described as "weak, anemic and nervous"; when she was seven, her parents limited her to one hour of piano playing a day because of her physical weakness; when she was 14, one of the reasons that her parents initially opposed study in Vienna was that she was "too young and weak"; and when she did go abroad, she spent her first four weeks in Germany taking the "cure." Julius Epstein stated decisively that she lacked the physical strength to be a concert pianist; Leschetizky expressed doubts as well. At various times she was diagnosed with anemia, dyspepsia, chronic constipation, frequent and violent headaches, fatigue, and curvature of the spine. Each diagnosis was followed by a recommendation that she lessen her musical activity or cease playing altogether. To ignore this advice, she was told, was to risk permanent physical damage or early death. While it is entirely possible that Fannie Blumenfeld was not physically robust, it is also true that physicians during this period generally viewed illness in a female not as a temporary condition and curable malady, but as a chronic condition that should preclude ambition. Women were assumed to be the weaker sex and thus more prone to fatigue and illness if they exerted themselves too strenuously. Sustained, demanding physical or mental activity could put them at risk and damage the delicate mechanism of reproduction, which was believed to be their primary reason for existence.[4]

Many adolescent girls, particularly in the years between 1870 and 1890, were also diagnosed with a disease known as "chlorosis."[5] The typical "chlorotic," like Fannie Blumenfeld, had been a sickly child and was a young unmarried woman between ages 14 or 15 and the early twenties. Characteristic symptoms included weakness, fatigue, moodiness and depression. Today experts speculate that the condition may have reflected traditions of sickliness and physical inactivity learned from older women, physicians' misunderstanding of menstruation, and perhaps avoidance of meat eating by some adolescent girls — all coinciding in many cases with iron-deficiency anemia. Sometimes a general loss of appetite extending beyond meat was observed in young women as well, leading some medical historians to note a similarity between a nineteenth-century diagnosis of chlorosis and a twentieth-century diagnosis of anorexia nervosa.[6] In the case of Fannie Blumenfeld, food does appear to have been an issue, at least on occasion. While attending Chicago's Dearborn Seminary in her early teens, her work at school and at the piano often left her exhausted and she would fall asleep on the couch before dinner. At such times her family would wake her with great difficulty, not wanting her to miss a meal. Several years later, when she was 15, she was described as being "of normal height but rather thin and scrawny." Sigmund Zeisler reported that what she needed when she was studying in Vienna was fresh air, light, and "an abundance of wholesome, palatable food to excite her poor appetite." In his later accounts of their European vacations he frequently noted that she had put on weight and often documented the number of pounds she had gained.

Chlorosis was not the only malady more frequently diagnosed in girls than in boys — curvature of the spine, or scoliosis, was as well. Many more girls than boys were treated at orthopedic institutions, especially in Germany during the period when Fannie Blumenfeld studied there.[7] It is remarkable that she persevered in the face of such overwhelmingly discouraging medical advice, especially since all of those in authority — parents, teachers, and physicians — predicted dire consequences if she ignored their advice.

In 1883, after five years of study, Fannie and her mother returned to the United States. On April 30, 1884, she gave a full recital at Chicago's Hershey Hall, assisted by her former teacher Karl Wolfsohn. She and her mother then established themselves in New York at the Belvedere Hotel, with hopes of launching her career. Although Fannie Bloomfield had acquired a fine reputation in Europe as one of Leschetizky's greatest pupils, late nineteenth-century North America was not particularly fertile ground for an aspiring concert pianist, and she began to despair about ever getting the opportunity to perform. John Freund, editor of *Musical America* and a personal friend, recalled that she "often wept in frustration at her inability to make a debut."[8]

The key to a breakthrough was gaining the support of one of the great piano manufacturers, who would subsidize an artist's tours in exchange for their performing on (and thus advertising) their instruments.[9] Bloomfield was having difficulty because most companies already had one or more distinguished artists representing them. Soon after her return from Europe, however, Freund persuaded Charles Keidel of the Knabe piano company to hear

Fannie Bloomfield-Zeisler in 1898. (New York Public Library.)

her play, despite Keidel's policy of not listening to what he termed "embryo artists." "I shall never forget the scene," wrote Freund, "when I brought Miss Fannie and her mother to the old Knabe warerooms on Fifth Avenue, and how Keidel, when he saw us entering the place, rushed into his private office and slammed the door. Quietly, I made one of the big grands ready to play. She hadn't been at it but a few minutes before the door of Keidel's private office opened and I saw him sticking his nose out. Bit by bit he came gradually forward. Then he sat down with his head in his hands, listening intently." As a result of this performance, Fannie Bloomfield was engaged by the Knabe piano company to give a recital at the Peabody Institute in Baltimore. Soon afterwards she presented a well-received New York debut and was offered what turned out to be a lifelong contract by Henry Wolfsohn, one of New York's most prominent agents.[10]

Bloomfield began to concertize in North America, performing to great critical acclaim in large cities and small towns. Noted essayist and music critic James Huneker wrote in 1885, "The music was fair until last night, when I heard for the first time a genius *Fannie Bloomfield* play as I never expected to hear a woman play or to hear the much abused Piano sing. Oh, it was superb, nothing superlative enough could describe it. It was *violin* playing on the Piano, so intense, so electric, so sweet and so masterly."[11]

In the same year that Fannie and her mother returned to the United States, Sigmund Zeisler emigrated from Bielitz, having received a degree in law and political science from the University of Vienna. Zeisler was a man of many interests. He wrote and lectured in the fields of art, music, literature, and science, and paid his way through Northwestern University at Evanston, Illinois, in part by writing music criticism for a German newspaper in Chicago. He earned an LL.B. from Northwestern after only a year, and was also awarded the prize for the best essay on an original thesis — a remarkable achievement given that he had only begun studying English the year before. Fannie Bloomfield and Sigmund Zeisler renewed the friendship they had begun in Europe and were married on October 18, 1885. Soon after, Zeisler gained prominence as one of the lawyers defending the anarchists charged in the wake of the 1886 bombing in Chicago's Haymarket Square. Even though his efforts to have the bombers acquitted were unsuccessful, he gained a reputation as one who was unafraid to take a stand if he believed a cause was just.[12]

Sigmund Zeisler did not marry with the idea of being the husband of a famous musician. Typical of the men of his generation, he assumed his wife would exchange her personal ambitions for the roles of wife and mother. Many women with distinguished concert careers in the late nineteenth and early twentieth centuries did, including Nettie Carpenter, Midge Wickham, Anna Senkrah, Lenore Jackson, Marie Hall and Amy Cheney Beach. All ceased performing regularly in public after they married.[13] Olga Samaroff observed, "I was brought up with the idea that I should fit myself for a public career but only undertake it 'if I had to.' This meant in plain English that if no stalwart male were at hand to relieve me of the necessity of making my living I might play in concerts and should be thoroughly prepared to do so, but there would be no question if I had the choice between matrimony and a career — I should marry."[14] The newspaper announcement of a woman musician's impending marriage was generally followed by a comment regarding her future professional plans. Often the notice reassured the public that she would not abandon her music but would shift most performances from the public stage to her private home.

Articles in late nineteenth-century music periodicals such as *Musical America* and *Musical Courier* reinforced the notion that true happiness lay in abandoning one's musical career for domesticity. "Are you content, artistic young woman, to give up your chances of a peaceful home life for the storm and stress of an artistic career?" asked the *Musical Courier* in 1898.[15] Two years later an article entitled "Why Artists Should Marry" stated unequivocally, "We believe that no success in art compensates for the absence of married love and a happy home."[16]

Even women with successful careers expressed the belief that the domestic setting was the appropriate outlet for their talents after marriage. "Don't give up music at the altar," advised *Etude* magazine in 1919, quoting musicians Antoinette Szumowska, Emma Ashford, Amy Cheney Beach, Mrs. Noah Brandt, Clara Clemens, Cecile Ayres de Horvath, Hildegard Hoffmann Huss, Louise Homer, Gloria Cotton Marshall, and Lily Strickland in their unanimous endorsement of the importance of music in the home. Although a number of these women were pursuing active concert careers, only Horvath explicitly distinguished between the amateur and the professional musician, asserting that it was wrong to expect the professionally trained woman to abandon her career after marriage.[17]

Such attitudes were slow to change. In 1936 the mother of violinist Yehudi Menuhin and his gifted pianist sister Hephzibah justified her reasons for discouraging her daughter's public career, while at the same time encouraging that of her son. "I always praised Hephzibah far more for a well-balanced, well-executed dinner cooked by her than for any concert she ever played with her brother.... Hephzibah yearns for Paris and solo recitals and a career of her own. I say it is better that she be happy than famous. I tell her that the only immortality to which a woman should aspire is that of a home and children."[18]

Some musicians chose marriage with every intention of giving up their career but found it impossible to do so. Pianist Olga Samaroff, for example, married conductor Leopold Stokowski in 1911 and announced that she would give up her career as a pianist and devote her time to fulfilling the role of conductor's wife, a decision reputedly endorsed by her husband. For two years she attended luncheons, teas, and after-concert suppers, kept track of the dates and events connected with them, ingratiated herself with women's committees and musical clubs, and in every way served as her husband's musical ambassador. "And I have been very happy," she reported. "I have been and I am — but my art is calling. I want to play again — I must."[19] In 1913 she returned to the concert stage, limiting herself to 40 concerts for the season, all in and around her home base of Philadelphia. She continued to perform every year for the next decade, although strains in the marriage caused her and her husband to divorce in 1923.

Within this context it is remarkable that Sigmund Zeisler, who married in 1885, wrote soon after, "There was a time when I had flattered myself with the hope that when once we were married, especially if we had a child, and when Fannie would have tasted the hardships and sacrifices of a professional career, she would give it up and be content with the life of a wife and mother. For several years I had done my utmost to persuade her in this direction. But when I discovered the truth that wherever nature plants an outstanding artistic gift, it plants right next to it an intense desire for its recognition, I became convinced that Fannie's gift was quite out of the ordinary and that her ambition was a perfectly natural passion for self-expression. Having seen the light I not only ceased my opposition to her professional career, but began to further it in every way that I could, realizing that this course was an essential condition to our continued happiness."

Thus Fannie Bloomfield and Sigmund Zeisler, two accomplished and ambitious professionals, began balancing the demands of career and family life, dealing with situations similar to those faced by professional couples today. The first major test occurred when Fannie decided in the spring of 1888 that she wanted to return to Vienna for a time to study with Leschetizky. Five years had passed since she had left Vienna; she feared that she was not growing as an artist and wanted to regain her self-confidence and immerse herself once again in the artistic atmosphere of Europe. Sigmund at first considered the idea a "bitter pill" for him to swallow. He could not leave his law office for an extended period, and they now had two-year-old Leonard to consider. Fannie proposed that the three of them go to Europe at the end of July 1888 with a nurse for the baby; Sigmund would stay as long as he could and then leave them in Vienna until Christmas. At first it seemed like a workable plan, but Fannie's mother could not decide whether to accompany them. Finally she proposed that she stay in Chicago with the baby. This would allow the couple to travel more freely, avoid the expense of traveling with a baby and a nurse, and give Fannie more time to study. These were persuasive arguments, and the Zeislers agreed.

The trip proved more difficult than anticipated, however, as the demands of career and family pulled Bloomfield-Zeisler in different directions. When

Fannie and Sigmund began the train ride to New York, "Fannie was dissolved in tears. Her heart was breaking at the thought of going away from her baby for five months." She became somewhat calmer when Sigmund diverted her with details of their itinerary and the idea that it would be a deferred wedding trip. Then upon arrival in New York they were greeted by a telegram saying that Fannie's mother had changed her mind and would soon join them, accompanied by the baby and his nurse. The family set out together. Things went smoothly at first, but after they had been traveling for a time Fannie's mother accused the nurse of theft. The police were summoned and proved the nurse's innocence. Understandably, however, the woman felt she could not stay on after such an accusation and quit. The baby was miserable without his familiar nurse, while Fannie and Sigmund were not only upset but had difficulty finding a replacement. All this happened just a week before Sigmund was scheduled to return to Chicago. The night of his departure Fannie wrote in her diary, "My heart went with him. It is killing me, I cannot stand it."[20] She took a couple of furnished rooms near Leschetizky's house in a suburb of Vienna. Her mother and baby stayed with a relative, and Fannie spent at least an hour with them every day.

The time in Vienna was productive musically. Fannie immediately started private lessons with Leschetizky, who treated her more like a colleague than a pupil. She attended master classes (one of her fellow students was Paderewski) as well as concerts, the theater, and the opera. She also served as a companion when Leschetizky's wife, Anna Essipoff, went to London for a brief concert tour. Essipoff served as both a support and a role model for Zeisler, including her on three of her London recitals and arranging for her to perform on one of the prestigious London Monday Popular Concerts. Essipoff also introduced her to many important musical figures in Leipzig and Berlin including Herman Wolff, who would later serve as Zeisler's European manager.[21]

In January 1889 when it was time to return to Chicago, Fannie's mother said she did not feel well enough to make the journey, and that it would be unwise for all of them to cross the ocean during the worst season of the year. She tried to persuade Fannie to wait, but Fannie had promised that she would be home after Christmas and did not want to break her word. After much anguished dithering (an entry in Fannie's diary at the time states, "Ma came and tortured me for a change"), Fannie cabled Sigmund for advice. He sailed two days later to accompany them on the trip home. Bertha remained undecided about whether to stay or go until, with Fannie's permission, Sigmund sent a note to his mother-in-law saying, "Cannot let you make us crazy any longer. Sailing tomorrow," and the four of them returned to Chicago. Clearly it was not easy to juggle everyone's priorities.

Fannie Bloomfield-Zeisler's return to North America was followed by three years of concertizing to great critical acclaim. Her appearances included a tour of New England with the Boston Symphony and one of the Middle West with the Chicago Orchestra (as it was then called) under the leadership of Theodore Thomas. She and Paderewski were the two featured pianists at the 1893 Chicago World's Fair.

During the 1892–93 season, the impresario Herman Wolff, who had been Anton Rubinstein's manager, urged Fannie to tour Europe the following concert season. It was a great temptation. Although she was considered by many to be the "greatest American woman pianist," she wanted to be accepted as one of the great pianists of the world irrespective of sex. In order to achieve this, she knew she had to perform in Europe and bring back a sheaf of laudatory reviews.

She was reluctant to go alone, but did not want Sigmund to feel he had to interrupt his work to accompany her. After many anxious talks, Sigmund persuaded her to let him go along. Only a few weeks before their scheduled departure, however, he was offered the position of Chief Assistant Corporation Counsel of the City of Chicago. The job was important to him and Fannie insisted he accept it, assuring him that she would find a friend or pupil to go with her or "conquer her timidity and go alone." She did find a friend to accompany her, but three days before her first Berlin concert her companion suddenly became ill and required major surgery. "Instead of having someone to cheer her up and drive away her nervousness," Sigmund later wrote, "Mrs. Zeisler had to spend hours every day at the hospital and to tremble for the life of her friend."

Despite this considerable distraction, Bloomfield-Zeisler's performances in various European capitals stunned the musical world. The reviewer for the Vienna *Tageblatt* reported, "Mrs. Zeisler, at her debut, created a furore, the same as she did in Berlin, as she is sure to do everywhere. She is a mighty virtuoso … who will always excite admiration and astonishment. Her playing possesses all the qualities to daze, excite and fascinate." One of the most remarkable events on this tour was the November 26, 1893, Dresden concert when Bloomfield-Zeisler performed concertos by Chopin and Anton Rubinstein, with Rubinstein himself in the audience. As a music editor of the *Chicago Tribune* proudly commented the next day, most cultured Germans had previously assumed that "crude America" had nothing to offer the world except "pork, grain and machinery," but this concert clearly proved otherwise. As the orchestra finished its opening piece, Rubinstein strode up the aisle and took a front-row seat that was in Bloomfield-Zeisler's line of sight every time she raised her eyes from the piano. During her performance of the Chopin concerto, "he sat with his eyes half closed, his head thrown slightly back, his body language indicating that nothing escaped him and that he approved of what he was hearing." When she began to play his own concerto in D minor, "He flushed, he shifted his position, he fidgeted during the entire first half of the first movement.... Soon he ... began nodding with the rhythm and 'beaming with delight.'" When the Chicago critic went backstage to express his congratulations after the performance, Rubinstein was thanking Bloomfield-Zeisler for her "superbly artistic" performance of both works. He later wrote that he had never heard his concerto played so beautifully.[22] American piano student and writer Amy Fay wrote of the performance, "She dashed it off like a mere bagatelle."[23]

Despite Bloomfield-Zeisler's unqualified European success, her husband noted that she seemed unable to savor her accomplishments. "If German public opinion had rejected her, if the German critics had damned her with faint praise she would have been cast into an abyss of despair.... But when day after day she read those critics' reviews in which she was raised to a pinnacle of fame, which proclaimed her the equal if not the superior of all pianists past and present, she was incapable of realizing that it was she who was being talked about." Her physical and emotional exhaustion were so great after a performance that she would frequently "fall into a heartbreaking crying spell" when she returned to her hotel room.

As the tour went on, Bloomfield-Zeisler felt increased anxiety as each sensational performance produced a spate of advance notices that served to raise expectations for the next one. World-famed musicians could be in the audience. Anton Bruckner and Johannes Brahms, for example, attended one performance. She knew that many pianists viewed her as a competitor and did not necessarily rejoice in her success. She feared that a prominent critic might decide to annihilate her just to show his independence of the German critics or because he could not resist the temptation to use a clever phrase. Thus, even though the tour was an enormous public success, she became increasingly isolated and exhausted until she finally collapsed and placed herself under the care of a physician in Vienna, who advised her to cancel her final engagements in order to avoid "serious consequences."[24]

Although Fannie and Sigmund exchanged letters daily,[25] she did not reveal her distress. Only when he read of her condition in a German newspaper at the Chicago Public Library on his way to work did Sigmund Zeisler learn of the seriousness of the situation. He became frightened and cabled her immediately, "Thoroughly alarmed. Insist cancellation of remaining engagements. Get well and come home. Promise accompany you next fall." To this he received the following reply two days later: "No cause for alarm. Nothing [the] matter except being alone. Will comply. Home soon." She returned home and performed no more that season, taking the luxury, for the first time in years, to rest and recuperate and spend time with her husband and son.[26]

The following season Fannie Bloomfield-Zeisler, accompanied by her husband, resumed her European tour, fulfilling many of the engagements she had canceled the previous year. Evidence suggests that Sigmund resigned his position as Chief Assistant Corporation Counsel for the City of Chicago in order to accompany her. The *Jewish Encyclopedia* states that he resigned the position after one year "on account of ill health," but *his* account makes no mention of his health at this time, although it does on other occasions.[27] Sigmund began a private legal practice after they returned from Europe, which he might well have done in order to give himself the flexibility to accompany her on future tours.

The couple was gone from September 1893 to January 1894, and this tour was also a huge success. She could have extended it with performances in England, but both were pulled by the need to return to Chicago. Fannie was "dreadfully homesick" for her son, and Sigmund was concerned about being away from his legal practice for so long. Bloomfield-Zeisler's triumphs in Europe generated much excitement in America. When she returned she was offered many engagements but postponed them all, choosing instead to "rest on her European laurels" until the following fall and devote her time to family, friends and students. She also turned her attentions to domestic concerns.

Bloomfield-Zeisler approached domesticity with the same energy and unconventionality that she evidenced in other areas of her life. Her husband reported that it was not unusual to find her "standing way up on a step-ladder with her head sticking in a cupboard, or her hands manipulating a curtain rod, or crouching or squatting under a sink, unscrewing a pipe and cleaning out a trap." She embarked on these tasks with complete disregard for dirt, dust, or danger to her hands, claiming that they "rested her from the brain work which wore out her nerves."

After eight months without concertizing, Bloomfield-Zeisler felt physically and psychologically rested and was eager to return to the stage. During the next season, 1895–96, she made 51 North American concert appearances, performing with symphony orchestras and giving recitals in almost all the larger cities east of Chicago. In November 1896, traveling with a Steinway concert grand, a piano tuner, her secretary, and her brother Sigmund, she embarked on a tour of the Pacific coast, performing in San Francisco, Sacramento, Oakland, San Jose, Portland, Tacoma, Seattle, and Spokane. During the seven recitals she gave in San Francisco, she displayed the remarkable size and range of her repertoire by performing seven entirely different programs. By February 1897 she was back in Chicago, devoting most of the rest of the year to her private life. On November 30, 1897, she gave birth to her second son, Paul.

Contemporary articles sentimentalized Bloomfield-Zeisler's motherhood, assuring readers that she was a "normal" woman despite her career. "Away from the concert room," effused William Armstrong in 1897, "Mrs. Bloomfield-Zeisler is first the mother, afterward the artist." Armstrong described the letters she received from her son while on tour as "so eloquent in their expression of childish loneliness that they brought tears to the eyes of strangers to whom his mother read them."[28]

The ideology of motherhood as woman's only true and noble destiny has been pervasive throughout American history. The issue gained particular prominence in the late nineteenth and early twentieth century, as the divorce rate quadrupled and the birth rate, especially among younger mothers, dropped to three children per family. Such figures caused conservative social critics to conclude that the American family was in crisis. The source of the crisis, they generally assumed, was the woman who selfishly put her own wants and needs above those of her loved ones. A widely discussed article in the *Atlantic Monthly* in 1907 described this "new woman" as a person with a "devouring ego" who worshipped "the brazen calf of Self." Instead of acknowledging that "Marriage is her work in the world," she has tried to enter the masculine realm with ambitions for education, careers and other public activity.[29]

Some women with successful careers did not have children. Of course, it is often impossible to know whether childlessness resulted from a conscious decision or happened naturally. Camilla Urso and Frederic Luer did not have children; nor did Maud Powell and Godfrey Turner. In Powell's case this was a conscious decision, although it may have been somewhat easier because she did not marry until she was 37. Nonetheless, she idealized the concept of motherhood and expressed regret that she had never had children.[30] Violinist Erica Morini felt that children and a career were incompatible. "I don't think it's possible for a woman to be a good mother and a good artist, too," she said.[31] Pianist Julie Rivé-King and her husband had no children, although in this case we know that it was not possible for them to do so. Frank King had contracted syphilis sometime during the Civil War and transmitted the disease to his wife. Although she was successfully treated, the resulting side effect was sterility.[32]

Other performers had children, but sometimes only one. Ethel Leginska lost custody of her son after her highly publicized divorce from Emerson Whithorne in 1917. Although it is impossible to reconstruct all of the details, her offer to give up her public career if she were awarded custody indicates that she struggled with the issue. Pianist Olga Samaroff and her husband had one daughter. But Samaroff spoke strongly about her intention to continue performing: "It would be wrong, I am sure, to give up my career. It would mean stifling something which is very much a part of me. I would be doing a violence to that something, you understand, and unfair to me as well as my child."[33]

It was important to Fannie Bloomfield-Zeisler that she successfully and simultaneously perform the roles of wife, mother, and artist. She frequently spoke of it in interviews, and one senses her need to reassure herself that she was not neglecting her domestic duties. In an article with the headline "Noted Pianiste Likes to Darn Hubby's Sox," she told a *Detroit News* reporter that when they were newlyweds she had darned all of Sigmund's socks and sewed on all of his buttons "just as carefully as if I could not play a note."[34] Journalists frequently held her up as an example for other women to emulate. In 1900, an article in the *Musical Courier* advised that some of the "restless and unhappy agitators" in the United States could find a solution to the "woman problem" by studying her life and career, describing her as one who "combines modesty with genius and tranquil domesticity with fame.... Fannie Bloomfield-Zeisler is a happy wife and mother. The home life of the pianist is as ideal as her public career is great."[35] Such articles about Bloomfield-Zeisler resemble those written about the feminist abolitionists of pre–Civil War America, when women's periodicals were filled with stories aimed at proving that strong-minded women could also be good wives and mothers, describing the feminists' well-ordered homes and well-behaved children. Historian Blanche Glassman Hersh has observed that these reformers also had a personal need to compensate for not devoting themselves exclusively to their families, although their guilt was diminished by the worthiness of their cause.[36]

Bloomfield-Zeisler clearly felt the pressure to be exemplary, and the tyranny of that ambition dramatically manifested itself during the birth of her second child. As Sigmund described it, Fannie had been in labor for more than eight hours, at home, with the doctor in attendance. During the whole time she never cried out, but "when the pain was the worst she pressed a napkin against her mouth to suppress her outcries." About an hour before the baby was born, Dr. Frankenthal, who had been "in the midst of a disquisition about the susceptibility of the average woman to pain during labor," dared her to go to the piano in the corner of the bedroom and play something. She accepted his challenge, got up, walked to the upright piano, and began to play. (She chose a piece for the left hand alone, since her right hand was still holding the "napkin" to her mouth.) She had two labor pains while she played, but did not stop, performing the piece "with all the dash and bravura, the technical perfection and the fiery temperament with which she had ever played it." Dr. Frankenthal frequently described this as the "most astounding experience in his life."

Barely five months after Paul's birth, Bloomfield-Zeisler returned to the concert stage. In February 1898 she performed in St. Louis, Kansas City, Omaha, and Des Moines. A few weeks later she filled seven engagements in the course of ten days, performing in Brooklyn, Cleveland, Auburn, N.Y., Hartford, Boston, and Toledo. In the spring of 1898 she played a series of concerts in England, even though it "nearly broke her heart" to leave her family. While in Europe she substituted for the ailing Paderewski at the prestigious Lower Rhine Music Festival, where she played concertos by Saint-Saëns, Chopin and Litolff. After these performances she had planned to return to England to fill several more engagements, but "an irresistible longing for home, especially for the baby," caused her to cancel them and return to Chicago at the beginning of June.

Bloomfield-Zeisler had always regretted that her first-born son had been an only child until he was 11 years old. Sigmund described Leonard as a sensitive child, "trembled over" by his mother and grandmother. His parents believed that he would have been better adjusted had he had a brother or sister for companionship. Fannie wanted very much for her second son, Paul, not to experience the same isolation, and so was happy when she became pregnant with her third child in December of 1898. Bloomfield-Zeisler concertized extensively in the months before the birth. There were New York recitals in February of 1899, an engagement in Atlanta in March, five concerts in five different Texas towns in April, and an appearance at the Albion, Michigan, Music Festival in May. Three months later, on August 23, 1899, she gave birth to her third son, Ernest. Although she had hoped for a girl, Bloomfield-Zeisler was overjoyed by his healthy arrival. She nursed Ernest for two months until the physician advised her to stop, saying that it was causing her to lose too much strength. Bloomfield-Zeisler acquiesced and stopped nursing, unlike the many other occasions when she chose to minimize the importance of a doctor's advice. She was soon concertizing again, receiving enthusiastic press notices for her performance of the Grieg piano concerto with the Boston Symphony barely three months after the birth, on December 1 and 2, 1899.

The year 1900 marked the twenty-fifth anniversary of Bloomfield-Zeisler's first public performance, an event commemorated on March 24 by a recital in Chicago. Before a capacity house, she played the same Beethoven Andante she had performed at her public debut on February 26, 1875, plus compositions by Schumann, Schubert, Chopin, and Rubinstein.[37] With floral tributes covering the stage and surrounded by an audience of personal friends and noted musicians, she received the admiration and appreciation of the crowd, responding to calls for pieces to be repeated as well as demands for many encores.

Bloomfield-Zeisler resumed her intense schedule of tours, performing 43 concerts in the United States during the 1900–01 season and 55 in 1901–02, keeping up this pace during the next two seasons as well. She continued to divide her time between concertizing and family life, scheduling her performance season so that she was home as much as possible. After the last concert on any tour she took the first train home, declining any social invitations in order to do so. She traveled all night by train if she was within reach of Chicago, and frequently traveled for two nights in a row in order to be with her family as quickly as possible.

Late in 1905 Fannie Bloomfield-Zeisler suffered a devastating personal loss. Pregnant with her fourth child, she was anticipating the birth with "an almost delirious joy," hoping that the child would be a long-hoped-for daughter. In November of 1905 she apparently strained herself when closing a heavy sliding door in her home. The next day she went into premature labor, and after 36 hours gave birth to an almost fully developed still-born girl. Bloomfield-Zeisler suffered major hemorrhaging and for a time lost consciousness. When she awoke and learned that she had lost a daughter she descended into "an indescribable despondency." She blamed herself for the death of the baby and remained in this state of melancholia for weeks.

When she had recovered enough to attempt to resume some of her activities, she experienced blurred vision, which her oculist said was caused by hemorrhages in both eyes. He told her that if she wanted to avoid total blindness, she must give her eyes a complete rest. She was confined for several months to a darkened room, the windows covered with heavy green shades which allowed no sunlight to enter. The doctor also advised that she might have to give up her profession, since the strain of reading music and the excitement of public performance might cause further hemorrhaging. As Bloomfield-Zeisler described it, "I was told that I would have to give up my work altogether, and made to sit in a dark room without anything to do. I could not read. I could not even touch a piano." The reason she could not recover, she believed, was "the inability to work" and "the thought that I was being robbed of my career by illness. For my temperament is such that I cannot live without my work."[38] When Bloomfield-Zeisler told the doctor that she could not imagine life without her music, he told her that he could not understand why. When she asked him to suggest how she should spend the rest of her life, he replied, "Buy a peach farm in Michigan and raise peaches." As Sigmund reported, "The oculist did not realize what his words meant to a person of Mrs. Zeisler's temperament, but the fact is that if he had thrown a bomb shell at her feet, it would not have had a more paralyzing effect." Although Bloomfield-Zeisler was suffering from the emotional aftermath of a miscarriage as well as from eye problems, the remedy that her doctor prescribed was the standard one during this period for women suffering from "nervous disorders." It was commonly termed the "rest cure."

The rest cure was extremely popular in America during the late nineteenth and early twentieth centuries. It evolved from the work of Dr. S. Weir Mitchell, who advised that the hysterical woman could be cured by allowing her "absolute rest" from her exertions. The patient was virtually placed in solitary confinement. She was required to spend days in a darkened room, where she was deprived of all physical and mental stimulation. (In severe cases, "absolute rest" meant that the patient was not even allowed to turn herself over in bed or to feed herself.)[39] In her 1892 short story *The Yellow Wallpaper*, Charlotte Perkins Gilman memorably immortalized the possible outcome of such a "cure" when she described her main character's gradual descent into madness. By the end of the novel, the woman is found crawling around on the floor of her yellow-walled room. Throughout the treatment she insists, without success, that the cure for her disorder is not rest, but instead work and stimulation.[40]

Bloomfield-Zeisler's rest cure was somewhat less draconic. She stopped making active use of her eyes; her secretary read her letters and she dictated the replies. The secretary read to her during the days and her husband read to her during the evenings. She never went near the piano, although she could have played by memory, saying hopelessly, "What is the use if I have to give up my career." When weather permitted, she took walks with her secretary, but rarely spoke. Sigmund told her that the doctor was being too pessimistic and that her eye troubles were related to the birth, from which she would fully recover, but she remained unresponsive. For many hours a day she either sat in a corner or lay brooding on her bed. Her sadness grew deeper from day to day until finally she ceased to speak at all.

On February 12, 1906, she went upstairs after breakfast. When Sigmund followed soon after, he could not find her. The family searched the house to no avail. With the help of a neighbor, Sigmund and his oldest son searched the neighborhood. With increasing fear, they walked along the nearby lake front. When they returned to the house and she had still not returned, Sigmund reluctantly decided to call the police, although he knew that if she were found unharmed, she would be angry at him for "acquainting the public with her private troubles." He notified authorities, and within an hour newsboys passed the house with "extras" announcing her disappearance and containing sensational speculations regarding its cause. Reporters gathered on the lawn. Then in midafternoon, about seven hours from the time her absence had been noted, she was spotted walking slowly toward the house. When eight-year-old Paul blurted out, "I am so glad you are back, Mother. Your picture is in the papers," she looked at her husband with "infinite pain and horror mixed with anger," went upstairs, and locked herself in her room. She finally allowed Sigmund's brother, a physician and close friend, to come in. She began to sob uncontrollably, explaining that she had left the house only because she wanted to be alone to think and had no idea that people had been worried for her safety.

The next day and for several days after, letters and telegrams poured in from friends and strangers who had read in the newspaper that she had suffered a nervous breakdown caused by overwork. One friend offered his home in Colorado Springs as a place to rest and recover. Within a few days Fannie Bloomfield-Zeisler, accompanied by a nurse, her oldest son, and a cook, set out for the Rockies.

The change proved beneficial and she began to improve. Sigmund had told his son and the nurse to try to persuade her to resume practicing, which she did after the first week. "From the moment Mrs. Zeisler began to play again her improvement made more rapid strides." Like the woman in *The Yellow*

Wallpaper, her cure was to be found in intellectual stimulation and not in total deprivation.

Exhibiting great sensitivity about his wife's psyche, Sigmund set in motion another event that helped restore her mental equilibrium. Within hours of her departure for Colorado Springs, he arranged for their youngest son, Ernest, to have a necessary and long-postponed hernia operation. He did not tell his wife about the surgery, and promised the boy that as soon as he felt well enough, they would both take the train to Colorado Springs and surprise his mother with his bravery. Fannie was told of the operation only hours before their train pulled into the station. The resulting relief and reunion accelerated the healing process. She began to focus less on the tragedy of the past and more on her hopes for the future.

A week later she wired her impresario that she was fully recovered and prepared to accept concert engagements for the following season. The family traveled to Europe for the summer. Sigmund noted that his wife returned from their trip 15 pounds heavier, and "in splendid health and exuberant spirits, impatient to get back to the concert platform."

Bloomfield-Zeisler continued to concertize almost every season until 1920, although in 1906 she began to limit the number of appearances, first to 30 per year and then, gradually, to 20, a decision precipitated by the emotional crisis as well as continued concern about her eyes. As she also explained in an interview, "My husband did not want me to be away from home so much, and neither did I. Our children are growing up, and we have a new house here, so I'm getting too fond of my home to spend much time away from it."[41]

The Zeislers celebrated birthdays and anniversaries with lavish enthusiasm. For Sigmund's fortieth birthday, Fannie threw a surprise party at which several of Chicago's best musicians dressed up as small boys and girls and performed a "children's symphony." She took part herself, holding a baby's milk bottle in one hand and a rattle in the other. For their twenty-fifth anniversary in October 1910, the entire 50' by 70' back lawn was covered with a hardwood floor over which was erected a canvas tent. Wreaths and garlands of fall leaves decorated the tent and a stage was built at one end. More than 200 guests were treated to a comic "mask" in celebration of the couple, after which caterers transformed the space into a dining room and everyone enjoyed a hot meal followed by dancing.

At their spacious home on Woodlawn Avenue, for more than 20 years the Zeislers entertained regularly in a manner reminiscent of the European salon. On the last Wednesday of each month they would be "at home." The Zeislers never knew how many guests would arrive, but by 9:30 or 10 in the evening the kitchen staff knew how much food to prepare — for 15 to 50 or sometimes 100 guests. The food was simple and usually combined with musical entertainment, a dramatic reading, or lively conversation on a current topic.

Sigmund Zeisler noted that one reason the Wednesday-night open houses were a particular source of satisfaction for his wife was that theirs was "the only home in which Gentiles and Jews met and mingled on a plane of perfect social equality." By furnishing such an opportunity, she felt she was doing her small part to help eliminate anti–Semitism. The belief that she could unite Jews and Gentiles through common cultural interest accords with the assimilationist leanings of many of the German Jews who immigrated to the United States in the nineteenth century.[42] The Zeislers took a secular approach to religion. Fannie Bloomfield-Zeisler gave concerts on Friday and Saturday, the Jewish Sabbath, observed Christmas as a day of gift giving, and was buried not in a Jewish ceremony but in one performed by the Chicago Ethical Society.[43] This behavior is consistent with that of the group of young American Jewish men and women who formed a kind of "intelligentsia" and were more likely to embrace secular philosophy than any organized religion.[44]

When Bloomfield-Zeisler's ethnicity was mentioned in contemporary articles, it was generally within the context of a physical description, assigning to her Jewishness an element of foreignness or exoticism. A reviewer in Grand Rapids, Michigan, for example, described her in 1890 as "a dark, slender Jewess, full of power and magnetism."[45] H. T. Parker, writing for the *Boston Transcript* in 1915, was more rhapsodic: "Some young artist, quick with memories of Rembrandt's pictures of Jewish women, ought to paint Mme. Bloomfield-Zeisler playing the piano, and it is easy to believe that the master himself would not have disclaimed her for a subject. As she sat yesterday afternoon in Jordan Hall, bent intently on the keyboard, she was pictorial indeed and rather in the fashion in which Rembrandt chose to limn and color his Jews. The sharp and strong Semitic profile; the deep-set and bright Semitic eyes; the full, hunched shoulders; the sinewy body; the dress rich in color and large flow of line; the whole impression of a vivid personality in vibrant play."[46]

For most years from 1889 to 1920, Fannie Bloomfield-Zeisler toured either in the United States or in Europe. Her American tour usually included an annual New York recital. Handwritten comments on many of the programs in her scrapbook indicate that she was frequently called upon to repeat pieces besides playing many encores.[47] Written annotations on a program from a Carnegie Hall recital given on January 26, 1907, for example, record that she repeated three of the advertised pieces in addition to performing *six* additional encores.[48] A recital on February 5, 1910, lasted a half-hour beyond its schedule; only when the lights were extinguished did the audience reluctantly depart.[49] Within this context, one should remember that the technology of recorded sound was still in its infancy in the early twentieth century. A live performance by a virtuoso of Bloomfield-Zeisler's stature was unique, and the only way one might hear a piece played in such a way again was to persuade the performer to repeat it.

On February 13, 1920, after an absence of several years from performing in New York, she played three major concertos in one concert, accompanied by an orchestra conducted by Victor Herbert. (The typical orchestral concert today features an instrumental soloist performing one concerto.) "Bloomfield-Zeisler Astounds New York" announced *Musical America*, giving an account of her brilliant interpretations of concertos by Mozart, Chopin, and Tchaikovsky. "The fire, color and Herculean power exhibited in [the Chopin concerto] was little short of overwhelming.... Only a few contemporary pianists are endowed with such a remarkable rhythmic faculty as this reincarnation of the old Fannie Zeisler." When the audience would not stop applauding, she followed these three large and demanding works with one of her most frequently performed encores with orchestra, the Scherzo by Litolff, which is characterized by rapid and dazzling fingerwork which she played with her usual "marvelous clarity, speed and polish."[50] Several days later she also performed in New York's Aeolian Hall with cellist Pablo Casals.[51]

Fannie Bloomfield-Zeisler was a celebrated professional pianist at a time when most women played the piano as a social grace. Having high standards, she felt strongly that music should not be trivialized — and not even an invitation from the White House caused her to compromise these principles. When a letter from Mrs. Theodore Roosevelt's secretary described as "a purely social affair" a "musicale" on which Bloomfield-Zeisler had been invited to perform, and added she might share the program with a singer who was "probably someone in the social circle," the pianist politely but decisively declined the invitation.[52]

Bloomfield-Zeisler insisted that her students be treated as serious professionals as well. When a Chicago matron requested that several of the pianist's advanced students donate their services, she responded that they should not be expected to perform without pay. "In fact it is against my principles to ask anybody who is worth-while hearing to do so," she responded, adding that if the lady could estimate a fee, she would do her best to persuade the students to accept the offer.[53]

Bloomfield-Zeisler believed that women were men's equals as musicians. In a lecture to the National Music Teachers Association in Detroit in 1890, she drew a distinction between the "reproductive" artist — the performer — and the "creative" artist — the composer. She acknowledged that women had proved their worth as performers but had yet to do so as composers. She reasoned, however, that this was through lack of opportunity and not lack of ability.[54] Acting on this belief, she served as an advocate for women composers by sometimes programming their pieces on her recitals. A New York program on November 17, 1915, for example, included pieces by Amy Cheney Beach, Mme. Signe Lund, Marie Prentner, and Cécile Chaminade. All four pieces had been dedicated to her by the composers — clear evidence that they were aware of her support. When a reporter questioned the wisdom of her programming these compositions, she replied, "People are apt to look askance if they see pieces by women on a program. I say ... if such things are never played, if artists will never bring them forward, they will always remain unknown. Yet these composers have their place and value." [55]

Bloomfield-Zeisler could not have accomplished all of this without help. When the children were small, one of her cousins lived with the family on a permanent basis and helped with housekeeping and child care.[56] When the boys were older, they attended boarding school and sometimes summer camp. Several letters that Bloomfield-Zeisler wrote to her two youngest sons at boarding school between 1910 and 1912 (Paul was 13 in 1910 and Ernest 11) show a typical mother fussing over their personal articles like pen nibs and suspenders, and urging them to remember to brush their teeth. Noting dryly on one occasion that she had received their "two laconic postals," she pleaded with them to write more often and tell her "everything" that happened. Although requests for frequent letters are not unusual among parents whose children are away at school, at one point she went so far as to ask twenty-five-year-old Leonard to enlist the help of an official at his brothers' school to make sure they wrote every other day. "Otherwise I will go frantic," she wrote, "and the little vacation which I need so badly will make me sick instead of resting me." Sometimes she told the boys that she would be unable to visit on a particular occasion because of another responsibility (the dressmaker was coming; she had to "do a stunt at the Book and Play Club" that evening; she had an inflamed elbow and was behind on her work). "We will make up for it when we are traveling together," she reassured them (and herself), referring to their summer trips to Europe or sometimes Mackinac Island, Michigan.

One must assume that at times her children disagreed with her priorities. It is difficult to believe, for example, that Ernest and Paul would think that a "stunt at the Book and Play Club" was more important than a visit with them. It is also true, however, that she was frequently torn between conflicting obligations. She spoke often of the tension, observing on one occasion that when a girl artist marries, she "assumes additional heavy burdens and is obliged to lead two entirely full lives — that is if she does her duty. In the case of the man who carries on a public career it makes little difference. He ... acquires in his wife someone who surrounds him with all of the comforts of domesticity and often stands between him and the unreasonableness of the outside world."[57]

When asked why she made the effort to lead "two entirely full lives," she explained, "From the beginning I felt somehow deep down, that I should realize my ambitions. There were heartaches and disappointments, but in my inner self I never faltered. It was that deep, underlying confidence, I suppose, which enabled me to keep my purpose.... It's part of me now, I guess, with all its work and study and travel and homesickness and stage frights and wooden smiles to audiences that are only blurs of faces. I must feed my ambitions occasionally. I think the desire is inherent; only in part is it acquired."[58] She also said she did it because she had no choice. "I play for the same reason that a drunkard drinks. I often feel that home life and its environments hold something that is lost — sacrificed — in living for the public, but I cannot give it up. I play because I must."[59]

Obviously her husband's help and support were essential to her success. She could probably have succeeded as a concert artist without them, but it was his willingness to accommodate her personal and professional needs in addition to his own that allowed her to fulfill the roles of artist, wife, and mother — and clearly all three roles were important to her. Sigmund altered the nature of his own career in favor of hers by resigning his position with the City of Chicago and maintaining a private legal practice which allowed him the flexibility to accompany her on some of her concert tours.[60] He sometimes put her needs above those of their children as well. In a letter she wrote to her sons at boarding school, Bloomfield-Zeisler explained that their father would be unable to visit them because he was "terribly busy and the few days that he will be away with me are positively all he can spare."[61] Sigmund's willingness to modify his own life in order to accommodate the needs and ambitions of his wife were particularly remarkable in the late nineteenth century.

February 25, 1925, marked the fiftieth anniversary of Fannie Bloomfield-Zeisler's first public performance and began a week of festivities in Chicago celebrating her life and career. She appeared as soloist with the Chicago Symphony with the proceeds of the concert going to establish a fund for the relief of needy musicians and their families. The enthusiastic sell-out crowd included prominent musicians from all over the country and the world. When Bloomfield-Zeisler appeared on stage, the members of the orchestra and the audience rose in her honor. Luncheons and public entertainments continued all week, culminating in a banquet attended by 400 people. Frederick Stock, conductor of the Chicago Symphony, introduced numerous speakers — newspaper critics, orchestra trustees, composers, students, a Steinway official — who all paid tribute to Bloomfield-Zeisler. After the speeches she rose and, "in a voice trembling with emotion," gave thanks to America, to Chicago, and to all of her friends and colleagues. The account in the *Chicago Musical Leader* noted that the crowd of well-wishers who surrounded her after the banquet included many distinguished women musicians who could have had successful careers but instead had "forsworn them to become domesticated."[62]

Fannie Bloomfield-Zeisler devoted much of her time during the rest of that year and the next to organizing the construction and dedication of a monument in Vienna honoring her teacher Theodor Leschetizky and was the principal speaker at the unveiling of the monument on September 26, 1926. During this European trip she began to exhibit shortness of breath and soon after her return to North America was diagnosed with a heart condition. After several months marked by seeming improvements followed by major setbacks, she died on August 18, 1927, at the age of 64.

"Perhaps the rarest thing about Madame Zeisler," read the eulogy at her memorial service, "is the fact that the same thoroughness which she devoted to all her professional work, was completely duplicated in all the other relations in her life.... For it is to be remembered that she lived as fully, and as rarely, the life of a wife and mother as she lived the life of the great artist.... Usually the artist finds it necessary to neglect all else for the sake of his art, to reduce domestic life to a mere incident ... and in the case of most of them, when they embrace the duties and happiness of domestic life, find it obligatory on them to sacrifice for that life any other career for which they may have been originally equipped by nature.... Because this is usually the case, we gaze with even more astonishment and admiration upon the wonderful and beautiful achievement of Mrs. Zeisler."

"A Gypsy Demon Possessed the Little Woman"

Ethel Leginska

Ethel Leginska pushed the boundaries of convention further than Fannie Bloomfield-Zeisler in both her professional and her personal life. She moved from a highly successful career as a pianist to the fields of composition and conducting, and from marriage and motherhood to the single careerism and outspoken feminism of the "new woman." Leginska belonged to the second generation of new women, who were educated in the 1890s and came into their own in the years immediately before and after World War I. While the previous generation of working women cultivated a sober style of dress and demeanor, and most often took up service professions such as teaching and social work, these later women placed more emphasis on self-fulfillment and frequently exhibited a more flamboyant personal style. Many moved easily in creative and artistic circles, rejected contemporary sexual conventions, and were at home in the Bohemian world of cities like New York, Paris, and Berlin.[1] Just as Bloomfield-Zeisler's experience illustrates public approval for the woman who managed to have a career while at the same time fulfilling her duties as a wife and mother, Leginska's underscores the premise that while wider opportunities appeared to be opening up for women in the early twentieth century, their possibilities were still constricted by prescribed gender roles.[2]

Ethel Leginska was born Ethel Annie Liggins in Hull, England, in 1886. Promoters changed her name early in her career because a foreign-sounding name was believed to contribute the cachet of continental sophistication to a musician's image. Like most successful concert artists, Leginska was a child prodigy — in her own words, "one of those horrid little nuisances, a wonder child" — born into a family she described as having no particular aptitude for music.[3] By the age of six she had already performed publicly. Her first teacher gave her a solid foundation in piano, encouraging her to improvise on a given theme and teaching her the basic elements of music theory and harmony. Later in life Leginska reminisced that her youth had been devoid of any "childish fun." [4]

The child's pianistic talents attracted the attention of Mary Emma Wilson, the wife of a local shipping magnate, who helped finance her musical education. When she was 11 Leginska received a scholarship to the Hoch Conservatory in Frankfurt; at 14 she began three years of study in Vienna with Theodor Leschetizky, who had also taught Fannie Bloomfield-Zeisler. (Leschetizky taught gifted pupils of both sexes, but evidence suggests that more were female than male.) He was so impressed with Leginska's talent that he taught her free of charge.[5] While in Vienna, Leginska met an American student, Emerson Whithorne, who was also studying piano, as well as composition and theory. Whithorne later wrote music criticism for *Musical America* and the *Pall Mall Gazette*, and his compositions were performed frequently in the 1920s and 1930s. After they married in 1907 he served as her concert manager from 1907 through 1909. [6] Their relationship was mutually beneficial professionally — Leginska frequently performed her husband's compositions, while he sometimes played the second piano part in two-piano pieces on her recitals.

By this time Ethel Leginska was already a popular performer in and around London, playing recitals and performing with major orchestras. A concert which included her performance of two piano concertos with the Queen's Hall Orchestra under the direction of Sir Henry Wood, was pronounced a "great success" by the *London Times* music reviewer, who reported enthusiastically that she played in "capital style."[7]

Leginska and Whithorne spent the first two years of their marriage in England, but undertook at least one trip to the United States in 1908 to visit Whithorne's native Cleveland. During this trip Leginska made her American debut in Cleveland's Hippodrome, a vaudeville theater. Her performance was sandwiched between a troupe of acrobats and a group of performing elephants. As the *Cleveland Plain Dealer* described the event on January 22, 1908, "Miss Ethel Leginska astonished Hippodrome audiences yesterday by her skill as a pianist.... The young woman's skill has stirred great enthusiasm and she was given several curtain calls.... The Gaudschmidts gave an excellent display of tumbling and athletic work.... The elephants continued to be a notable feature of the bill, and their antics seem not to pall."[8] While it was not unusual for vaudeville shows to include a combination of "highbrow" and "lowbrow" acts, it *was* somewhat unusual for a strictly "serious" instrumentalist to perform in vaudeville.[9]

The couple returned to England in early 1908, and in September of that year Leginska gave birth to a son, Cedric. For a brief time she combined the roles of wife, mother, and concert artist, but this appears to have been a difficult period in her life. Only a month after Cedric was born, Leginska embarked on a series of eight London recitals, each one devoted to the music of a different country or region. On November 19, 1908, she presented a recital of German music; in December, American music including pieces by her husband; in January, 1909, Polish, Bohemian, and Hungarian piano music; and on later programs, works by French, British, Italian, and Scandinavian composers. The series required her to perform a completely different program every month and to learn many pieces outside the standard piano repertoire. The recitals would have presented a challenge under any circumstances, and the stresses of public and private life apparently took their toll. The *London Times* noted after the first recital that by the end of the program "she was so tired that both her memory and her fingers failed her."[10] On February 9, 1909, Leginska failed to appear for her scheduled fourth recital. She was missing for four days until identified by the landlord of a Birmingham boardinghouse who recognized her from a newspaper photograph and telegraphed her husband. Leginska's father told reporters that his daughter's disappearance had been the result of a "lapse of memory caused by overwork."[11] The press referred to this and similar episodes she experienced later in her career as "nervous breakdowns."

Leginska continued to perform, however, making highly successful appearances in England and in major European cities including Paris, Berlin, Vienna, and Petrograd (St. Petersburg). In Berlin, where audiences were notoriously critical, a reviewer pronounced her technique "extraordinary," and described her musical conception as "profound and imbued with the personal element of the born artist."[12]

Leginska and her husband separated in 1910. Although neither spoke publicly of the reasons, Leginska frequently expressed strong opinions about combining a career with marriage and children. Men, she noted, wasted no time on self-sacrifice, which she viewed as an "over-rated and, in the long run, usually wasteful virtue." She said that a woman should not "surrender herself body and soul" to a husband and family, adding that a husband and children would respect a wife and mother more if she were allowed to pursue her own interests in addition to theirs. Leginska doubted, however, that this balance was feasible for performing artists, observing that "women who achieve great names in arts do receive much adulation and attention from men, but these men do not want them for wives. The great men want little girls.... They want their women to be unselfish, and it is impossible for a woman with a career to be unselfish."[13]

After the separation, Whithorne remained in England for a time as correspondent for the American weekly *Musical America*. Their son Cedric may have spent a brief period with his mother, but before long he was sent to Cleveland to be cared for by his paternal grandparents.[14] Leginska shifted her base of operation to the United States and settled in New York.

Although she had performed to great critical acclaim in England and Europe, when Leginska arrived in New York she was almost completely unknown and had very little money. She prepared for her debut by depriving herself of most social contacts and devoting all her time to practice and teaching. As she related years later, "When I first came to America, for one year I closeted myself in a studio at Carnegie Hall, gave lessons every morning and practiced every night until 10 o'clock. I was very young and I liked the companionship of merry people, but I denied myself all these things so as not to be diverted. Again, I wanted to save my money for my concert season that was to come the following year." For 14 months the only people to whom she spoke regularly were her students and an occasional tradesperson.[15]

Her New York debut took place in Aeolian Hall on January 21, 1913.[16] In a recital devoted to the works of Beethoven, Brahms, Chopin, and Liszt, Leginska impressed the critics and captivated the audience. She was pronounced "an artist of unusual gifts and attainments" and praised for her "fiery temperament," "controlled strength," and the "brilliance and facility of her technique." Hailed by critics as the "newest musical sensation," she was enthusiastically compared to Paderewski and Rubinstein.[17] Seven engagements followed with the orchestra of the Symphony Society of New York, with which she performed in various cities in New York State and Ohio between January and late February 1913. Her orchestral appearances in New York City and Brooklyn fueled requests for another full recital, which she presented on March 19 in the much larger Carnegie Hall. Her busy and successful year ended with yet another Carnegie Hall recital in December 1913, where she presented works by Bach, Scarlatti, Mozart, Weber, Schubert, Mendelssohn, Chopin, Schumann, Liszt, Reger, MacDowell, Ravel, Cyril Scott, and Debussy. The *New York Times* reported that she played with "exquisite beauty." [18]

Leginska allowed herself at least one diversionary break during the summer of 1913, when she toured as pianist for modern dancer Ruth St. Denis. Dancers like St. Denis and Isadora Duncan customarily hired classically trained musicians to accompany their performances, intending their dance to be a visual representation of the music. St. Denis, who described Leginska as "one of the most intense personalities I have ever come across," provided a comical picture of their Bohemian travels: "Father, Ethel Leginska and I went off in Buzz's [St. Denis's brother] glorified wreck of a car to play in Maine. We got our luggage strapped to the back of this terrible contraption and my colored maid, Mary, strapped to a seat on the side of the car. We had part of a windshield and no top. Some of the car's innards could be seen from the front; Buzz had painted the wheels red in spite of the bilious green upholstery. Poor Mary clutched to her seat as though her last moment had come, but Ethel loved it; and Buzz, who found her quite the lady of his heart, was in transports of delight at being able to carry her along at forty miles an hour…. Our Maine concertizing was very al fresco. Ethel pounded and I danced and Buzz watered the car."[19]

Following this unconventional interlude Leginska toured extensively in North America, performing both solo recitals and concertos with orchestra. Like other major artists, she kept up a tireless pace. Between October 26 and November 14, 1917, for example, she performed in Des Moines, St. Paul, Winnipeg, Calgary, Duluth, and Kansas City.[20] She also had a prodigious repertoire. One of her scrapbooks contains a list of "master composer" recitals she gave between November 1915 and March 1916; every month she presented at least one complete recital of the works of a major composer. In a five-month period she gave eight recitals which featured the music of Brahms, Chopin, Bach, Beethoven, Macdowell, Schubert, Schumann, and Liszt.[21]

Ethel Leginska made a dramatic impression both on and off the stage. One interviewer described her as communicating an "undeniably hypnotic effect," while another observed that after only five minutes it was clear that she possessed "vitality, forcefulness [and] vividness burning like a flame; there is intellect of the type usually described as 'masculine' in that tiny, very feminine person." A newspaper critic reported that when she performed Liszt's Hungarian Fantasy, it was as if "a gypsy demon possessed the little woman, who played with a reckless daring which took the breath quite away from the listeners as well as the orchestra."[22]

Aware of her power to impress, Leginska experimented deliberately and dramatically with different ways of presenting herself as a female virtuoso in a male-dominated field. While most women concert artists of the period wore elaborate evening gowns, as early as 1909 Leginska sometimes performed in a feminized version of male concert attire — a dark dress or skirt and jacket with a touch of white at the neck. She explained that this costume gave her freedom of movement, kept her warm in drafty concert halls, and allowed her to stop thinking about her appearance and concentrate on her art.[23] Her hairstyle was also the subject of much comment, as she wore it short and bobbed in the style fashionable during World War I; critics also observed that the cut resembled that worn by Liszt and Paderewski. Photographs of Leginska provide intriguing examples of one woman musician's experimentation with image. In a photo from the 1910s she sits in profile, looking like a plump, beruffled country maid. In another from the same period she faces the camera wearing an early version of her tailored costume. In a picture from 1917, at the height of her pianistic career, she again stands in profile, wearing a diaphanous dress, eyes lowered and gazing demurely at a drooping flower. And as a conductor in the 1920s, in direct contrast to the passive image with the flower, she boldly faces the camera dressed in a tuxedo and vest.[24]

Leginska's stage dress resembled the comfortable and practical attire worn by her contemporaries in other professions, such as writers Willa Cather and Gertrude Stein, painters Frida Kahlo and Romaine Brooks, and physician Mary Walker. These and other women of the period used male attire both to free

Changing images: publicity photos of Ethel Leginska as pianist (left) and as conductor (right). (Unidentified newspaper clippings, New York Public Library, Ethel Leginska clipping file.)

themselves from the constraints of restrictive female dress and to convey their seriousness about their work. As Leginska herself said, "My outward appearance expresses my desire to do a man's-size work in the world." By modifying their dress, these women sought to alter gender expectations.[25]

Some reporters expressed discomfort with Leginska's costume and coiffure. A 1915 headline in the *New York Press* announced, "Energetic English Pianiste Tries Hard as She Can to Be Like a Man; Wears Short Hair, Mannish Suit, with Long Sleeves and Something Suspiciously Like a Skirt, Thus Ridding Herself of Frills."[26] A Boston writer observed that her choice of severe black dress, short hair and large steel shoe-buckles revealed an "imposing personality.... It is always a question whether a woman taking a man's place should be met with the discreet courtesy due to her sex or as a man."[27] Such criticism was consistent with the newly conceptualized "science" of "sexology," which attributed violations of gender rules to organic disorders. Within this context Viennese neurologist Krafft-Ebing pronounced it "abnormal" for women to

prefer male garments, stigmatizing women who did so as analogous to effemi-
nate men.[28]

Ironically, Leginska claimed to see her dress not as a method of appearing mannish, but instead as a way to *eliminate* gender from her performance
and serve simply as the conduit through which the music flowed. This was not
lost on one critic, who observed that, dressed completely in black, with black
hair, she appeared to be "an integral part of the big black instrument on which
she plays," and that her habit of sitting almost with her back to the audience
allowed listeners to focus more completely on the music. "What I may call her
'human personality' has nothing to do with her art, at least as far as the eye
of the hearer is concerned."[29] This approach was in direct contrast to that of
the early male virtuosos, whose flamboyance drew attention to themselves as
personalities, or the elaborately dressed women virtuosos, whose gowns emphasized their femininity. Yet in combination with her youth, Leginska made the
severe purity of her devotion to the music a source of drama.

Leginska was diminutive in size and looked much younger than her
chronological age, a fact she probably exploited, knowing that an appearance
of precocity made her seem more remarkable. In 1915, when she was 29, a Dayton reviewer referred to her as a "very young protegee" who played with the
"enthusiasm of youth" and "the gladness of the child." In the same year another
called her a "little miss in short skirts and with hair bobbed," noting (ironically) how remarkable it was that she could combine "all the fire and abandon
of youth" with "the care and thoughtfulness and understanding of a mature
artist." A Buffalo critic observed in 1916, when she was 30, that "this splendid
young woman has talents far beyond what one would expect in one so fragile
in appearance and so young." Robert Kelly of the *Detroit News* described her,
when she was 37, as "a slip of a girl in whom glowed the spark of a genius."
And a reporter in Racine, Wisconsin, estimated her to be in her early twenties when she performed there in 1929 — she was in fact 43.[30]

Leginska often dramatized her virtuosity by performing on a darkened
stage with only her hands illuminated. The effect of the lighting, the dress,
the hair, and the youthfulness, combined with her remarkable playing, left
audiences spellbound. "When she seated herself at the piano, the instrument
seemed disproportionately, cruelly large. Her hair, bobbed Galahad-like, to stop
at the shoulders, her long manlike gown, her air of absorption, were all sug-
gestive of a female Liszt, unspoiled as yet by mannerisms. With the passing of
the evening, this figure frequently silhouetted against its background along
with the green, and the American Beauty roses that provided a touch of con-
trasting richness to an essential somberness; and as the eyes and brain of the
spectator and listener succumbed to the hypnotic influence of the decorative
scheme, and to the light, and to the music of the piano, there were moments
when the predominating consciousness was of a boyish, half-hidden face, a

white collar, and two agile hands that performed with uncanny dexterity and eloquence."[31]

Leginska's personal style was so distinctive that it inspired young girls with musical aspirations to imitate her. Critic James Huneker described an audience of such girls at one of her performances in New York in 1919: "The hall was full of little Ethel Leginskas with Buster Brown coiffures, full of suppressed technique and boiling over with enthusiasm."[32] The December 27, 1919, issue of *Musical America* includes a photograph of Leginska and five young girls having tea; all are identically clad in dark, tailored dresses with white collars and all sport similar bobbed haircuts. The text speculates whether the picture should be captioned "The Bobbed-Hair Damozels," "The New Day in Feminism," or "Aftermath of Suffrage." The Leginska phenomenon was so widespread that actress/comedienne Gertrude Hoffman performed an imitation of "the Paderewski of women pianists" on her cross-country vaudeville tour.[33]

Leginska reinforced her image of independence with outspoken comments on many "feminist" issues, frequently stating that a woman's only chance to succeed was "to stand on her own two feet and emulate man." Unlike Fannie

Ethel Leginska with a group of enthusiastic young followers. ("Ethel Leginska Makes Converts to a Quaint Cause," *Musical America* 31, December 27, 1919.)

Bloomfield-Zeisler, who sought to reassure the public that she did not neglect her domestic duties, Leginska declared that women should not allow themselves to be diverted by "trifles, societal, sartorial or domestic" while men single-mindedly pursued their goals. She criticized the superficial education of girls, saying that they should be taught to excel in one thing instead of being encouraged to dabble in many. When she was a child, Leginska recalled, she was often told that something she wanted to do wasn't "proper" for little girls. "Men have never been put off with such an unreasonable reason — they wouldn't stand for it. Because women haven't done something in the past, it is supposed to be reason enough why they shouldn't do it in the future.... We will never be original, do great work, until we get some courage and daring, and trust our own way instead of the eternal beaten paths on which we are always asked to poke along."[34]

Leginska's behavior often matched her assertive rhetoric. On one occasion early in her career, she was taken backstage to meet the legendary pianist Vladimir de Pachmann. As she described it, the famous artist "lifted his hand to my mouth in order that I might have the honor of kissing it. Being not at all inclined to avail myself of this opportunity, I gave him instead a good British handshake. With a howl of indignation he went hopping about the room, first on one foot, then on the other, exclaiming 'She bruk' my wrist! She bruk' my wrist!' while a circle of doting de Pachmann enthusiasts glared at me for my 'gross affront to the master.'"[35]

Leginska's ideas about dress, hair, and career issues were consistent with the image of the "New Woman" of the 1910s and 1920s — a style which rejected fashion in favor of comfort and practicality, endorsed financial independence from male relatives, affected emancipated habits like smoking and using bold language, and asserted women's rights to the same privileges enjoyed by men. While the generation of feminists born between 1850 and 1900 often endorsed the notion that women were superior in virtue to men, those of Leginska's generation fought for absolute equality. "They wished to be as successful, as political, as sexual as men. Their mannish bob, cigarette smoking, boyish figures, symbolized their rejection of gender distinctions."[36] As one Bostonian noted approvingly, "Mme. Leginska has an atmosphere about her which is truly twentieth-century, and the very opposite of Jenny Lind — twentieth-century science, twentieth-century art, and twentieth-century emancipation of woman."[37]

Sometimes Leginska revealed an acerbic quality with interviewers whose questions she considered obvious or boring. On one occasion she spun an elaborate tale about how she had once disguised herself as a boy, and traveled from France to Vienna, earning subsistence money by doing odd jobs along the way. On another, when asked what advice she would give the aspiring young concert pianist, she satirized the standard answer given girls considering a musical career: "Suffice it to say that the young musician who has ambition to some time become world renowned will find no rosy path before him. Boys, in particular — unless they have assurance that theirs is an unusual talent — should not plan to make the public concert stage their life's work. For when the 'One Girl' comes into a boy's life, he will realize it is better to be a good plumber with an assured income than a mediocre musician with no future prospects. No career, however famous, can ever compensate for having missed the great opportunity that comes but once to every man and every woman."[38] Apparently the reporter did not realize she was speaking tongue in cheek.

Leginska's avowed certitude in choosing public performance over domesticity seemingly faltered in 1917 when, at the height of her pianistic career, she sued her husband for divorce and custody of their son. Newspaper headlines — "Actress and Pianiste in Divorce Triangle" and "Wife Accuses Stage Beauty" — hyped the legal battle between the famous pianist, her prominent composer-husband, and Martha Hedman, the beautiful actress with whom he was frequently seen. Whithorne countercharged that Leginska had been romantically involved with Oliver Denton, another prominent pianist.[39]

Leginska's North American public was startled to learn that she was married. A newspaper headline summed up the clash of image and reality: "Demon Gypsy Announces Marriage in Divorce Court."[40] Her youthful appearance and outspoken feminism had contributed to the impression that she was single, and Leginska had done nothing to dispel this impression. According to one reporter, "only a few of her most intimate friends knew the celebrated pianist was married, and many of her friends and admirers of her art were astonished to learn that she not only had a husband but also a son." Another startled critic, who had obviously thought her to be much younger, reported with amazement that Leginska was "not only not a child" but a wife and mother as well.[41]

It is unclear why Leginska chose to sue for divorce and especially for custody at this particular time. She had not lived with Emerson Whithorne since 1910, nor with her son for almost as long, and she was clearly out of touch with Cedric. One of the lawyers representing the boy's grandparents at the custody hearing stated that although Leginska had performed in Cleveland a number of times during the past several years, she had never attempted to visit him. When Leginska encountered Cedric in court for the first time, she asked for a kiss and approached the eight year old with gifts of candy and, most inappropriately, a toy rattle. He burst into tears and clung to his grandmother. While it seems doubtful that Leginska should have been awarded custody, the fact that she sued shows that, at least briefly, she had second thoughts regarding motherhood. At one point in the trial she promised to stop performing in public if the boy lived with her, assuring the court that she could earn $300 a week if she devoted herself exclusively to teaching.[42]

In the courtroom drama, Leginska's personal style and profession were used in attempts to discredit her. A friend of Emerson Whithorne testified that he had tried his best to prevent the marriage because he had been concerned that she was "so much afflicted with the artistic temperament." And a hostile attorney asked Leginska whether she was "addicted to the cigaret habit." The judge awarded custody of the boy to his grandparents.[43]

At the close of the 1918 concert season, with her fame as a pianist undimmed, Leginska declared a self-imposed sabbatical from performing. She cited the performance anxiety that had always plagued her and the sheer exhaustion of having concertized and toured, almost without interruption, for the past seven seasons.[44] The custody battle provides additional evidence that, at the age of 32, Ethel Leginska was reevaluating her priorities. She told the press she planned to concentrate her energies on teaching and on the formal study of composition, commenting that her previous inattention to composition was the result of "the conventional status of women in musical activities" rather than any "deficiency of creative impulse" in herself.[45]

Leginska was sufficiently well known that her possible shift from performer to composer elicited an editorial in the *Christian Science Monitor*, which questioned the wisdom of "giving up an assured career for a problematical one." The piece noted that many people were impatient for her to finish her "experiments at the writing desk" and return to her "triumphs at the keyboard."[46] Nonetheless, Leginska shifted her attention from performance to composition.

For an aspiring composer, these were heady years to live in New York. The city was becoming the capital of American culture and the nation's music business. Even as international influences excited artists and intellectuals, American composers were experimenting with new rhythms and harmonies to create a uniquely "American" style. Aaron Copland recalled it as "the intoxicating world of trying anything."[47]

Public awareness of "new music" began in 1915 with the "futurist" compositions of iconoclast Leo Ornstein, a composer who seemed pivotal at the time but has since receded into obscurity. In addition to the works of Ornstein, New York audiences attended the premieres of works by Schoenberg and Stravinsky, American composers Henry Cowell, Carl Ruggles, Charles Seeger, Ruth Crawford, and Charles Griffes, and European émigrés Edgar Varese and Ernest Bloch. All contributed musical ideas to the avant-garde explosion.

Ethel Leginska figured prominently within this musical scene. She studied composition with Ernest Bloch; she performed with Leo Ornstein; she lived and taught in Greenwich Village; she was a member of the board of directors of the International Composers Guild, an organization founded by Edgar Varese in 1921 to promote performances of new music. Leginska composed music for voice, orchestra, small chamber ensembles, and piano. Many of her instrumental works were performed by mainstream ensembles soon after

their composition, although they remained unpublished and most of the man-
uscripts have not survived. Her tone poem for orchestra, "Beyond the Fields
We Know," for example, was performed by the New York Symphony in February 1922. Her "Four Poems After Tagore" was played by the London String
Quartet in June 1921 and the New York String Quartet in March 1925. Her
compositions were also performed by Pro-Musica, another prominent group
that presented avant-garde music in New York between 1923 and 1930.[48] Well-
known singers such as soprano Nina Morgana, baritone Arthur Middleton,
and Metropolitan Opera tenor Rafael Diaz performed Leginska's songs. Some
of her songs and piano music were published by major firms such as Schirmer
and the John Church Company.[49]

Leginska's compositional style was, for the most part, explicitly "modern"
and avant-garde. As she remarked in 1924, "We are living in a period that
demands an idiom of its own."[50] One reviewer described her piano solo "Dance
of a Puppet" as "angular, mechanical, brittle and biting," with "startling and
puzzling" dynamic effects, and "clashing major and minor seconds [which] are
frequently shocking to the Romantic ear." Another stated that her "Gargoyles
of Notre Dame" "strayed so far afield from the beaten paths of music that they
became bizarre and bewildering." Her performance (with the People's Orchestra of Boston) of her "Two Short Pieces for Orchestra" impressed one listener
as both "gossamer" and "bizarre ... frankly dissonant, but expressively so."[51]

Some placed her in the category of new composers who tried to be modern for modern's sake. Daniel Gregory Mason, a composer and professor of
music at Columbia University from 1905 to 1942, wrote, "The struggle to be
'modern' and 'original' preoccupies almost everyone, and beautiful melodic
ideas ... are dismissed by people like Salzedo, Gautier, Loeffler, Bloch, Bauer
and Leginska as 'old-fashioned.'" Mason went on to say that while it was permissible to present simple musical thoughts in new ways, it was unacceptable
merely to "willfully multiply oddities."[52]

During this period of exploration Leginska participated in a wide variety
of musical activities. She was one of only two women (the other was Germaine
Tailleferre) who served on the advisory committee of the International Composers Guild, considered by some to be the musical equivalent of Alfred
Stieglitz's Gallery 291. (Stieglitz attended many of the Guild's concerts.) Leginska was one of only two women (again the other was Tailleferre) whose compositions were performed by Pro-Musica.[53] Leginska also devoted much of her
time to teaching, as she had throughout her career. Between 1919 and 1922
several of her most gifted students gave debut recitals in New York and Boston.
Whenever a student performed, the fact that she was a "student of Leginska"
featured prominently in both the advertising and the reviews. Leginska also
investigated the possibility of a full-time teaching position, writing David
Mannes of Manhattan's Mannes School of Music to inquire about openings.[54]

Although she did not perform as a soloist during this period, Leginska took part in numerous chamber music concerts, including several with cellist Hans Kindler and others with the San Francisco Chamber Music Society and the New York String Quartet. She also performed with Leo Ornstein on at least one documented occasion, when they presented the premiere of his Sonata for Two Pianos on March 7, 1923.[55]

During these years Leginska began the formal study of orchestral conducting. She explained in 1923 that she had originally intended to study conducting as a way to learn more about the various instruments so that she could more skillfully compose for them. Before long, however, conducting became the more compelling activity.[56] She also believed it was necessary to move beyond the mastery of one musical instrument in order to be a truly great musician: "Being a pianist is nothing. I have always said that. Think of what Liszt accomplished. He was first a pianist, then a composer, and he ended his career as the greatest conductor of the age."[57]

Historically, the shift from instrumental soloist to conductor has been relatively common among male instrumentalists. In the nineteenth century, pianists Franz Liszt, Hans von Bülow and Anton Rubinstein did considerable conducting. In the twentieth century, pianists Leonard Bernstein, Daniel Barenboim, André Previn and Vladimir Ashkenazy; violinists Yehudi Menuhin and Pinchas Zuckerman; cellists Pablo Casals and Mstislav Rostropovitch all began their careers as instrumentalists and then shifted, at least in part, to orchestral conducting. For pianists in particular it seems a logical move. Since the instrument, like an orchestra, is capable of playing many musical lines simultaneously, pianists become accustomed to conceptualizing their music in orchestral terms. As Leginska commented, "I think of the piano as orchestral; it seems to me there is a growing tendency to make it like an orchestra."[58]

For part of the 1923 season Leginska studied conducting with Eugene Goossens in London and Robert Heger in Munich. Three years later Goossens expressed a chauvinistic view of women conductors, saying, rather ominously for Leginska, "To conduct a very large orchestra entails endurance and nerve strain for which a woman is not physically fitted. A conductor must have a forceful personality also. I have met few women musicians with a personality sufficiently forceful to ensure the control of a very large orchestra either of men only, or men and women, or of women."[59]

In 1924 Leginska appeared as guest conductor with major orchestras in Munich, Paris, London, and Berlin. She secured conducting engagements by shrewdly drawing upon contacts she had developed during her years as a pianist and in most cases, by agreeing to perform a piano concerto on the program she conducted.[60] In a manner similar to the style later revived by Leonard Bernstein, she would generally conduct from the piano. Typically she included one of her own compositions on the program.

Ethel Leginska made her American conducting debut with the New York Symphony at Carnegie Hall on January 9, 1925, in performances of a Wagner overture, a Bach piano concerto, Beethoven's Seventh Symphony, and her own "Four Poems After Tagore." It was the first time a woman had conducted a major American symphony orchestra. The concert was well attended, in spite of being outside the regular symphony series.[61]

The size of the audience boded well for Leginska, since she faced formidable competition for concertgoers' attention that week. On January 3 Wilhelm Furtwängler conducted what one reviewer described as "the most important New York podium debut since Mahler and Toscanini arrived at the Metropolitan Opera." On January 6 Leopold Stokowski conducted a performance of the Philadelphia Orchestra. On January 8 Igor Stravinsky made his American debut conducting a program of his own works. The entire New York season was notable for its plethora of big-name conductors, which also included Willem Mengelberg, Ernst von Dohnanyi, Walter Damrosch, Serge Koussevitzky, Otto Klemperer, and Fritz Reiner. [62]

Not surprisingly, Leginska's presence on the podium raised many eyebrows. As the *New York Sun* reported wryly the next day, "The intermission gave everyone time to discuss the new successor of Stransky, Bodanzky, Stravinsky, Damrosch, Van Hoogstraten, Mengelberg, Golschmann and Henry Hadley. There was much talk." One critic observed that her appearance had "occasioned curiosity, skepticism, and even some hardly suppressed merriment on the part of certain scoffing and uncavalierly males." Another noted, however, that there were many who "came to ridicule and stayed to admire." A third overheard a "thoughtful gentleman" report to his companion after the performance, "My worst fears have been by no means realized."[63] Of course we have no way of directly judging Leginska's performance as a conductor, but we *can* compare her background and experience to that of other conductors of the period.

Most nineteenth- and early twentieth-century conductors had no formal training in conducting, although all had studied music in some form. As previously noted, some were instrumentalists: Toscanini was a cellist, Hans Richter and Arthur Nikisch were violinists, and Gustav Mahler and Willem Mengelberg were pianists. Others, like Bruno Walter and Erich Kleiber, had worked as opera coaches or choral directors, while still others, like Wilhelm Furtwängler, had studied composition.[64] And conductors don't agree on what constitutes appropriate training anyway. Some feel strongly that one can learn basic technique from a book or in the classroom; others are equally convinced that the only way to learn to conduct is by actually conducting. Eugène Bigot, for example, who conducted prominent groups in Paris in the period between 1913 and 1947 and taught conducting at the Paris Conservatory, maintained that "beating time without an orchestra will aid the student to learn to conduct about as much as fingering an imaginary instrument will enable a violinist to play Paganini."[65]

The early musical training of most illustrious conductors was actually quite similar to Leginska's. Gustav Mahler, for example, entered the Vienna Conservatory at 15, where he studied piano with Julius Epstein. There was, however, one critical difference — the male musician almost always had a mentor who helped him obtain his first opportunities to conduct. Mahler and Epstein, for example, developed a close personal and professional relationship. Two years after Mahler graduated from the conservatory, Epstein helped him obtain his first conducting position, although Mahler was only 20 years old and had no prior conducting experience. This beginning post involved leading an orchestra of 15 players performing popular operettas at an Austrian spa. The job gave Mahler confidence as well as experience. He wrote on a job application soon afterwards, "I have acquired sufficient insight to know that I am capable of filling such a position in any theater whatever." Toscanini was equally inexperienced when he conducted for the first time at age 19. Plucked from the cello section of his touring opera company orchestra as a last-minute replacement for the scheduled conductor, he directed *Aida* without a rehearsal.[66]

Starting as novices, most conductors began with deficiencies and improved their conducting skills on the job. Berta Geissmar, a close friend and secretarial assistant to conductor Wilhelm Furtwängler, observed, "While Furtwängler was learning, he was often handicapped by conflicts between technique and vision.... He gesticulated in all directions, shook his head constantly, walked about his rostrum, made faces when something went wrong, stamped, sang, shouted, and even spat." She described his beat as "an absolute nightmare to all players until they get used to it." A member of the London Philharmonic Orchestra once commented in frustration that Furtwängler's baton descended "only after the thirteenth preliminary wiggle."[67]

Reviews of Leginska's conducting debut ranged from patronizing to cautiously positive. Olin Downes of the *New York Times* reported that Leginska showed "enthusiasm for her task," and that her interpretive ideas were clear, "at least to herself." Downes sarcastically concluded, "It is to be hoped that later in the season Miss Leginska will give a piano recital." The *New York Herald Tribune* reported that although Leginska probably would not claim to be more than an "earnest student of the conductor's art," it was "at least to her credit that nothing very serious occurred to mar the performance for which she so energetically beat time, indicated entrances, and communicated her ideas of expression." Frank Warren of the *New York Evening World*, adopting a patronizing tone, gamely acknowledged that "the aspirant did a very good job. She knew the music and she got her own effects from the band." Three reviewers speculated that because the program contained pieces already familiar to the orchestra, the men could have performed without any conductor at all — an extremely peevish comment given that most orchestras of the period performed familiar works from the standard repertoire.[68]

The audience applauded enthusiastically at the end of the performance and Leginska tried repeatedly to make the orchestra rise and bow with her — a standard gesture of mutual respect between conductor and orchestra. But, as Olin Downes described it, "those astute gentlemen preferred that she alone should receive credit for the performance and remained obstinately seated." Frank Warren observed that the men of the orchestra assumed a "coy attitude, refusing to rise on any occasion when requested, leaving all the glory to the conductor." The men's failure to rise could indeed have been a gesture of tribute or respect, but in this context it could equally well have expressed discomfort at being led by a woman and signified an attempt to disassociate themselves from the performance.

Leginska served as a guest conductor with the New York Symphony — that is, one who leads the ensemble for one or more concerts in place of the regular or permanent leader. A few weeks after her appearance, an article in *Musical America* discussed the challenges of such a position, noting that a guest conductor usually has few opportunities to rehearse the group before the actual performance. "To win a new orchestra is no easy task," the writer observed, "and few conductors succeed in giving finished performances at their first guest appearances." Esteemed conductor Wilhelm Furtwängler stated that it was difficult to do one's best when facing a "strange orchestra which may be antagonistic," adding that "your degree of success depends largely on your ability to gain the respect of your men, to make them feel your interpretations."[69]

Less than three weeks after Leginska risked her reputation at her conducting debut, her prestige suffered lasting damage in a well publicized incident that branded her as a temperamental artist who could not be relied upon to show up for a scheduled performance. She was to give a piano recital at Carnegie Hall on January 27, 1925. With 2,000 people assembled, in a situation similar to that which had occurred in London 15 years earlier, she failed to appear. "Leginska Not Found; Nerves Are Blamed," announced the front page of the *New York Times* the next day. The paper speculated that when she doubted her ability to play the difficult program (one she had successfully performed before, it should be noted), she "became a little girl again and just ran away." This analysis is consistent with the contemporary view of the "hysterical" woman as one whose responses could be traced, in part, to her immature and childlike personality. Beliefs that women were weak and capricious, with limited capacity to think and to concentrate, led naturally to notions that "hysterical women were, in effect, children, and ill-behaved, difficult children at that."[70]

Though it is impossible to know what went through Leginska's mind before this recital, it is easy to imagine that she had misgivings about walking onto the same stage where, just 18 days earlier, she had been greeted with "skepticism" and "hardly suppressed merriment." Leginska's personal scrapbook contains only one reference to this incident, a clipping from the *London Weekly Dispatch* which says artists should be excused their occasional idiosyncrasies. "For the true artist has of necessity an unconventional mind.... The art which amazes and enchants us comes from a mind which perceives aspects of things that escape the rest of us. The owners of these minds may be — must be — allowed eccentricities."[71]

Leginska continued to conduct, but shifted her base of operation from New York to Boston. During the 1925-26 season she appeared at least five times as guest conductor of the People's Symphony, an organization composed partially of former members of the Boston Symphony who had left that group when the orchestra was forbidden to unionize. The People's Symphony was not the primary source of employment for its members, most of whom had other music jobs in theaters and hotels. The men were paid for rehearsals, but these were generally limited to three because of the necessity to pay union scale. The orchestra raised most of its money from ticket sales and kept ticket prices deliberately low so that more people could attend.[72] Leginska received no pay for her guest conducting beyond "enhancing her prestige as an orchestra leader." In many of the concerts, she performed a piano concerto while conducting from the keyboard, and frequently included one of her own compositions on the program. So she often served in a triple capacity as conductor, pianist and composer.[73]

Reviews of Leginska and the People's Orchestra were cautiously positive. The critic from the *Christian Science Monitor* observed that she "made an excellent impression. Obviously she knew what she was about; clearly she had definite notions of what she wanted, and the means to impress her desires on the players." The review described her as "both graceful and dynamic," but expressed discomfort at what were judged to be extravagant physical gestures. But the reviewer for the *Musical Courier* stated that the public was "handicapped by an unexplainable distaste for women as orchestral leaders."[74]

Whatever the ambivalence of reviewers, Bostonians flocked to the concerts. The size of the audience increased with each of her appearances, and by the fourth the theater was so full that all the standing room was taken and chairs were added to the orchestra pit. As the *Christian Science Monitor* reported, "It was little wonder that enthusiasm ran high in the audience, for Leginska is herself an enthusiast; she revels in her music; she believes the orchestra is capable of great things, and she fires them with her own enthusiasm."[75]

Leginska also resumed her performance of solo recitals in 1925, although she occasionally exhibited signs of performance anxiety. On at least two occasions in the fall of 1925 and winter of 1926, one at Washington Irving High

School in New York and the other in Evansville, Indiana, she failed to appear for scheduled performances. She also showed signs of what the *New York Times* termed "Gotham temperament" when she expressed displeasure at the cab, the hall, and the piano in Evansville.[76] Most of her 1925 performances proceeded without incident, however, including an extensive tour of the West, with appearances in Phoenix, San Francisco, Casper, Bozeman, Helena, Denver, Pueblo, and Long Beach.[77]

Leginska's western tour included a highly acclaimed appearance as guest conductor of the Hollywood Bowl Orchestra on August 5, 1925. (Other guest conductors that summer had included Fritz Reiner, Pierre Monteux, Sir Henry Wood, and Howard Hanson.) Again she served in a triple capacity as conductor, pianist, and composer. Thirty thousand people attended the concert; traffic was so heavy that the performance began a half-hour late because the members of the orchestra could not get to the amphitheater. "As the evening went on, the applause grew into a veritable ovation, culminating with cheers and bravos when Mme. Leginska took her bow after playing the Weber concerto for piano and conducting simultaneously." The audience recalled her nine times, even though it was late in the evening when the program ended. An insider's account suggests that Leginska's success was hard won. Hollywood Bowl historian Grace Koopal writes that while the conductor "electrified the audience," she had also "enraged the orchestra in a dramatic example of 'Women's Lib,'" exhibiting a "tempestuous fighting spirit, even resorting to profanity at rehearsals.... The night of her program she coped more than adequately with ... the ninety rebellious

Ethel Leginska. (New York Public Library.)

musicians under her baton." Koopal also noted that Leginska paved the way for Antonia Brico, who would conduct the Bowl orchestra in 1930. "Remembering [Leginska's] virtuosity, the men treated a later woman conductor with more respect."[78]

Almost a year to the day after Leginska had made her Carnegie Hall conducting debut she again performed in New York, in January 1926, conducting an orchestra made up of 80 members of the New York Philharmonic. Given her previous willingness to conduct without pay, it is possible that she organized the concert and paid the musicians herself. Leonard Liebling of the *New York American* reported that although she displayed no "new interpretive revelation," she nonetheless performed in a "straightforward, meritorious and musical way."[79]

A review of this concert by Olga Samaroff, a celebrated pianist who had been the wife of conductor Leopold Stokowski, stands out because she was probably the only person capable of judging the performance from the multiple perspectives of pianist, conductor, and woman virtuoso. Samaroff noted that Leginska's conducting was of interest not only because of her (Leginska's) personality, but also as an indication of how far a woman could go in the field of conducting. "There seems to be no logical reason why the same gifts of artistic intuition, intellectual grasp, emotional intensity and musicianship which would enable a woman to master the role of Isolde should not, with sufficient specialized training and experience, enable her to conduct an orchestral work.... What remains to be seen is whether some mystery of sex psychology would stand in the way of her dominating the whole situation, not in scattered guest performances, but in assuming a regular conductor's position and meeting its terrific demands. Miss Leginska is probably the only woman today who could furnish the answer to that question if given an opportunity. Last night she proved that a woman can conduct."[80]

At the close of the 1925–26 concert season, Leginska announced that she would concentrate all of her energies on conducting. In December 1925, she had advertised her availability as a guest or permanent conductor. In April 1926, she told the press she would no longer give solo piano recitals, and would perform as a pianist only with chamber ensembles and with orchestras when she played and conducted a piano concerto from the instrument. She cited nerves as the primary reason. "The public will soon forget me as a pianist and I shall be glad. No one knows how I have suffered for the past seventeen years every time I have been obliged to face an audience. I have no regrets. Concert playing may be spectacular, but the great art is in composing and conducting. I am never frightened when I conduct."[81]

Although Leginska had guest conducted the People's Orchestra with increasing success and must have hoped to be named permanent conductor, at the end of the 1925-26 season the organization awarded the post to another guest conductor, Stuart Mason. Boston's musical grapevine speculated about her reaction. "There is an opinion about that I am sulking over something," she responded in June of 1926 when asked about her future plans. "That's rubbish. I am perfectly happy."[82] There are no guarantees, of course, that *anyone* will be offered a position as conductor just because he or she wants it. Even Leonard Bernstein had to wait 15 years between his conducting debut and his permanent appointment with the New York Philharmonic.[83] Nonetheless, it must have been a grave disappointment for Leginska.

She approached the situation with characteristic determination and energy. If there was no existing orchestra that would have her, she would start one. For six months she worked to organize her own Boston Philharmonic Orchestra, securing financial backing, assembling the musicians, buying and studying the music to be performed, and managing the business side of the organization. As the *Boston Globe* reported, "The Boston Symphony Orchestra was the creation of one man, Major Higginson.... The Boston Philharmonic Orchestra ... will be the creation of one woman, Ethel Leginska."[84] The group consisted of 90 men, 25 of whom had been members of the People's Orchestra. On October 24, 1926, an audience of 5,000 braved the rainy and windy streets to attend the first concert, which included performances of Beethoven's Fifth Symphony and Liszt's Hungarian Fantasy for piano and orchestra, with Leginska conducting from the piano.[85] The reviewer for the *Boston Post*, who admitted that he had come to the concert in a mood "rather too skeptical," pronounced the group "an excellent orchestra," and reported that the audience received the performance with "a tumult of applause." "It is strange," he mused, "what the energy of one small woman can bring to pass."[86]

Leginska still exuded charisma. One reporter described her as having the same "mysterious charm and dash" possessed by French tennis champion Suzanne Lenglen, magician Harry Houdini, and baseball player Babe Ruth, concluding, "One doesn't need intimate acquaintance with music or tennis or home runs to feel the quality which these stars exude."[87] Leginska introduced novelty into the programs in order to appeal to her large and diverse audiences. In April 1927, for example, she performed Beethoven's third piano concerto with orchestra, playing the second and third movements in person, but substituting a "mechanical recording" she had made previously for the first. One reviewer remarked that using the recording had added an element of suspense to the performance, as both the audience and the orchestra wondered whether the recording or the orchestra would finish first.[88]

Leginska's Boston Philharmonic gave six concerts during the 1926–27 season, laboring under the acoustical disadvantages of cavernous Mechanics Hall, which caused the sound to dissipate and the musicians to appear "almost as though through the wrong end of a spyglass."[89] As with the People's Orchestra, the necessity to pay union scale limited rehearsals to three before each performance. Also, as with the People's Orchestra, ticket prices were kept low. About 16,000 men, women, and children attended the first four concerts, many paying as little as 25 cents for admission.

Leginska tried to establish the Philharmonic as a permanent orchestra in Boston, but even though she had commitments from at least 35 sponsors, money remained the obstacle. As in many of her previous situations, she conducted without pay. "I don't want to make any money of art," she declared. "I won't starve, and physical things mean very little to me." She repeatedly appealed for funds in newspapers and symphony programs. On the last concert of the season, April 10, 1927, the members of the orchestra performed without pay in a gesture of tribute to her efforts. After the performance, Leginska thanked the audience for its support, saying she hoped that they would come back to hear the orchestra "next year and the year after that and forever." Financial difficulties proved insurmountable, though, and this proved to be their last performance.[90]

Leginska's money troubles were by no means unique, as almost every American symphony orchestra had financial problems in the 1920s. Unionization had resulted in rising salaries for the musicians; conductors' salaries had increased; available philanthropic resources had shrunk after World War I; and the rising costs in general after the war took their toll. In most major cities, a wealthy individual or group of guarantors absorbed the deficits. Henry Harkness Flagler contributed $100,000 annually to the New York Symphony for ten years; Edward Bok contributed $100,000 to the Philadelphia Orchestra; W. A. Clark Jr. gave $543,000 over a three-year period to the Los Angeles Symphony and guaranteed the deficit after that. In February 1924, prominent patrons of American symphony orchestras met in New York to discuss how "big business methods" could be applied to their organizations.[91] Leginska's orchestra, however, had no rescuer.

While Leginska's Boston Philharmonic struggled for survival in 1927, she was asked by a group of women from the Massachusetts State Federation of Women's Clubs to conduct their newly formed Boston Women's Symphony (or Orchestra — the name varied). The ensemble consisted of trained women musicians from the Boston area ranging in age from 14 to 65. She accepted the offer, again serving without pay.[92]

The eclectic nature of the previous jobs held by members of the Boston Women's Symphony underscores how few opportunities existed for "serious" women instrumentalists. Concertmaster Mabel Farrar, for instance, had begun her professional career at 14, playing in a movie house for 50 cents a night. She had also performed in vaudeville and on the radio and had been a member of the Cleveland Orchestra. Trombone player Edith Swan had played with the Fadettes Orchestra as well as at Chatauquas and lyceums. French-horn player Suzanne Howitt had tried unsuccessfully to support herself by playing in vaudeville. Many members of the symphony were quite young. One reviewer observed that, with so many young players, to call it a "women's orchestra" was a "futuristic fantasy."[93]

Their first concert took place on March 23, 1927, in Boston's Jordan Hall, with Leginska as conductor and Lucille Oliver as piano soloist. *Musical America* reported that Leginska conducted with her "usual magnetism and fire," while the orchestra responded with "warm tone quality and expressive playing." It added that the ensemble was "an organization that can vie for excellence with its brother symphonic associations."[94]

In 1928 Leginska took the women's orchestra on a tour of New England and the Mid-Atlantic states. Between October 28 and December 8, they gave 52 concerts. A partial list of concert dates gives an idea of the tour's hectic pace:

Amherst, MA	Oct. 28	Lynchburg, VA	Nov. 1
Millersville, PA (aft.)	Oct. 29	Farmville, VA (aft.)	Nov. 2
Coatsville, PA (eve.)	Oct. 29	Farmville, VA (eve.)	Nov. 2
Shippensburg, PA (aft.)	Oct. 30	Hampton, VA	Nov. 3
Penn Hall, PA (eve.)	Oct. 30	Washington, D.C.	Nov. 4
Harrisburg, PA	Oct. 31	Washington, D.C.	Nov. 5

On some days the group performed both a matinee in one town and an evening performance in another.[95] By way of comparison, a union contract for the 1921–22 tour of the (male) New York Symphony limited the group to no more than seven concerts and rehearsals per week.[96]

The Boston Women's Symphony received more universally favorable reviews than previous orchestras conducted by Leginska. After a 1928 performance in Washington, the *Evening Star* pronounced the concert a "rare musical treat," praising the group for its fine balance and ensemble and Leginska for her "purposeful and highly effective" conducting. The next night the *Star* described the orchestra as "one of the finest ever heard in the National Capital," saying that Washington could now join Boston, Chicago and New York in acclaiming Leginska a genius as a conductor as well as a pianist.[97]

Several factors contributed to the orchestra's high quality and favorable reception. Leginska was the permanent conductor, not a guest; the musicians had played together for more than two years and rehearsed frequently; and the women in the group accepted her as their conductor in a way that many men in other orchestras had not. It is also possible that reviewers felt more comfortable watching a woman conduct a group of women than a group of men.

Leginska tried to ensure the orchestra's survival by making it indispensable to the musical life of Boston. She suggested that they give concerts in Boston on the Saturday nights when the regular Boston Symphony was away

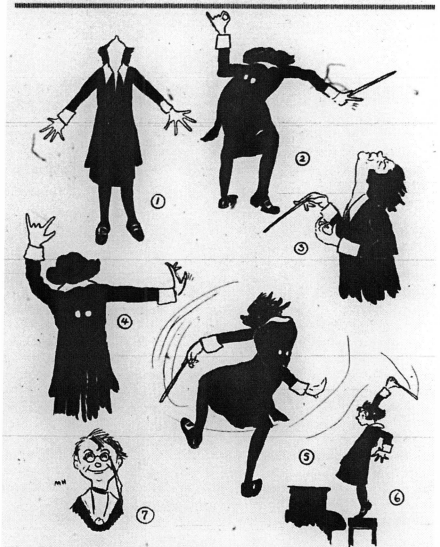

"Our Foolish Correspondent" Gives Impressions of Ethel Leginska, the Country's Most Noted Skirted Conductor, in Her Arduous and Versatile Duties With the New Boston Philharmonic

Cartoon of Ethel Leginska conducting, January 1927. The caption reads, "'Our Foolish Correspondent' gives Impressions of Ethel Leginska, the Country's Most Noted Skirted Conductor, in Her Arduous and Versatile Duties With the New Boston Philharmonic." ("City of Cabots Views Its Dynamic New Leader," *Musical America* 45, January 22, 1927, p. 4.)

on tour.[98] She outlined plans for a new opera company, Opera in English, for which the Women's Orchestra would provide instrumental accompaniment. She planned to approach local music teachers to identify advanced singers for the solos, organize local choral groups to sing the choral parts, and identify young art students to design the sets, scenery and costumes. Yet finances remained shaky in spite of her efforts. The program for February 17, 1929 — the first concert of the Boston Women's Orchestra's third season — contained the inevitable appeal for financial support, explaining that the more money that came in, the less the orchestra would have to rely on touring. Nevertheless, in October 1929 the orchestra embarked on its second extended tour, performing 75 concerts in ten weeks. In the fall of 1930 the group continued its intense pace by touring for another ten weeks, in cities in the Midwest and South.

From 1927 to 1929 Leginska also served as conductor of the Woman's Symphony of Chicago, an organization that was founded in 1925 and lasted until 1948. The group flourished under her leadership, and she led them in performances of many standard orchestral works as well as compositions by contemporary composers such as Debussy and Stravinsky. Leginska played a major role in establishing the orchestra as "one of the principal musical ensembles of the city." Attendance increased to such an extent that the concerts were moved from the Goodman Theatre to the larger and more prominent Orchestra Hall.[99] In 1929 Leginska was succeeded by conductor Ebba Sundstrom, who had served as concertmistress and assistant conductor. Leginska was apparently unable to continue her association with the Chicago group because her Boston commitments, particularly the Boston Women's Symphony, made it impossible for her to do both.[100]

During the early 1930s Leginska served as guest conductor with a number of orchestras including the London Symphony, the Havana (Cuba) Philharmonic, and the Dallas Symphony. The Dallas appearance included the first local performance of Beethoven's Ninth Symphony. A photograph in the *Dallas Morning News* showed the orchestra's regular conductor, Dr. Paul Van Katwijk, graciously handing Leginska his baton as if it were the key to the city. The caption read, "Conductor Relinquishes Baton to Guest Maestra."[101]

Leginska also conducted several operas in the late 1920s and early 1930s. They included a performance of *Madame Butterfly* by the San Carlo Opera Company at the Boston Opera House on October 21, 1927, *Rigoletto* by the National Opera Company in Boston on December 27, 1928, and von Suppe's comic opera *Boccaccio* in New York by the Charles L. Wagner Opera Company on November 17, 1931.[102] On January 10, 1933, she conducted another production of *Madame Butterfly*, this time in Havana, Cuba. She organized a company of 150 Cuban singers and an orchestra of 75 and rehearsed the groups for a full two months prior to the performance. On November 23, 1935, Leginska produced and conducted a performance of her own opera, *Gale*, with the Chicago City Opera Company, contributing $4,000 of her own money to stage the event.

Leginska's shift to opera is significant. Many of the women who have made names for themselves as conductors — Sarah Caldwell, Eve Queler, Judith Somogi and Sian Edwards are examples — shifted or drifted into this particular specialty. Judith Somogi joked that this was the best route for the woman conductor, since by conducting from the orchestra pit, she could not be seen by the audience.[103] Although the comment was made in jest, there is some truth in it. As long as she remained out of sight, gender was not a major consideration for the people viewing and judging the performance.

In 1932 Leginska formed what would be her last woman's orchestra, based in New York and variously called by the press the Woman's Symphony or National Women's Symphony. The group made its first and last public appearance on March 12, 1932. W. J. Henderson, one of New York's most prominent, albeit elderly, critics, described the occasion with a detached amusement similar to that used by John Sullivan Dwight almost one hundred years earlier: "They marched ceremoniously to the stage, all attired in black and white collars, after the fashion of their conductor, and they made a sober and even Puritan picture. Where Miss Leginska found them all can only be conjectured.... On the whole, the first concert of this new orchestra was distinctly worth while. The girls really knew how to count their rests.... She might possibly have got on as well without quite so much conducting — leaping to her feet after every piano passage, even beating time with one hand sometimes while she was playing with the other. She had our sympathy and admiration. In spite of the manifest anxiety of the occasion she gave a pretty smooth and pleasing keyboard performance.... It is hardly necessary to add that Miss Leginska exhibited a fine confidence and a comfortable competence with the baton.... The National Women's Symphony Orchestra ... went at its program in a workwomanlike manner." He ended by saying that he hoped that the musicians would find favor with the public and not be regarded "merely as a passing curiosity."[104]

Henderson's condescension reflects the trend identified by Carroll Smith-Rosenberg, who observed that in the 1930s, society was far more judgmental about the idea of broader public roles for women than it had been in the 1910s and 1920s. While in the earlier decades of the twentieth century women were allowed more freedom to pursue their interests and talents regardless of gender, by the 1930s such women were perceived as having "masculine" interests and were thus judged to be "unnatural." As this happened, women who pursued unconventional careers occupied positions further and further from the mainstream and assumed increasingly marginal roles.[105] This pattern was certainly true of Leginska, who became less and less involved with orchestras within the musical establishment until almost the only orchestras she conducted were those she organized herself.

Faced with the lack of a permanent conducting position and the uncertainty of a future piecing together a succession of guest appearances, Ethel Leginska moved to Los Angeles in 1940, at the age of 54. She lived and taught piano there until her death in 1970. During this entire 30-year period, she never performed in public as a soloist. And she never conducted, either, except to direct temporary groups she hired in order to provide her students with the experience of playing a concerto with an orchestra.

The timing of Leginska's shift from conducting to teaching is ironic, since many new American orchestras were founded in the 1920s and 1930s. According to a 1939 survey, the number of symphony orchestras in the United States had increased from 17 before World War I to 270 after. Most Americans automatically assumed that European men were the only ones capable of conducting these orchestras. Music critics lamented the dearth of conductors in America and wondered where symphony directors would find capable leaders once the supply of available European men had been exhausted.[106] Indeed, there was widespread prejudice against American conductors regardless of their gender.

Leginska had always enjoyed teaching and had taught throughout her career. "I don't know why teaching is considered by so many to be drudgery," she observed in 1919. "To me it is most interesting. I find the same joy in diagnosing and prescribing for a pupil's difficulties that a physician finds in prescribing for a patient."[107] She wanted to teach the best. Her reaction the first time she heard a recording of the young Glenn Gould was, "Who is that lad? He should study with *me*."[108]

As with many a virtuoso-turned-teacher, she was not an easy taskmaster. She expected the same total dedication from her students that she required of herself. Marilyn Neeley, now a professor of piano at the Catholic University of America in Washington, D.C., studied with Leginska in the 1940s. "You had to want to play every phrase more beautifully than it had ever been played," she reminisced. "I have such mixed feelings about all of those years.... I don't have happy memories of my childhood ... week after week of hearing the word 'no'; living in fear from one lesson to the next.... You had to perform to a certain standard and you never quite knew what that standard was; Leginska was the arbiter of that standard."[109] Lisa Sitjar studied with Leginska for a number of years beginning in 1963 when she was seven years old (Leginska was then 77). Sitjar, who now works in New York as an editor and freelance pianist, remembers a period of time when she had as many as six lessons a week, some lasting as long as four hours. Leginska's teaching often involved concentrating on one piece of music until she felt it had been mastered. Sitjar recalls studying one particular Chopin mazurka almost exclusively for six months.[110] Despite the rigor, Leginska's students remember her with admiration as someone who not only provided them with excellent musical training but also influenced them in a broader sense, sharing with them her enthusiasm for literature, the visual arts and other subjects as well.

Leginska approached teaching with the seriousness and innovation that she had invested in her other musical endeavors. In 1943 she formed New Ventures in Music, an organization which annually presented her students in an ambitious series of recitals. The first year 20 students presented programs which featured the 24 preludes and fugues from the first volume of Bach's Well-Tempered Clavier. The next year 37 young pianists presented all of the 24 preludes and fugues from the second volume. In subsequent years New Ventures presented sets of recitals which included all 32 piano sonatas and 21 sets of variations by Beethoven, the entire piano solo works of Chopin, and the complete solo works for piano by Schumann.[111] Each student contributed by performing one or more pieces. Any piece unknown to the students was presented by Leginska's secretary and assistant, Lucille Oliver.

Once a year Leginska also featured her students in a concerto concert. She hired about 30 professional musicians (including some from the Los Angeles Symphony) to form a temporary orchestra which she conducted while the students performed the solo piano parts. These concerts took place in the Wilshire-Ebell Theater, a well-known recital hall in Los Angeles which seats about 1,300 people. Leginska also periodically traveled to New York with students who gave debut recitals. On January 5, 1944, for example, seven of her students ranging in age from eight to 12 performed works by Bach, Beethoven, Chopin, Griffes, Liszt, and Leginska at a series of Town Hall recitals. The last program featured the students playing piano concertos, accompanied by a small orchestra that Leginska conducted.[112] She frequently wrote to well-known musicians — mostly conductors — in advance of these performances, inviting them to attend in the hope that they might be able to help the young artists later on in their careers.[113]

Leginska operated in total autonomy for the entire 30 years she taught private lessons in Los Angeles. She did not belong to any organizations of music teachers. She did not participate in the established musical activities of the city. She did not socialize or associate with any of the many illustrious musicians who were based in the city at the time.

Ethel Leginska's death on February 26, 1970, went unannounced in all the major newspapers including the *Los Angeles Times*. Two days later, the *Times* included an obituary which consisted of her name and the cemetery where she was to be buried. On March 1 another obituary identified her as a "pianist, composer, conductor, teacher" and gave the time and place of her funeral.[114] The absence of a larger story was due in part to the death several months earlier of her friend and longtime companion, Lucille Oliver, since Oliver had handled all of Leginska's correspondence and publicity. Nonetheless, the lack of a full obituary provides evidence of the relative obscurity in which she lived her last decades.

There are a number of ways to view Leginska's experience. One is to use Carolyn Heilbrun's term "thwarted life," since she was unable to achieve her goal for reasons of gender and not lack of ability.[115] Here was a musician who possessed phenomenal talent, organizational skill, and practical experience. She achieved prominence as a conductor in a period of American music history when communities were founding new orchestras and searching for people to conduct them; nonetheless, she was unable to obtain a position. Another view, however, was expressed by journalist Helen De Motte of the *Richmond News Leader*, who described her as "a personality undaunted by difficulties, by adverse criticism, by ridicule, by misunderstanding; holding always to an ideal, looking beyond the confines of the present for its realization; never replying to her critics, never answering the challenge of her detractors, never explaining to her inquisitors. She has simply gone on her way as she saw it, making no claims, [and] said to us one day, very simply, 'It is what I have always wanted to do. I like to play, yes; but the orchestra seems to release something in me that has never before found expression.'"[116]

"Why Not Dr. Brico?"

Antonia Brico

The experience of Antonia Brico further illustrates the phenomenon described by historian Carroll Smith-Rosenberg: developments in the early twentieth century which appeared to be broadening opportunities for women, were beginning to disappear by the 1930s.[1] Brico knew early on that her ambition was to conduct. As a child watching Sunday afternoon concerts in the park, she was fascinated by what seemed the conductor's magical ability to make the music happen. After graduating from the University of California at Berkeley in 1923, Brico studied conducting in Germany and became the first American of either sex to graduate from the Master School of Conducting of the Berlin State Academy of Music.[2] Yet she never found a permanent position leading a professional orchestra, and by the 1950s earned her living in relative obscurity directing amateur ensembles and teaching piano. Although she frequently stated that she was not a "woman conductor," but rather a "conductor who happens to be a woman," much of her public reputation focused on gender and not conducting.[3] When folk singer Judy Collins, who studied piano with Brico in the 1960s, made a much-publicized 1974 documentary about Brico's efforts to be accepted as a conductor,[4] her newly found fame again centered on her career difficulties from a feminist perspective.

Antonia Brico was born in Rotterdam, Netherlands, on June 26, 1902. She had no memory of her parents, who placed her with another family when she was two years old because they could not afford to keep her. Eventually she was adopted by foster parents in Amsterdam — uneducated people who were well meaning but temperamentally unsuited to dealing with the bright, intense, emotionally vulnerable girl. Brico later described her foster mother as a "very stern, typical Dutch woman who was not given to affection [or] demonstrativeness" but "spankings, beatings and pinchings." Her foster father, who was a baker, treated her more gently. He never struck her, Brico said, but never hugged her either, and his way of dealing with family tensions was to withdraw physically and psychologically. Brico remembered her childhood bitterly

124

and was haunted all her life by the early absence of physical contact and emotional attachment.[5] She would compensate in later life by repeatedly forming adoring attachments to strong male figures including conductor Paul Steindorf, in later life, Finnish composer Jean Sibelius and celebrated doctor and musician Albert Schweitzer.[6]

In 1906, when Brico was five, the family immigrated to the United States and settled in California. Her foster father had originally bought tickets for Australia, but changed his plans when he learned of the 1906 San Francisco earthquake. "Where there's an earthquake or a national calamity there's work," he reasoned, and traded in his tickets to Australia. The family lived in Oakland for a year and then moved to St. Helena, a small town in California's wine country. Brico's foster parents bought her a piano when she was ten, primarily because the doctor suggested piano playing as a remedy to stop the child from biting her fingernails. She took lessons from the twelve-year-old girl across the street.

Brico loved music and she loved school, turning to them in part as an escape from her unhappiness at home. She remembered being frequently punished, especially for playing the piano too early in the morning, and for reading too much which her foster mother derided as "swallowing books whole." Punishment usually consisted of spankings or being forced to eat foods she disliked.

Brico's foster mother developed an interest in spiritualism and took Antonia along to meetings and séances. The people there were kind to her and asked her to play hymns and solos on the piano. She loved the praise and hugs she got afterwards. Sometimes one of the spiritualists told her they saw a famous musician such as Liszt or Beethoven standing behind her when she played and predicted that she would become a famous musician, and she believed them. Her foster mother moved from spiritualism to astrology, tea-leaf reading, card reading, and theosophy. Brico continued to accompany her to meetings, fascinated by the people and the ideas. Her interest in these subjects stayed with her. Years later at the University of California at Berkeley, she studied Asian philosophy and religion as well as music.

By the time Brico was 13 she was accompanying music groups in school; she sight-read easily and was in great demand for her playing ability. She also began to study with a more advanced piano teacher. About this time Brico's foster mother realized that her daughter's talents could be lucrative and sought to put her on the vaudeville circuit. Brico rebelled when she learned that this would mean missing school but was nonetheless taken to San Francisco, where she performed at amateur nights in a vaudeville theater. The experience was traumatic. After the amateurs had performed, a master of ceremonies held his hand over the head of each performer and the audience registered its approval or disapproval with cheers or boos. Since Brico played classical music — generally not much of a crowd-pleaser — she was almost always loudly booed. Not surprisingly, she remembered the experience as "a very emotionally disturbing thing." Brico did get positive reinforcement from her high school choral director, however, who praised her musical ability and advised her to attend college — a goal her parents did not have for her.

Brico also began to work in the local Woolworth's store, where she discovered that she was a born salesperson. The store manager moved her from place to place around the store, pushing items that had not sold well. She particularly liked to sell sheet music, and she would demonstrate a piece on the piano, adding variations and embellishments for her own amusement. Sometimes customers would try to return the music several days later, saying that it didn't sound the same when they played it at home. Brico would then explain the store policy against returning merchandise.

After graduating from high school, Brico secretly registered at Berkeley with some of the money she had earned. Her foster mother, who did not understand her desire for a college education and wanted her to become a stenographer, evicted her when she found out. Brico was taken in by the parents of friends, who also supported her during her first year in college. When that family moved to Los Angeles in her second year, she lived with the president of the local Theosophical Society. Such benefactors proved the first in a series who came to her aid throughout her life. Brico's energy, talent, enthusiasm, and salesmanship apparently made people want to help her.

Brico first manifested her interest in conducting when she saw German conductor Paul Steindorf lead Sunday afternoon band concerts in the park. When she was about 13 she attended her first symphony concert. "I was so completely in a state of shock over this tremendous amount of sound that was engineered by one person," she recalled. Paul Steindorf taught at Berkeley and she later studied piano with him there. She developed a serious crush on him and would wait on street corners so that they would just happen to take the same street car. His response when she confessed her ambition to be a conductor was, "No, no, that's too difficult. [You will] never [be] able to do that. That's just because you love me." "No, no," she countered. "That is because I want to be a conductor." Although he tried to discourage her from wasting her time, he allowed her to play the piano for several of his choral society productions. Their performance of music such as Verdi's *Requiem* and Mozart's *Marriage of Figaro* provided her with valuable experience playing and rehearsing large works.

While at Berkeley, Brico was befriended and supported by a number of prominent people, including violinists Mildred and Cedric Wright, Dean of Women Lucy Ward Stebbins, and Walter Feiner, who was first cellist with the San Francisco Symphony. All nurtured her musically, financially, and emotionally. She also won a scholarship to attend master classes with Sigismund Stojowski, who had been a colleague and student of Paderewski. When Stojowski left Berkeley, he offered her his assistance if she ever came to New York. She did, and for a time helped support herself by babysitting for his three children. (She said that his pet name for her was Cheretska, which means "daughter" in Polish.) Brico enrolled in conducting classes at what is now the Juilliard School, but this displeased Stojowski, who said it was ridiculous because there was no future for a woman in conducting. Antonia Brico was at a crossroads — she knew what she wanted but had neither the way nor the means to obtain it.

While attending classes in Hindu religion and philosophy, Brico met yet another wealthy benefactor who helped her trace her birth family in Holland and encouraged her to go back and meet them. She learned that her natural father was Italian and her mother Dutch and that her father had been a pianist. She also learned her given name, Antonia Brico, and began using it instead of Wilhelmina Wolthus, the name given her by her adoptive parents. When Brico went to Holland she was met in Rotterdam by her Uncle Theo, who was nine years her senior. She was struck by how similar they were in personality — both "very dramatic and very musical and affectionate." Although he was married, they were attracted to each other. At first Brico interpreted her strong feelings as being caused by their blood relationship — he was the first such relative she had met and she always idealized such situations. But she began to feel there was more to it as they attended concerts and took long walks together. Theo apparently grew uncomfortable with the closeness of their friendship and distanced himself from her.

When Brico returned to the United States she toured the Southwest for a time as accompanist for two singers, a Native American man and woman known professionally as Princess Chanina and Prince Ahskananton. They were protégés of American composer Charles Wakefield Cadman, a fascinating but largely forgotten figure who used his versions of Native American musical themes in an attempt to write authentically "American" music. Brico had not, however, abandoned her plans to study conducting, and was once again helped financially by Lucy Ward Stebbins.

Armed with three letters of introduction from noted California musicians who attested to her talent, she set out for Germany and Bayreuth to study with conductor Karl Muck, who accepted her as a pupil and gave her tickets to all the Bayreuth performances, many of which he conducted. At Bayreuth the orchestra was concealed from the audience by a covered orchestra pit, so that the instrumentalists would not distract the audience's attention from the drama on the stage. Muck allowed Brico into the pit to watch him conduct. The orchestra of 130 was huge, with seven harps, eight horns, 24 first violins, 18 second violins, and other instrument groups larger than those in the standard orchestra. Years later, Brico described her reaction to hearing these musicians: "I was emotionally, absolutely shattered." When asked why Muck took such an interest in her, she speculated that he was "intrigued" by her enthusiasm, her youth, and her ardor. During the following year, Muck coached her in opera conducting. She wanted to continue, but he felt that she needed more formal schooling and advised her to enter the Master School of Conducting at the Berlin Academy of Music. There she studied with Julius Prüwer, the conductor of the Berlin Philharmonic's popular concerts.

In 1929 Antonia Brico became the first American to graduate from the Berlin Academy. Karl Muck pronounced her "highly musically talented; gifted with a will of iron diligence concerning her studies; a person who has made enormous progress." He also described her as modest, simple, frugal, and full of a burning ambition to achieve the highest artistic goals. Julius Prüwer wrote that she was "strongly talented" and possessed "extraordinary diligence. She is an outstandingly serious person with unimpeachable character; it would be a big mistake not to allow her to continue her education."[7]

Brico's studies in Berlin culminated in a performance conducting the Berlin Philharmonic on January 10, 1930. For the program she chose a Handel concerto grosso, Gluck-Mottl's Ballet Suite No. 1, two songs by Beethoven, and Dvorak's Symphony in D minor.[8] The German critics gave her high praise. The reviewer for the *Allemeine Zeitung* wrote that she possessed "more ability, cleverness and musicianship than certain of her male colleagues who bore us in Berlin." "Miss Brico triumphs as conductor," reported the *New York Times*, adding that the "performance of the San Francisco girl" elicited "thunderous applause and many floral tributes."[9]

Brico's return to California was marked by an appearance with the San Francisco Symphony Orchestra. In an article entitled "U. of C. Co-ed Wins Triumph in San Francisco Concert," music critic for the *San Francisco Examiner*, Redfern Mason, described her as a "director at once dynamic, imaginative and authoritative.... All the signs indicate that this young woman will be one more eminent leader in a generation where the genus [i.e., woman] is sparsely represented."[10] She returned to Germany in 1931 for a performance with the Hamburg Philharmonic. Her teacher Karl Muck was in the audience and she described the experience as "the greatest moment of her life."[11] This appearance was followed by others in Berlin, Vienna, Austria, Poland, Paris, and London — a tour that was sponsored by the City of San Francisco and the University of California at Berkeley. During the 1931–32 season she served as conductor for the Riga, Latvia, municipal orchestra.[12]

Brico returned to the United States, where she remained active as a conductor in the early 1930s. Ironically, she owed much of her employment to the Great Depression, since she primarily conducted government-sponsored orchestras of unemployed musicians. In March of 1932 the Musicians' Emergency Aid formed a symphony orchestra of 200 known as the Musicians' Symphony Orchestra, which presented five concerts per week "at popular prices" at New York's Metropolitan Opera House. The orchestra committee planned for "at least one conductor of national or international fame" to lead the group in each concert, and Sir Thomas Beecham, Walter Damrosch, Sandor Harmati, and Arturo Toscanini were among those who conducted during the first season.[13] Antonia Brico was one of the featured conductors during the second season, leading the group in performances of works by Beethoven, Strauss, Prokofiev, and Tchaikovsky.[14] Jean Lyon of the *New York Sun*, who had reviewed concerts conducted by Ethel Leginska, reported that despite talk that the men of the orchestra were "just a

Early publicity photo of Antonia Brico. (Colorado Historical Society.)

trifle resentful of having a woman conductor," Brico had learned to accept this attitude and aimed to dispel it "within the first few seconds after she has taken up the baton."[15]

The following summer Brico conducted two series of "pops" concerts, one with the Musicians' Symphony in White Plains, New York, and another in Buffalo.[16] It is possible that organizers found it easier to assign her pops venues. At the very least it must have been a bit of a comedown, since the audience sat at tables where they could eat, drink, and chat during the performances. Brico's sense of fun was also in evidence, though. When Westchester County officials refused a permit for the sale of beer at the White Plains concerts, she insisted that the musicians be served beer during one of the afternoon rehearsals.[17]

This government-subsidized activity continued through the depression.

In 1934 and 1935 Brico guest conducted many concerts of the New York Civic Orchestra, an organization sponsored by the New York State Civil Works Administration and the City of New York. For a time she conducted three concerts a week, one at the Natural History Museum in Manhattan and two at the Brooklyn Academy of Music. She made $32 a week. As she reminisced with enthusiasm, "For me it was first class! It gave me an opportunity to conduct every single week, three concerts, and to prepare three different programs; I was just thrilled to death.... Every day I had rehearsals." For four months in 1938 she also conducted the Bay Region Symphony Orchestra in San Francisco. This group was another of the 38 American symphony orchestras that were part of the Federal Music Project of the Works Progress Administration, formed to provide work for unemployed musicians. The people of San Francisco and Oakland flocked to hear her conduct one sold-out performance after another. Admission was ten cents per person, and these concerts, known as the Dime Symphony Concerts, drew as many as 10,000 people at a time in San Francisco's vast civic auditorium.[18]

Brico frequently denied being a feminist, stating that her primary interest was music and not gender. When asked by a reporter in 1933 if she had any notion of forming a women's orchestra, she answered emphatically, "No! I am interested only in musicians, whether they be men or women. It is my lot to be a woman. I want to conduct orchestras."[19] Nonetheless, since she had yet to secure a permanent conducting position and the country's economic situation was unpromising, Brico formed a women's orchestra, stating that her three goals were to provide employment for out-of-work women musicians, to offer training opportunities to women with latent talents, and to give high-caliber, reasonably priced concerts to the public. Brico must have known about Leginska's similar activities only a few years earlier: but if she did, she never alluded to them in public interviews.[20]

Brico did not think small when she sought sponsors for her group. Knowing that a prominent name would help with marketing and fund-raising, she arranged through a friend in the U.S. State Department to have tea with First Lady Eleanor Roosevelt, who consented to lend her name to the project. Mrs. Roosevelt thought the enterprise of sufficient merit to devote part of one of her daily "My Day" newspaper columns to its promotion.[21] Then, with the help of friends and "everybody who knows somebody," Brico amassed a list of sponsors that included the crème de la crème of New York and Washington society, including Mrs. James Roosevelt, Mrs. Walter Naumberg, Mrs. Godfrey S. Rockefeller, Mrs. Avery Rockefeller, and Mrs. Cornelius Vanderbilt. The New York Women's Symphony gave its New York debut at Town Hall on February 18, 1935.[22]

As with Leginska's women's orchestra, most of the members were young — in their middle twenties, with a few in their early forties. Although the group had 80 members, only about 50 of them could attend the three rehearsals a week for six weeks before the first performance. Many players had other jobs and were free only for evening sessions. Besides, they received no pay for rehearsals. The resulting unevenness in the quality of performance was a perpetual source of frustration for Brico.[23]

The first concert of the New York Women's Symphony was for invited guests only, and to the embarrassment of the organizers who had anticipated a small turnout, considerably more people arrived than there were seats to accommodate them. The result was that many wealthy and prominent matrons had to be turned away after having dismissed

Early publicity photo of Antonia Brico. (Colorado Historical Society.)

their chauffeurs with instructions to return when the concert was over. The *New Yorker* magazine pronounced the first concert a success, even though the "new organization, naturally, isn't yet fused into a unit but, ably led by Miss Brico, it came through triumphantly."[24] There was only one drawback in the press coverage — support of the event by so many wealthy society women caused some reporters to trivialize it. The *New York Times*, for example, described the efforts of a group of young "debutantes" to advertise the performance by walking up and down Park Avenue near the Ritz Tower Hotel carrying placards. "That was what the girls were standing out in the snow for, taking the winds of March with beauty, like figureheads on the prow of a gallant, though storm-driven flotilla — doing their best for music, art, culture and the advancement of Woman."[25]

The orchestra gave three more performances that season and received generally positive reviews, although critics were more likely to give unqualified praise to Brico than to the group as a whole. Gone was the mocking tone used to describe Leginska, as were derogatory comments about the extravagance of gesture on the podium, although it is probable that Brico's gestures were in fact more conservative than Leginska's, since her mentor, Karl Muck, was known for his restrained conducting style. Some critics were still dubious, however, like the incorrigible W. J. Henderson of the *New York Sun*, who asked his readers, "Why does a woman take up the study of the bassoon?" while proclaiming solemnly in the next line, "We should not object to her or to any player in an orchestra because she wears skirts."[26]

At the end of their first season the Women's Symphony sought federal funding from the newly formed Federal Music Project of the WPA. The chairman of the orchestra's executive board argued that the group provided work for a large number of struggling, unemployed professional musicians, noting that most members of the group were contributing to their own support as well as that of their parents, husbands, and children.[27] Not surprisingly, given the government's preference for helping unemployed men, the WPA did not fund the women's orchestra and in the wake of this failure the orchestra suffered financial and organizational problems.[28]

Concert attendance remained high, though, and in its second season the New York Women's Symphony moved its concerts from Town Hall to the much larger Carnegie Hall. The list of sponsors continued to include visible and wealthy patrons of the arts.[29] Reviews of the group were favorable but read like faint praise because they invariably contained a comment about how much the group had improved since its last performance. But Brico's conducting continued to elicit unqualified admiration. *Musical America*, for instance, stated that she had "developed her art and is today a conductor truly worthy of appearing in any symphonic series. Her beat is firm, her rhythmic sense certain, and she has genuine authority over her players."[30]

In 1936 Brico changed the name of the orchestra to the Brico Symphony and admitted several men to the organization. She explained to the press that while she had been "accused of being a feminist," she had already proved that women could hold their own in the orchestra and it was now time to move on. "Musically, I consider women neither inferior nor superior to men," she stated. "I believe equally in their potentialities and desire only that their opportunities should be equal and that talent should be accredited justly."[31] At the sight of the four males, the *Times* reviewer commented, "The male musicians might have felt a bit embarrassed ... but the four scattered players were so well hidden behind the rows of ladies in front of them that if there were any blushes no one in the audience was the wiser."[32] An article in the *Cincinnati Enquirer* announced the inclusion of men in the group with the headline, "Maestra Disbands her Amazons and Gives the Boys a Chance to Play."[33]

The climax of the orchestra's third season was a performance of American composer Horatio Parker's "Hora Novissima." For Brico it was a tremendous undertaking, requiring the rehearsal and coordination of five separate choral groups (of which she was also the regular director) in addition to the hundred-piece orchestra. She even rehearsed different sections of the orchestra in her apartment in the afternoons. "I would have, like the horns one hour and the trombones another hour and the strings another hour, and the violas one hour and the violins another hour." Brico imbued both vocalists and instrumentalists with "her own fire and vision," and reviews document that the audience was both enthusiastic and deeply moved.[34] The physical and emotional letdown she experienced after this performance was enormous. After a celebratory reception, a friend took her to her hotel, where she cried for most of the night. For days afterwards she was exhausted and despondent, sobbing to her friend, "It's over and I can't hear it again."

In the late 1930s Brico appeared several times with her Brico Symphony and also as guest conductor with a number of prominent orchestras, including the Los Angeles Symphony, the Detroit Symphony, and the New York Philharmonic in 1938. For the New York Philharmonic appearance she chose the Sibelius First Symphony, Beethoven's Lenore Overture, Tchaikowsky's *Romeo and Juliet*, Liszt's Mephisto Waltz, and Wagner's *Die Meistersinger*. She confessed to a friend that the musicians played so beautifully that she had very little to criticize or change, but that she still stopped them occasionally, "just to make the rehearsal last a little longer."[35]

By this time she had a manager, Wilmore Powers, whose most bankable star was Romanian composer and conductor Georges Enesco. In 1940 Powers had arranged for Enesco to give many performances in North America, but the authorities refused to allow the musician to leave Romania. One of his scheduled performances was with the Denver Symphony, and as Powers scrambled to fill Enesco's various commitments, he proposed to the Denver Civic Symphony Association that Antonia Brico appear in his place. The president, Mrs. George Cranmer, was an independent sort who was struck by the idea of Brico conducting. She agreed to the arrangement without consulting the orchestra's board of directors, and this made Brico's relations with the symphony board tenuous from the start. Thus began a series of events that changed the course of Brico's life and career.

On December 10, 1940, Brico conducted the Denver orchestra in a highly successful performance that included the Sibelius First Symphony. She was a sensation: according to all accounts the public loved her, the musicians loved her, and the critics waxed eloquent. On the day after the concert John C. Kendel of the *Denver Post* called her a "first-class conductor" whose performance "not only justified fully her advance notices but went far beyond them." He praised her as a "distinct personality dependent only upon her ability and vast musical knowledge for her success on the podium...; every nuance and phrase was carefully worked out." At the end of the program the audience cheered and gave her a standing ovation. Kendel concluded: "When a Denver audience gives vent to 'bravos' and 'huzzas' at a symphony concert, that is news indeed." Anne Stein Roth of the *Rocky Mountain News* wrote, "Her decisive beat had the strength born of conviction, and it commanded the unfailing cooperation of every musician."[36] Brico was wined and dined by Denver society. The concert was such a success that she was immediately engaged to conduct two more during the next season. One would be a performance of the massive Brahms *German Requiem*; the other would include Rachmaninoff's second piano concerto, with her friend and former teacher Simon Barer as piano soloist. Brico was ecstatic and amid the euphoria heard suggestions that if she moved to Denver she would probably be appointed permanent conductor. Enticed by the possibility of a permanent conducting position, supportive friends and benefactors, a less expensive city, and a more congenial climate, Antonia Brico moved to Denver in 1941.

The two concerts for which she had been engaged went well and she slowly began to attract piano students. (Like Leginska, Brico relied upon piano teaching as a "day job" to pay the bills.) It became apparent almost immediately, however, that many of those who had embraced her warmly as a guest conductor were not at all sure they wanted to give her the appointment on a permanent basis. The year before the decision was to be made, the orchestra had a series of guest conductors, of which Brico was one. From this group the symphony board and the musicians would choose their permanent conductor. By this point the issue had become highly politicized — there were pro–Brico and anti–Brico factions and much behind-the-scenes maneuvering. In the end, the board and the musicians played it safe and, in 1945, chose Saul Caston as permanent conductor of the Denver Symphony.

Brico was devastated, although she probably saw it coming. She was also desperate to conduct and devised a plan to get endorsements from well-known musicians to use as references in her efforts to obtain a position. When she asked pianist Artur Rubinstein if he would write her a letter of recommendation, Rubinstein was receptive but said that he wanted to watch her rehearse first. So Brico arranged to be in New York when Rubinstein was there to perform. She hired 60 New York musicians (this was not an established group accustomed to playing together, but 60 assorted musicians), rented Carnegie Hall, and held a rehearsal of the Brahms Second Symphony before an invited audience which included Rubinstein and Bruno Walter. This was not just a run-through of the piece, but a rehearsal in which she stopped the musicians in order to correct or change things or to try a different interpretation. Thus she could demonstrate her ability to shape and interpret the music. Rubinstein was much impressed with her performance, and Bruno Walter wrote, "I have heard an orchestra rehearsal of Brahms Second Symphony conducted by Miss Antonia Brico, and the impression was extremely favorable. Miss Brico without any doubt is a born conductor. She not only has the technical skill, but what matters more, the most important quality of a conductor, the 'power of communication,' both with regard to her orchestra and her listeners. I do not hesitate despite the general prejudice against women conductors to believe in a successful career of [sic] this exceptionally gifted musician."[37] From this and similar testimonials, Brico crafted a brochure which she sent to people she knew who might be in a position to help her. Jean Sibelius, for example, whom she had met in 1937, helped her get several appearances with the Helsinki Symphony in 1946, and Bruno Walter helped her obtain an engagement with the London Philharmonic. She conducted several performances in Yugoslavia and Holland as well.

Her base of operation, though, remained Denver, where she continued to support herself teaching piano and conducting church choirs. (She was ecumenical in this regard: at various times she conducted at Trinity Methodist Church, an African-American Baptist church, a Greek Orthodox church, and a Unitarian church.) She also conducted a number of amateur orchestras, including the Boulder Symphony, the Boise (Idaho) Symphony, and for more than 20 years the Denver Businessman's Orchestra, which was later renamed the Brico Symphony.

For a musician of Brico's ability and experience, a lifetime of such piecework was galling. In Boise, for instance, the strictly amateur orchestra was small, consisting of nine first violins, nine second violins, five or six celli, five or six string basses, three clarinets, one or two oboes, two bassoons, two flutes, four trumpets, two trombones, two horns and two percussionists. A letter from the group in October 1958 attempted to buck her up with the news that turnouts for rehearsals had been somewhat better that year, although many members of the orchestra were teachers with time commitments that conflicted with rehearsals. The letter also asked Brico if she could provide them with a new photo — "one sort of happy-like — as we said, the one that has been used is so stern-looking ... one sort of on the glamorous side." Another letter from this period asked her to fill in as guest conductor of the Cheyenne, Wyoming, orchestra for the fall season while their permanent conductor, Will Schwartz, was in the hospital. The combination of being passed over for permanent positions, having constantly to deal with the mediocre playing and absenteeism in amateur groups, and being taken for granted as always available to fill in on a temporary basis began to take its toll. Brico wrote a friend in November 1960, "My artistic life has been full of hurt and frustration and deep anguish over the fate that has made me a conductor of volunteer groups most of my life — you often told me you understand my deep passion for symphony and my anguish and torture over not hearing what I really want to."[38]

The major portion of Brico's conducting energies during the 1950s and 1960s went into leading the Denver Businessman's Orchestra. Despite its name, this group was a mixed orchestra, with about half the members being women. The group gave its first concert in 1948 and offered four programs each season. Before December 1955 the orchestra had seven guest conductors; after that, Brico served as permanent conductor. The organization included music teachers, lawyers, doctors, geologists, physicists, accountants, salesmen, office workers, farmers, and music students and was strictly amateur in the sense that no one was paid to rehearse or perform. Guest soloists received an honorarium only if the treasury was sufficiently full. Over the years, the group experienced various trials. It rehearsed in a variety of places, including the state armory, a church sanctuary (while preparing the Saint-Saëns Organ Symphony), a church basement, the Disabled American Veterans Assembly Hall, a commercial garage, and the Pillar of Fire Church building in downtown Denver. If necessary, depending upon the location of the rehearsal, each musician brought his or her own chair and music stand. The group also endured more than its share of nuisances and harassment, such as having to plug up the vents at the Disabled American Veterans hall so that card players in the barroom would not be disturbed by the music, and having to compete with car radios turned up full volume on the streets outside the Pillar of Fire Church.[39]

Despite these problems, during the years that Brico conducted the Denver Businessman's Orchestra (the name was changed to the Brico Symphony in her honor in 1966), she tackled some of the most difficult works in the orchestral literature, making no concessions to the amateur status of the group. One performance featured Mahler's Resurrection Symphony, augmented by a chorus of 150 from the Cheyenne (Wyoming) Symphony Choral Society. The group also performed a concert version of Beethoven's opera *Fidelio*, as well as Mahler's *Kindertotenlieder*, Brahms's Fourth Symphony, and Verdi's *Requiem*. In 1960 the group performed two sold-out performances of Stravinsky's *Petrouchka* with the Denver Civic Ballet. As Wayne Johnson of the *Denver Post* said with reference to the 1962 performance of the Resurrection Symphony, "This spring, as she has in many past springs, Brico has assembled hundreds of amateur musicians, and by means of her hard work, forceful personality, and superb musicianship, she molded them into a unified ensemble capable of giving professional polish to the performance of an extremely difficult work."[40]

During the years Brico lived in Denver, the Denver Symphony Orchestra had a series of permanent conductors: Saul Caston served from 1945 to 1964, Vladimir Golschmann from 1964 to 1970, Brian Priestman from 1970 to 1978,

Gaetano Delogu from 1979 to 1986, and Phillippe Entrement from 1986 to 1989.[41] Each time the position became vacant, the idea of appointing Brico invariably surfaced. The issue was particularly public and rancorous prior to the appointment of Vladimir Golschmann in 1964. Both large newspapers in the Denver area, the *Post* and the *Rocky Mountain News*, carried editorials and letters discussing the issue of Brico and the conductorship, including a debate about whether or not the amateur Denver Businessman's Orchestra was superior to the professional Denver Symphony. "It is understandable how the idea of the superiority of the Businessman's Orchestra got started," wrote Wayne Johnson in the *Denver Post* on June 2, 1963. "A sense of musical excitement pervades every concert given by Dr. Brico and her players, and it is precisely this excitement that has been noticeably missing from the [Denver] Symphony concerts in recent years," Johnson explained, although he went on to argue that with the "right conductor" the Denver Symphony was "capable of creating a refined and precise musical excitement that simply is not within the competence of the Businessman's Orchestra players." Yet Johnson asserted that it would be pointless to include Brico as one of the five guest conductors from which a permanent one would be chosen: "My opposition has nothing to do with Brico's personality or musicianship, but rather with the fact that Dr. Brico has about as much chance of being named the new permanent conductor of the Denver Symphony as I have of taking Leonard Bernstein's place with the [New York] Philharmonic."[42] Marjorie Barrett of the *Rocky Mountain News* posed the question, "Why Not Dr. Brico to Head Denver Symphony?" Noting that Vladimir Golschmann was the person most frequently mentioned for the position and that he had made a "big hit" with his "continental charm" at a recent Denver party, Barrett nonetheless argued: "Few of the men being considered for the post of permanent conductor of the Denver Symphony Orchestra can boast the background, training or experience of Dr. Brico."[43] By this time, however, Brico had lived in Denver for 20 years. She had long since ceased to be the exotic, dynamic guest conductor from New York, and had become, at least to some, a local eccentric who taught piano.

Antonia Brico lived in relative obscurity until 1974, when one of her former piano students, folk singer Judy Collins, who grew up in Denver, coproduced a documentary film about her, *Antonia: Portrait of the Woman*. With poignance and humor the film chronicled her musical life and frustration. When it was nominated for an Academy Award for the best documentary, it began to attract audiences, and Brico made headlines once again.

After the film was released, Brico experienced a flurry of activity. She was invited to conduct the Oakland Symphony in Berkeley. The concert sold out. Next came the Hollywood Bowl, then a weekend of Mostly Mozart concerts at New York's Lincoln Center. When the weekend quickly sold out, another was scheduled and that sold out as well. Engagements in Washington, Spokane, and Columbia, Missouri, followed. "And finally," she said with an air of triumph, "the Denver Symphony. At last." Brico's resurrected career held a certain irony, however, since it focused more on her gender than on her conducting, celebrating her as a victim rather than as a musician.[44]

After the initial flood of conducting invitations which followed the opening of the film, Brico was asked to participate in occasional conferences on college campuses. These events, usually sponsored by women's studies groups and not music departments, echoed the message of the film. A typical format for these conferences was that of the one hosted by the University of Illinois. First came a showing of the film, *Antonia: Portrait of the Woman*, followed by Brico presenting a workshop on conducting, then a lecture on "her music, her friends, and her life." After this, Brico and others participated in a panel discussion of the subject, "Is there a Feminine Aesthetic?" The last session consisted of a performance of Brico conducting the National Women's Music Festival Orchestra.[45]

Brico expressed discomfort with the extent to which the film revealed her emotional anguish. In what she referred to as "the famous kitchen scene," she almost breaks down crying as she says to Judy Collins, "Judy, I'm only speaking to you, my friend. I'm not telling anyone else about my heartbreak. But why should I only conduct four or five times a year when I have the energy to conduct four or five times a month?" The scene is emotionally wrenching, and Brico said afterwards, "If I'd had any idea about the distribution, the reviews, the Oscar nomination ... I would have been unable to express myself as well."[46]

Nonetheless, Antonia Brico felt vindicated by the notoriety the film brought her. "Everything's happening so quickly," she said in an interview in 1975. "Right now I'm so happy, so happy every day ... now, I have some goals, and the more I conduct, the more I recognize that my passionate desire is to conduct more opera. I also want to conduct the New York Philharmonic, and I want to conduct in Germany, France, Sweden, Holland, but that'll come in time.... This morning, when the emotions began to build, I said to myself, now come on Brico, get hold of yourself. Just say, I'm here. I'm in the Kennedy Center. I'm conducting. I'm doing what I want to do. I'm consistent. That's all I want. That's all I've ever wanted."[47]

But gradually the conducting and speaking engagements decreased and Brico's life again receded into relative anonymity in Denver. She was, after all, 72 years old in 1974, and there were limits to her ability to begin again. Brico remained independent and productive as a teacher until the last two years of her life, which were spent in a Denver nursing home. She died in 1989.[48]

Late in life Antonia Brico expressed bitterness about her thwarted ambitions — her frustration and anguish at rarely being able to hear what she imagined. Nonetheless, her perseverance and visibility helped establish a climate in Denver that allowed the next generation of gifted women to be successful.

From 1983 to 1992 JoAnn Falletta served as conductor of the Denver Chamber Orchestra, and in 1993 Marin Alsop was appointed principal conductor of the Colorado Symphony Orchestra, a group rebuilt from the former Denver Symphony. While this is not the legacy Antonia Brico would have chosen for herself, it is nonetheless significant.

"Playing with Style"

The Late Twentieth Century

Many issues which dominated the lives and careers of women instrumentalists in the nineteenth and early twentieth centuries continued to do so throughout the rest of the twentieth and into the twenty-first. Gender still plays a major role in determining the instrument a woman is likely to play, the nature of her acceptance as an instrumentalist or conductor, decisions about marriage and motherhood, and her onstage presentation of self. The subjects of late twentieth-century conferences on women and music bear this out. In the fall of 1989, for instance, a Juilliard symposium entitled "Women in Music: Choices and Chances" featured 11 prominent women musicians speaking about the ways in which gender had influenced their lives and careers. In May 1997 the Tenth International Congress on Women in Music in Los Angeles dealt with these issues as well. Jeannie Pool, founder and organizer, noted that she had chosen the word "congress" because this group's gatherings resemble a "congress" that took place in 1893 at the World Columbian Exposition in Chicago, the first world's fair to have a pavilion that celebrated women's contributions to the arts. "We're still raising many of the same issues at the end of the twentieth century," she observed.[1] What has changed and what remains the same?

Women have continued and expanded their strong presence as instrumental soloists. Pianists Rosalyn Tureck, Ruth Laredo, and Ursula Oppens, violinists Erica Morini and Nadja Salerno-Sonnenberg, flutists Paula Robison and Eugenia Zuckerman, cellists Jacquelyn du Pré and Ofra Hornoy are just a few of the women who have continued the legacy begun by Teresa Carreño, Camilla Urso, Julie Rivé-King, Maud Powell, and Fannie Bloomfield-Zeisler. The public has long since abandoned the notion that womanhood and virtuosity are mutually exclusive; admiration has replaced mockery and bewilderment when a woman musician exhibits strength and assertiveness. Richard Dyer of the *Boston Globe* described a 1997 performance by pianist Ursula Oppens as "musically assured and ... utterly fearless in attack.... She let the fugue erupt in all its ruly and unruly energy, playing with absolute control and equal abandon." Gordon Sparber of the *Washington Post* described the "gutsiness" of flutist Paula Robison's playing: "Such fierce power from a flutist forces a listener to sit up and take notice."[2] In these and most other contemporary reviews, the emphasis is on the performance of the music and the mastery of the performer, and mastery is an admirable quality, regardless of gender.

Women today have a better chance of being admitted to symphony orchestras, although unconditional acceptance has been gradual. The Cleveland Orchestra's inclusion of four women in 1923 was the subject of much comment. When the San Francisco Symphony admitted four women violinists and a cellist in 1925, *Etude* magazine commended conductor Alfred Hertz for his

Vienna Philharmonic admitted its first woman in 1997. (c. *The New Yorker* Collection, 1997, Roz Chast from cartoonbank.com. All Rights Reserved.)

"courage." Other ensembles exhibited similar acts of courage. The Philadelphia Orchestra included harpist Edna Philipps in 1930 and cellist Elsa Hilger in 1935. When the Pittsburgh Orchestra appointed Ellen Stone Bogoda first horn in 1937 it marked the first time an American symphony orchestra had appointed a woman brass player to an orchestra not composed entirely of women.[3] When Doriot Anthony Dwyer became the first flutist of the Boston Symphony Orchestra in 1952 she was the first woman to occupy a principal position in one of the top five American orchestras.[4]

When World War II depleted the male ranks of American orchestras, the percentage of women in major orchestras increased slightly, from two percent in 1942 to eight percent in 1948. By 1948 there were 109 women in America's 15 major orchestras and this number did not decrease significantly amid growing pressures for female domesticity in the 1950s: in 1953 these same 15 orchestras still contained 100 women musicians.[5] By the mid-1960s women's membership in symphony orchestras accounted for 28 percent of the musicians under regular contract in major, regional, and metropolitan American orchestras. By 1975 this number had increased to 35 percent. According to the American Symphony Orchestra League, the proportion of women musicians in large American orchestras (those with budgets of $1 million or more) had reached 39 percent by 1989. This steady increase was due in part to the practice of "blind auditions," a procedure implemented by most orchestras during the 1960s and 1970s in response to legal pressures and union demands. In a blind audition, the musician trying out for a position performs behind a screen so that the judges cannot see the applicant, although the screen is usually removed for the very last stages of the process. A study of hiring patterns by U.S. orchestras from 1970 to 1996 revealed that *before* the use of screens fewer than 10 percent of hires were women, whereas by 1996, at top orchestras using screens, the percentage had increased to 35.[6]

While women's membership in American orchestras has increased, the likelihood that these women will play particular instruments has changed very little. An examination of orchestral membership lists from the 1940s to the 1980s provides a fairly accurate picture of the instruments women have played and continue to play in American symphony orchestras (see Table 1).[7] Even in the 1980s, fewer than 15 percent of the orchestra members who played percussion instruments, the string bass, or the "heavier brasses" (any but the French horn) were women. In the woodwind sections women substantially increased their representation as oboists, English horn players, and bassoonists between the 1940s and the 1980s. Female participation as violinists, violists, and cellists was already high and increased slightly. And women continued to predominate in the traditional female specialties. Sixty-one percent of the flutists in these orchestras were women in the 1980s, as were 60 percent of the keyboard players and 90 percent of the harpists.

Decade	1940s	1950s	1960s	1970s	1980s
Number of Orchestras	47	63	36	49	44
Violin	46	44	41	57	53
Viola	33	29	34	36	45
Cello	44	47	45	55	53
String Bass	23	14	13	16	14
Flute/Piccolo	44	43	44	54	61
Clarinet	14	10	9	16	12
Oboe/English Horn	3	21	19	30	41
Bassoon	19	14	12	22	36
Trumpet	8	5	2	5	5
Trombone	6	5	4	2	3
French Horn	18	14	12	16	27
Tuba	7	2	0	0	2
Percussion	13	9	14	12	6
Keyboard	64	64	42	54	60
Harp	80	89	82	88	90

Table 1. Instrumental Players in Selected American Symphony Orchestras: Percentage Female

These patterns are likely to continue if music school enrollments are an indication of future trends. The Berklee College of Music in Boston reported in 1990 that only about 16 percent of its students were women. Of these, about 43 percent were singers and 27 percent pianists. Only seven percent were studying saxophone, three percent string bass, and just two percent brass instruments.[8] At the New England Conservatory during the same period, ten of the 13 student horn players were women but only one of 20 trumpet players; there were no women studying trombone or tuba. Ann Gilbert found similar results in 1994 when she compared the instrumental majors of the males and females enrolled at four music conservatories.[9] However, the number of women brass players with positions in American and European orchestras has increased. According to Maureen Horgan, a prominent Boston-based freelance trombonist, 53 women have held such positions since 1950, and a quarter of these women occupied the first chair.[10]

Isolated incidents reveal that gender-based attitudes about musical instruments still exist. The September 16, 1990, issue of *The New Yorker* magazine announced a performance of a piece for trombone and orchestra featuring solo trombonist Ava Ordman. The author felt obliged to add: "Those who find themselves a little startled by the prospect of a female trombone soloist may be assured that times are, however tardily, changing."[11] A 1991 incident at Boston University provides another example. At a master class in March of that year, trumpeter Rolf Smedvig, former principal trumpet of the Boston Symphony Orchestra and cofounder of the popular Empire Brass, criticized a performance by three undergraduate women in terms that they and others in the room found sexist and demeaning. Smedvig remarked that women's problems with brass instruments originated in their passive nature and told them they "sounded like women." The students complained to the head of the chamber music program, who convened a forum to discuss women, brass-playing and sexism. Although the forum was ostensibly organized to defuse tensions, it had the opposite effect. While Smedvig, who was among the panelists, retreated from the language he had used in the class (which was on tape), he still maintained that women lacked the physical endurance required to play brasses and questioned whether women were capable of sustaining the climaxes of major symphonies such as those by Bruckner and Mahler or of creating the "animal expression" required to perform Stravinsky's *Rite of Spring*. The dean of Boston University's School for the Arts observed that it was a matter of perception, and that people are thought to be capable of doing only what others are accustomed to seeing them do. In an article in the *Boston Globe* describing the incident, Susan Slaughter, principal trumpet of the St. Louis Symphony, similarly noted that it was cultural conditioning that caused some women to avoid playing brasses. "You cannot ask a question with a brass instrument; you must always be making statements. And to make a statement one has to be confident and 100 percent sure of yourself [sic]."[12]

While Smedvig's comments were similar to those voiced in the nineteenth century, the reactions to them were not. The students complained and their complaint was taken seriously; the university convened a forum; the story was covered in the *Boston Globe*; and the reporter interviewed a woman brass player in a major American orchestra. While these responses do not negate the fact that the incident took place, they indicate that such remarks do not always go unchallenged.

Presentation of self remains an issue for both soloists and ensemble players. While most musicians would agree that they want their musical performance to be judged in gender-neutral fashion, many disagree on the extent to which they emphasize gender in their onstage appearance. Pianist Rosalyn Tureck, for example, generally opted for dark, conservative garb, much like Ethel Leginska, so as not to distract from the music.[13] Violinist Anne-Sophie Mutter, on the other hand, favors fashionable, low-cut, off-the-shoulder designer gowns. "Never in my life would I go onstage in a dress which is not beautiful," she stated in 1988, voicing a sentiment similar to that of Maud Powell.[14]

Presentation of self has remained a persistent issue for orchestra members as well. The concerts of early women's orchestras were considered novelties as much as serious musical performances. When the Vienna Ladies Orchestra performed in North America in 1871, the *Dwight's* reviewer noted that for the first half of the program the musicians dressed in "purest white." They changed their gowns during the intermission and reappeared in dresses described by the disgruntled reviewer as "very ugly green and purple ones."[15] More than 60 years later, when the Fadettes Orchestra toured North America in 1937, the members wore identical gowns of "shimmering pale blue."[16] When the performers were women the audience expected to see, as well as hear, something beautiful. For many, this expectation has not changed.

In a 1996 piece entitled, "Playing with Style," Paula Deitz of *The New Yorker* discussed appropriate dress for women in symphony orchestras. She quoted Nancy Mehta, wife of Zubin Mehta, music director of the New York Philharmonic from 1978 to 1991, as advocating a uniform, especially since she predicted that by the twenty-first century the women in these groups would outnumber the men. "If men can accept a uniform in lieu of a variety of dress suits, why shouldn't women," she asked. The article, however, features drawings of suggested symphony attire by designers Giorgio Armani, Gianni Versace, Ralph Lauren, and Isaac Mizrahi. Each drawing portrays a young woman of model slimness wearing a body-clinging black and white dress; each garment is cut to reveal either shoulders, arms, décolletage, or leg. One woman holds a flute, two hold violins, and one holds a bassoon-like object; but if it is a bassoon, it is drawn as half the size of the actual instrument.[17] These late twentieth-century alternatives to concert dress share many of the disadvantages of their nineteenth-century predecessors, even though they represent a radical departure from the cumbersome, fussy gowns of the earlier era. The garments are not designed for the actual physical activity of playing a variety of instruments, nor would they provide warmth in drafty concert halls. Most obviously, the gowns would only look good on a woman who was tall, slender, and beautiful.

Conducting posts remains elusive for women, although this too is slowly changing. In 1990, seven of 91 major American symphony orchestras had a woman conductor, although a woman had yet to be appointed music director of one of these groups.[18] By 1998, four women had been appointed music director of American symphony orchestras: Catherine Comet, Gisele Ben-Dor, Marin Alsop, and JoAnn Falletta. In May 1998 Falletta became national news when she accepted a three-year appointment as conductor and music director of the Buffalo Philharmonic. The *Buffalo News* reported that Falletta had "dazzled musicians and audiences" during her two guest appearances the previous winter and was definitely the person to guide the orchestra "as it moves into the twenty-first century."[19]

Falletta came to learn the continuing influence of gender on her way to

JoAnn Falletta, Conductor. (Photograph by Jim Bush.)

achieving this prestigious appointment. As she grew up in New York, her parents frequently took her and her sister to orchestra concerts and by the time she was ten she knew she wanted to be a conductor. Like Antonia Brico, she was intrigued with the person on the podium who appeared to make it all happen, and by age 13 she was studying orchestral scores and attending rehearsals. Falletta's parents did not realize that her conducting ambition was unusual for a girl, and she says that she never made the connection that the person on the podium was always a man.[20]

When Falletta announced her career goal to the faculty at the Mannes School of Music they were dubious. "They told me, in the kindest way possible, that women didn't conduct, except perhaps choral music. It wasn't that they told me I wouldn't be allowed to try — only that they wanted to save me from a course of study that, as they saw it, would probably bring me frustration." And Falletta initially did experience frustration. Diminutive and soft spoken, she was not given to the grand gestures and, in her words, "macho conducting style" that people were accustomed to seeing. She understood this in a new light while studying with Korean conductor Sung Kwak, who taught her by example that a conductor could wield power not only by exhibiting tyrannical behavior but also through the "dignity of his approach."[21]

One advantage women conductors of the modern era have over their predecessors is an awareness of gender-related styles of communication. Falletta credits one of her Juilliard teachers, Jorge Mester (who had never taught a woman conductor before Falletta), with helping her realize that she would have to overcome certain tendencies originating in her traditional Italian upbringing in order to succeed. He analyzed her body language and her patterns of verbal communication, knowing that these affected her ability to command respect. Mester observed, for instance, that Falletta was more apologetic than the other five (male) students in his class. "The five young men would say, 'Let's start from (rehearsal) letter C,' and she would say, 'Please, let's just take letter C.'" And rather than looking directly into a player's eyes, she would cast her head downward, which undermined her authority." Mester acknowledged that it was accepted in our culture for women to be "nurturing, understanding, and self-effacing," but understood that a woman assuming a leadership role must combine these characteristics with "assertiveness, intelligence and problem-solving skills": a balance that he believed Falletta had achieved. [22]

Like Leginska and Brico, Falletta gained experience conducting ensembles she organized herself. While an undergraduate at Mannes she conducted the Jamaica (New York) Symphony, a small group of elderly instrumentalists who played together for their own enjoyment. She persuaded some of her fellow college students to join the ensemble and gradually molded it into a cohesive unit. Within a few years the group was renamed the Queens Philharmonic, gave five concerts a year, and paid its players a salary.[23]

Before and after completing her doctorate in conducting from Juilliard in 1989, JoAnn Falletta gradually assumed the musical directorships of the Queens Philharmonic from 1978 to 1991, the Denver Chamber Orchestra from 1983 to 1992, the San Francisco Women's Philharmonic from 1986 to 1996, the Virginia Symphony since 1991, and the Long Beach Symphony since 1989. In May 1998 she was appointed music director of the Buffalo Philharmonic beginning with the 1998-99 season.[24]

Despite her obvious successes, JoAnn Falletta considers her image when she takes the podium. Although she generally chooses a version of concert attire similar to that devised by Leginska, she varies her dress according to her estimate of how conservative the region is where she is performing. When conducting the Bay Area Women's Philharmonic and the Denver Chamber Orchestra, she wears tails. In Long Beach she has experimented with tails or skirts or black and white outfits. And when making guest appearances in the South, she sticks to dresses "to avoid appearing masculine." Even so, her choices have spurred occasional comments in the press. A San Francisco reviewer speculated in 1990 on what "psychosexual message" Falletta sought to convey when wearing a tuxedo.[25] The comment bears a striking resemblance to a description of Ethel Leginska in the 1920s as one who "perhaps intentionally leaves to the imagination of her audience whether she is a girl or a boy."[26]

Marin Alsop, another conductor who has achieved prominence in the modern era, has also had to overcome resistance in pursuit of her career. Her parents were both musicians — her father was concertmaster of the New York City Ballet Orchestra and her mother a cellist in the same group. Alsop began to play the violin at six and by age seven was playing in the Juilliard Youth Orchestra. Her fascination with conducting began when she attended a Young People's Concert given by Leonard Bernstein in the 1950s. She later said that she was captivated first by his personality and then by his conducting. "I sat in the second row," she recalled, "and that experience stayed with me. I immediately knew this was it; this was what I wanted to do." At age 12 Alsop explained to one of her Juilliard teachers that she wanted to be a conductor and was told, "Girls don't do that." When her father learned of the incident, he went out and bought her a box of batons.[27]

After Marin Alsop received a bachelor's degree in violin from Juilliard, she applied to the school's graduate conducting program and was rejected twice. She responded by attending as many concerts as she could. When she observed a conductor whose techniques she admired, she asked him for private lessons. In this way she studied with Eduardo Mata, Karl Richter, Gustav Meier, Harold Faberman, Walter Hendl, and Carl Bamberger. Bamberger would arrange his living room like an orchestra and have her conduct the furniture. She supported herself by freelancing as a violinist, an experience that included playing violin backup on a few Billy Joel albums and on a commercial for Kentucky Fried Chicken. She also started two ensembles in Manhattan in order to give herself opportunities to conduct. In 1981 she founded what may well be the only all-string swing band, the fourteen-piece String Fever, immersing herself in jazz and learning as she went along. In 1983 she formed a fifty-piece chamber orchestra, Concordia, which eventually had its own series at Lincoln Center.[28]

Alsop was rejected four times before being admitted to the conducting program at Tanglewood, although she blames herself for some of the problem, since she missed deadlines and submitted incomplete application materials. Finally in 1988, Alsop was awarded Tanglewood's Leonard Bernstein Conducting Fellowship. The year also fortuitously saw Bernstein's seventieth birthday. Alsop captivated Bernstein when she conducted his birthday concert, and as the press documented "Lenny-mania" that summer, it seemed that whenever he appeared before a camera he had his arm around Marin Alsop.[29]

The next summer Alsop won Tanglewood's Koussevitzky Conducting Prize, which led to music directorships of the Eugene (Oregon) Symphony and the Long Island Philharmonic. In 1993 she was appointed conductor of the Colorado Symphony; her title was changed to music director in 1995. Ironically, Alsop now leads the successor organization to the debt-laden Denver Symphony, which folded in 1989, the year of Antonia Brico's death. And in 1996 she was named to the creative-conductor chair of the St. Louis Symphony, with the goals of devising innovative programming and assuring the continuation of the orchestra's commitment to American music. (An example of her innovation was the program "Radio Rhapsody," which was a re-creation of a Paul Whiteman radio show.)

Reviews of Alsop's performances show that things have changed since Leginska conducted the New York Symphony in 1925. Writing for the *New York Times* in 1994, Robert Schwarz described Alsop performing with the St. Louis Symphony as a "muscular, kinetic presence, unafraid of sweeping gestures and emotive expressions." The chairman of the Colorado Symphony's

Marin Alsop and Leonard Bernstein at Tanglewood, 1988. (Photograph by Walter H. Scott.)

board stated in 1995: "Each time Marin takes the podium, a new sense of excitement flows through our growing audience." Charles Staff of the *Indianapolis Star* wrote in June, 1998, "Alsop doesn't just understand Gershwin's language. She speaks it and with her body language — not just her baton — she imparts the meaning to the musicians who pass it on to the audience." Reviews express genuine admiration and respect with none of the snideness and innuendo that greeted Ethel Leginska and, to a lesser extent, Antonia Brico when they conducted their orchestras.[30]

Presentation of self remains a concern, however, for women conductors. While some adopt a tailored look similar to that of Leginska and Brico, others experiment with their image. As Diane Wittry, music director and conductor of the Symphony of Southeast Texas in Beaumont, explained in 1994, "Because I am not of the customary gender, I chose to start a new tradition of my own. Elegant gowns, skirts and blouses, especially selected for each concert. Long, flowing outfits with sequins and lace. And who says a conductor must always wear black? I began to mingle silver and gold with the standard black and white, adding a touch of pizzazz and excitement to our stage. We even toyed with the idea of a marketing campaign called 'Dress the Conductor,' in which local fashion stores would select attire for each concert.

Marin Alsop in concert. (Photography by Catherine Byrd, courtesy Michael Schmidt Artists International, Inc.)

Throughout the years, we have kept concertgoers guessing. 'What are you going to wear?' they all ask me. 'Come to the next concert and find out,' I reply. Ticket sales have increased dramatically."[31]

Wittry's desire to assert rather than underplay her femininity is shared by other women conductors. "Your appearance defines your attitude on the job," says Sian Edwards, the first woman to be named by the Los Angeles Philharmonic to lead subscription concerts. Wanting to dress comfortably and yet "look different from a man," Edwards chooses from a selection of evening trousers and colored blouses. "In my work, there's always the woman thing," says Iona Brown, director of the Academy of St. Martin-in-the-Fields in London, but Brown refuses to use male dress as a means to impose her authority. "I absolutely do not want to convey a masculine image," she says. "I like being feminine and want to look feminine. I love compliments on my appearance." Marin Alsop always wears pants when she conducts, although she offsets the severity of her tuxedo with a brightly colored silk blouse, saying that she strives to "maintain a balance between the masculine and the feminine."[32] Gisele Ben-Dor experiments with various looks — she feels too casual if she wears a short jacket while everyone else is in tails, but feels that wearing tails makes her look like a "little man."[33] Despite the increased chances that women will conduct, they continue to wrestle with the image they convey.

The trend to assert the sexuality of women musicians is evident in the marketing of compact discs. In one catalog violinist Nadja Salerno-Sonnenberg, clad in the briefest of black dresses, leans forward on her chair with nary a violin in sight. Young English violinist Pip Clarke appears to be topless in some of her publicity stills, clasping her violin against her chest in the afternoon sunlight, lips slightly parted.[34] Ofra Hornoy reclines on a couch, gently embracing her cello. Michala Petri, a recorder soloist whose image was relatively natural and unaffected until she began recording for RCA, was photographed in a strapless gown and heavy red lipstick for the cover of her recording of Telemann sonatas. Violinist Anne Akiko Meyers viewed her first CD cover as a "disaster — too much makeup, too much hair. My family didn't even recognize me."[35] Similar methods are also used to market small instrumental ensembles. The three attractive members of the Eroica Trio pose in graceful, low-cut gowns. Two women's groups which have achieved acclaim in the 1990s are called the Medieval Baebes and Bimbetta.

"I'm so glad I'm not a beauty," stated Ethel Leginska in the late 1920s, expressing her belief that physical beauty would handicap her chances of success.[36] Violinist Anne-Sophie Mutter, dubbed the "strapless violinist" by *Vanity Fair* and considered a beautiful woman, echoed a version of this sentiment nearly 70 years later. "Sometimes if you are very ugly it's easier to be taken seriously as someone with brains and with abilities than if you look more or less good and are in the public eye," she observed.[37] Conductor JoAnn Falletta muses, "If having a soloist who looks young and exciting and off-beat and interesting attracts people who otherwise might not have come to a concert or who might not otherwise have bought a record, then the result is good. But, it worries me a little bit because we may be marketing something that is not really the core of what the art form is. And we may be creating false expectations. When people get to the concert and they hear the Bruch violin concerto and it's not what they thought it was going to be, then they have to deal with the disillusionment. Obviously, these people are selling tickets and selling records, but whether they are creating a long-term audience for the arts, I'm not sure."[38]

As music critic Jamie James has observed, "There is nothing new in using Barnum-like hype to sell serious music performed by musicians of either sex. Paganini and Liszt became the musical idols of their day in part because of their canny exploitation of their compelling looks and stage personalities. Jenny Lind was managed by P. T. Barnum himself and Louis Moreau Gottschalk was one of the country's first matinee idols. And during the recording era, it has never hurt to have a pretty or at least interesting face to put on the cover. Van Cliburn's phenomenal success may be attributed at least in small measure to his dewy-eyed good looks, which incited young girls to pursue him like a pop star,"[39] just as they have more recently the dashing Irish pianist Barry Douglas, the winner of the Tchaikovsky Competition in 1986. The marketing of male musicians, however, allows for a wider variety of images. Tall, dark, and handsome Barry Douglas stands in front of the grand piano exuding a brooding sensitivity. Members of the now middle-aged Canadian Brass casually stroll together near the Great Wall of China. At least where marketing is concerned, men can be intense, sensitive, casual or middle-aged, while it is preferable for women to be young and beautiful.

9

Conclusion

The women's lives we have examined form a rough continuum. Fannie Bloomfield-Zeisler combined women's traditional roles of wife and mother with success as a piano virtuoso. Ethel Leginska went beyond the bounds of convention by rejecting traditional domesticity and seeking a career as a conductor. Antonia Brico worked single-mindedly toward her goal, uninterrupted by domestic detours, but her progress was still constrained by prescribed gender roles. Not until the late twentieth century did women like JoAnn Falletta and Marin Alsop successfully break down barriers to become music directors of major American symphony orchestras. Also in the modern era, women have assumed positions of leadership as first-chair players, although they still are only somewhat more likely to play instruments traditionally thought inappropriate for women.

Newspaper accounts no longer automatically label a woman's apparent performance anxiety a nervous breakdown, and in fact most statistical data on performance-related stress among musicians do not distinguish between males and females. Psychologists and physicians in the late twentieth century are more likely to suggest treatments such as cognitive behavior therapy or beta blockers than the "rest cure."[1]

These changes, however, must not obscure the reality that the stereotypical notions which limited women's musical growth in the mid–nineteenth century continue to do so today, though in attenuated form. The instruments women commonly play are still those that allow them to look graceful. Relatively few women have been vouchsafed the opportunity to conduct, and those who have succeeded have done so only by persisting in the face of repeated rejection. Women who have become successful instrumentalists and conductors still must deal with issues of presentation of self and the gender message they convey when performing.

Choices and trade-offs regarding marriage and family continue to pose problems for women musicians, as they do for women in all professions. Among women musicians who marry, however, their managers are no longer the usual choice. Some marry fellow musicians, but many marry professionals who exercise flexibility in a manner similar to that of Sigmund Zeisler. Catherine Comet, for instance, who served as conductor of the Grand Rapids Symphony from 1986 to 1997, is married to an academic whose moves have sometimes been dictated by *her* opportunities. Conductor Victoria Bond and her lawyer husband have spent much of their marriage commuting between New York and the cities where she has had jobs. Children pose further complications whose solutions vary. JoAnn Falletta has reported wishing to have children but being concerned about when to take the time off to do so. Bond and her husband concluded that children and a conducting career were incompatible, especially since the couple lived apart so much of the year. And Catherine Comet stopped conducting for several years when her daughter was very young.[2]

When Comet's daughter was five years old, she took her to a concert by the St. Louis Symphony, where she served as assistant conductor. When conductor Leonard Slatkin walked on stage, young Caroline piped up in amazement, "Mommy, it's a man!" This, too, represents a transition to a time when no one notices a difference at all. JoAnn Falletta observed: "It's very satisfying to see an orchestra stop thinking of you as a woman conductor and start thinking of you as a conductor. I'm at the point now where I can feel when it happens. It may be in the second rehearsal or the third rehearsal, but it happens whether it's Mexico or Germany or Italy. That's a good feeling."[3]

Notes

1. *"Whence Comes the Lady Tympanist?"*

1. "A Monster Concert by Young Ladies," *Dwight's Journal of Music* 3 (August 6, 1853): 142. The phrase "monster concert" refers to the large number of instrumentalists on stage, not to the participants.

2. George P. Upton, *Woman in Music: An Essay* (Boston: James R. Osgood and Co., 1880), 18.

3. T.L. Krebs, "Women as Musicians," *Sewanee Review* 2 (November 1893): 76. See Julia Eklund Koza, "Music and the Feminine Sphere: Images of Women as Musicians in *Godey's Lady's Book*, 1830–1877," *Musical Quarterly* 75 (Summer 1991): 103–129, for a discussion of why music seemed particularly suitable for women and how this was expressed in the fiction of one of the most popular periodicals of the period.

4. Charles E. Rosenberg, *No Other Gods: On Science and American Social Thought* (Baltimore: Johns Hopkins University Press, 1976), 55.

5. Since deeper instruments were also larger and more ungainly, it is difficult to separate issues of size and pitch. The aversion to deep tones produced by female performers was obvious, however, in the case of singers. A *New York Tribune* reviewer, describing a recital by a woman who possessed an extraordinarily wide vocal range, wrote in 1853, "The idea of a woman's voice is feminine; anything below that is disgusting: it is as bad as a bride with a beard on her chin and an oath in her mouth.... We hear a great deal about Woman's sphere. That sphere exists in music, and it is in the soprano region of the voice." ("Black Swan," *Dwight's Journal of Music* 3 [April 9, 1853]: 2.) Music critic Robert Grau observed in 1916 that no contralto had gained the public adulation and popularity achieved by the sopranos. (Robert Grau, "A Strange Public Aversion to Contraltos as Compared with the Sopranos of Great Fame," *Musician* 21 [November 1916]: 694.)

6. Philip Hale, *Musical Record*, June 1, 1900, 240.

7. "The New Woman in Music," *Musical America* 9 (April 28, 1906): 8.

8. Cynthia Eagle Russett, *Sexual Science: The Victorian Construction of Womanhood* (Cambridge, Mass.: Harvard University Press, 1989), 29–30.

9. "Fannie Bloomfield-Zeisler," *Musical Courier,* December 28, 1898, p. 40.

10. "Minnie Coons," *Musical Courier*, January 31, 1906, p. 24.

11. Olga Samaroff Stokowski, "Women in Music," *Music Clubs Magazine* 17 (September-October 1937): 7–9, 12. A rare example of a reviewer invoking male attributes in a positive way is Philip Hale's enthusiastic pronouncement, "Mrs. Zeisler played

like a man: not like a little man, but like a robust and bearded creature rejoicing in his strength." The Hale article is contained on Microfilm Reel #3315 at the American Jewish Archives in Cincinnati. The archive has two reels of film which contain clippings from two of Fannie Bloomfield-Zeisler's scrapbooks. Cited hereafter as FBZ-AJA 3315 and FBZ-AJA 3316. Philip Hale, "Fannie Bloomfield Zeisler," *Boston Journal*, American Jewish Archives, Cincinnati, FBZ-AJA 3315.

12. Peter G. Filene, *Him/Her/Self: Sex Roles in Modern America* (Baltimore: Johns Hopkins University Press, 1986), 69ff. See also Peter N. Stearns, *Be a Man: Males in Modern Society* (New York: Holmes and Meier, 1979), 49ff.

13. "Fannie Bloomfield-Zeisler," *Musical Courier*, January 3, 1900, p. 18.

14. Judith Tick, "Passed Away Is the Piano Girl: Changes in American Musical Life, 1870–1900," in *Women Making Music: The Western Art Tradition, 1150–1950*, ed. Jane Bowers and Judith Tick (Urbana: University of Illinois Press, 1986), 328.

15. Karen Shaffer and Neva Garner Greenwood, *Maud Powell: Pioneer American Violinist* (Arlington, Va.: Maud Powell Foundation; Ames, Iowa: Iowa State University Press, 1988), 16.

16. Tick, "Passed Away," 328. See also "Mr. Eichberg's Violin Classes," *Dwight's Journal of Music* 39 (January 4, 1879): 7.

17. Raymond Morin, *The Worcester Music Festival, Its Background and History, 1855–1945* (Worcester, Mass.: Worcester County Music Association, 1946), 42–43, quoted in Christine Ammer, *Unsung: A History of Women in American Music* (Westport, Conn.: Greenwood, 1980), 30.

18. "The Symphony Society," *New York Times*, January 20, 1889, 3. Quoted in Shaffer and Greenwood, *Maud Powell*, 113.

19. "Florence Austin, A Violin Virtuosa," *Musical Courier*, November 1910, p. 19.

20. Shaffer and Greenwood, *Maud Powell*, 148ff.

21. Dee Garrison, *Apostles of Culture: The Public Librarian and American Society* (New York: Free Press, 1979), 177.

22. Krebs, "Women," 80–81.

23. The *Ladies Home Journal* pictured active and athletic women in its late nineteenth- and early twentieth-century issues. Recommended out-door sports for girls included bicycling, gymnastics, badminton, tennis, and golf. Fashion pages showed clothes for these activities: divided skirts, sports frocks, looser corsets, and lightweight girdles. (Mary P. Ryan, *Womanhood in America: From Colonial Times to the Present* [New York: Franklin Watts, 1983], 211–212.)

24. E. Van der Straeten, *The Techniques of Violoncello Playing* (London: The Strad, 1915), 19. Quoted in Elizabeth Cowling, *The Cello* (New York: Charles Scribner's Sons, 1983), 179.

25. "Elsa Reugger," *Musical Courier*, November 12, 1902, p. 27.

26. Quoted in Judith Tick, *American Women Composers Before 1870* (Ann Arbor: UMI Research, 1983), 28.

27. Sidney Lanier, *Music and Poetry: Essays Upon Some Aspects and Interrelations of the Two Arts* (New York: C. Scribner's Sons, 1898), 39.

28. Leon Vallas, *Claude Debussy: His Life and Works* (New York: Dover, 1973), 162.

29. James Barron, "A Sax Craze Inspired by the Simpsons," *New York Times*, January 14, 1996, sec. 4, p. 2.

30. Alice Kessler-Harris, *Out to Work: A History of Wage-Earning Women in the United States* (New York: Oxford University Press, 1982), 101–102.

31. Garrison, *Apostles of Culture*, 184.

32. Ralph Korn, *How to Organize the Amateur Band and Orchestra* (New York: Greenberg, 1928), 42.

33. Mary L. Stoltzfus, "Eve in the Ensemble," *Musical Courier,* December 1, 1947, p. 9.

34. "Orchestral Women," *Scientific American* 73 (November 23, 1895): 327.

35. Kessler-Harris, *Out to Work*, 186–187.

36. Lanier, *Music and Poetry*, 39; Frederique Joanne Petrides, "Women in Orchestras," *Etude* 56 (July 1938): 429–430.

37. According to one source, he later vindicated himself: when he founded the American Symphony Orchestra in 1962, he included many women, blacks, and members of other minority groups. (Jan Bell Groh, *Evening the Score: Women in Music and the Legacy of Frederique Petrides* [Fayetteville: University of Arkansas Press, 1991], 60.)

38. W. J. Henderson, "Music and Musicians," *New York Sun*, November 16, 1935, 9.

39. These groups were generally segregated by color. For information on black women's groups, see D. Antoinette Handy, *Black Women in American Bands and Orchestras* (Metuchen, N.J.: Scarecrow Press, 1981); on white women's groups, see Christine Ammer, *Unsung: A History of Women in American Music* (Westport, Conn.: Greenwood, 1980), 99–109, and Carol Neuls-Bates, "Women's Orchestras in the United States, 1925–45," in *Women Making Music: The Western Art Tradition, 1150–1950*, ed. Jane Bowers and Judith Tick (Urbana: University of Illinois Press, 1986), 349–369. See also D. Antoinette Handy, "Black Women and American Orchestras: An Update," in *New Perspectives on Music: Essays in Honor of Eileen Southern*, edited by Josephine Wright. (Warren, Mich.: Harmonie Park Press, 1992), 451–462, and Josephine Wright: "Black Women in Classical Music in Boston During the Late Nineteenth Century: Profiles of Leadership," in *New Perspectives on Music: Essays in Honor of Eileen Southern*, edited by Josephine Wright. (Warren, Mich.: Harmonie Park Press, 1992), 373–408.

40. Tick, "Passed Away," 329–332; Carol Neuls-Bates, "Women's Orchestras," 349–369.

41. Tick, "Passed Away," 332–333.

42. "Vienna Lady Orchestra," *New York Times*, September 13, 1871, 5.

43. "World of Music," *Etude* 34 (April 1916): 320; Z.A.S., "Salt Lake Women Give Worthy Orchestral Concert," *Musical America* 22 (May 22, 1915): 27.

44. Reprinted as "Vienna Lady Orchestra," *Dwight's Journal of Music* 31 (September 23, 1871): 104.

45. "World of Music," *Etude* 34 (April 1916): 320; "Salt Lake Women," 27.

46. "Vienna Lady Orchestra," *New York Times*, September 13, 1871, 5.

47. "Leginska, Guest Conductor of Chicago Woman's Symphony, to Play Solo," *Musical Courier*, April 28, 1927, pp. 32–33.

48. A.K.C., "Woman's Symphony of Chicago Completes Successful Season," *Musical Courier*, May 24, 1930, p. 16.

49. "When Women Blow Horns," *Literary Digest* 113 (April 2, 1932): 19–20.

There are two types of double-bass bow. One is constructed like a modern cello bow and is held in an overhand position. The other is larger and grasped by the end, almost like a saw. "Bow" in *New Grove Dictionary of Music and Musicians*, Stanley Sadie, ed. (London: Macmillan, 1980).

50. Tick, "Passed Away," 329; Ammer, *Unsung*, 103.

51. Lois Banner, *American Beauty* (New York: Knopf, 1983), 121–125.

52. Douglas Gilbert, *American Vaudeville: Its Life and Times* (New York: Dover, 1963), 395–410.

53. Blanche Naylor, *The Anthology of the Fadettes* (Boston: The Author, 1941?), 8, 18.

54. "The Saxonians," Flyer, William Miles' Personal Collection, Mt. Pleasant, Mich.

55. Joseph E. Maddy and T. P. Giddings, *Instrumental Techniques for Orchestra and Band* (Cincinnati: Willis Music Co., 1926), 3.

56. David Macleod, *Building Character in the American Boy: The Boy Scouts, YMCA, and Their Forerunners, 1870–1920* (Madison: University of Wisconsin Press, 1983), 47.

57. Harold Randolph, "The Feminization of Music," in Music Teachers National Association, *Papers and Proceedings of the 44th Annual Meeting* (New York, 1922), 200.

58. See Julia Eklund Koza, "The 'Missing Males' and Other Gender Issues in Music Education: Evidence from the *Music Supervisors' Journal*, 1914–1924," *Journal of Research in Music Education* 41 (Fall 1993): 212–232, for an analysis of gender-related references. Koza found that the journal included many articles which discussed music in the education of boys, career opportunities in music for males, and many other related subjects. By contrast, the journal paid little attention to girls and their interests and problems.

59. Londa Schiebinger, *The Mind Has No Sex?* (Cambridge, Mass.: Harvard University Press, 1989), 118.

60. Kessler-Harris, *Out to Work*, 117.

61. "Leginska Conducts Last of Three Concerts of People's Symphony," *Musical Courier*, November 26, 1925, p. 24, quoted in Neuls-Bates, "Women's Orchestras," 357.

62. "When Women Blow Horns," 19–20.

63. Adam Lesinsky, "Give the Girls a Chance," *School Musician* 1 (February 1930): 7.

64. "Chicago Holds Her Solo Contest," *School Musician* 1 (January 1930): 18.

65. Edwin Franko Goldman, *Band Betterment: Suggestions and Advice to Bands, Bandmasters and Band-players* (New York: Carl Fischer, 1934), 14–15. See also Edwin Barnes, *Music As an Educational Asset* (Philadelphia: Theodore Presser, 1927), 46.

66. Lesinsky, "Give the Girls," 7; Franklyn Wiltse, "Girls!" *School Musician* 4 (April 1933): 8.

67. Wiltse, "Girls!", 8.

68. Joe Berryman, "The Bugle-Lyra in the Girls' Drum Corps," *School Musician* 8 (March 1937): 18.

69. "Pretty Girls with Flashing Batons," *School Musician* 12 (February 1941): 28; Ray W. Dutcher, "Eastside High School Augments its Band with Flag Twirlers," *School Musician* 12 (February 1941): 17.

70. Roy R. Coates, "Put the Girls to Work in a Drum Corps," *School Musician* 8 (September 1937): 8; P. E. Laubach, "Girls," *School Musician* 11 (January 1940): 8.

71. Lesinsky, "Give the Girls," 7; "Lads of the Third Division," *School Musician* 6 (February 1935): 23; "Beauty Plus," *School Musician* 6 (January 1935): 27.

72. Raymond Paige, "Why Not Women in Orchestras?" *Etude* 70 (January 1952): 14–15.

73. Barbara Sicherman, "Working It Out: Gender, Profession and Reform in the Career of Alice Hamilton," in Noralee Frankel and Nancy S. Dye, eds., *Gender, Class, Race and Reform in the Progressive Era* (Lexington: University Press of Kentucky, 1991), 128.

2. *"He Is Himself a Grand Piano"*

1. Marcia J. Citron, *Gender and the Musical Canon* (New York: Cambridge, 1993), 57.

2. *The New Grove Dictionary of Music and Musicians,* s.v. "Schumann, Clara." A startling example of the mishandling a woman's compositional talent was experienced by Amy Cheney (later Amy Beach), whose parents were advised that they should not seek formal instruction for their talented daughter, but instead have her teach herself by studying the music of great composers. They followed this advice. See Adrienne Fried Block, *Amy Beach: Passionate Victorian* (New York: Oxford University Press, 1998), 40–41.

3. Mary Ann Feldman, "George Upton: Journalist, Music Critic and Mentor to Early Chicago" (Ph.D. diss., Univ. of Minnesota, 1983), 262–263.

4. Fanny Bloomfield-Zeisler, "Woman in Music," *Music Teachers National Association: Official Report of Annual Meeting,* 1890, pp. 38–44.

5. Eleanor Perenyi, *Liszt: The Artist as Romantic Hero* (Boston: Little, Brown, 1974), 3.

6. *The New Grove Dictionary of Music and Musicians,* s.v. "Liszt."

7. Cited in S. Frederick Starr, *Bamboula: The Life and Times of Louis Moreau Gottschalk* (New York: Oxford University Press, 1995), 53.

8. R. Allen Lott, "The American Concert Tours of Leopold de Meyer, Henri Herz and Sigismund Thalberg" (Ph.D. diss., City University of New York, 1986); see also names of individual virtuosos in *New Grove Dictionary of Music and Musicians.*

9. Lott, "American Concert Tours," 583–584.

10. Catherine Drinker Bowen, *"Free Artist": The Story of Anton and Nicholas Rubinstein* (New York: Random House, 1939), 231.

11. Cited in Lott, "American Concert Tours," 358.

12. Cited in Arthur Loesser, *Men, Women and Pianos* (New York: Simon and Schuster, 1954), 515.

13. Adam Zamoyski, *Paderewski* (New York: Atheneum, 1982), 85.

14. Rom Landau, *Ignace Paderewski, Musician and Statesman* (New York: Thomas Y. Crowell, 1934), 77.

15. Lott, "American Concert Tours," 55.

16. George P. Upton, *Musical Memories: My Recollections of Celebrities of the Half-Century 1850–1900* (Chicago: A. C. McClurg, 1908), 79–80.

17. Arnold T. Schwab, *James Gibbons Huneker: Critic of the Seven Arts* (Stanford: Stanford University Press, 1963), 62–63.

18. Untitled article, *Guardian*, May 4, 1898, FBZ-AJA 3315.

19. Fanny Marks Siebels, *Wishes Are Horses: Montgomery, Alabama's First Lady of the Violin* (New York: Exposition Press, 1958), 84; Joseph Horowitz, *Understanding Toscanini: How He Became an American Culture-God and Helped Create a New Audience for Old Music* (Minneapolis: University of Minnesota Press, 1987), 22; Landau, *Ignace Paderewski*, 77; Adam Zamoyski, *Paderewski* (New York: Atheneum, 1982), 91.

20. Philip Hale, untitled review, *Musical Record*, June 1, 1900, p. 240.

21. "Virtuosos and Virtuosity," *Dwight's Journal of Music* 25 (September 22, 1855): 193.

22. *New Grove Dictionary of American Music*, s.v. "Lind, Jenny." See also Adrienne Fried Block, "Two Virtuoso Performers in Boston: Jenny Lind and Camilla Urso," in *New Perspectives in Music: Essays in Honor of Eileen Southern* (Warren, Mich.: Harmonie Park Press, 1992), 355–371.

23. Upton, *Musical Memories*, 20–24.

24. Gladys Denny Schultz, *Jenny Lind, the Swedish Nightingale* (Philadelphia: Lippincott, 1962), 219–220.

25. Quoted in Schultz, *Jenny Lind*, 209.

26. Lucy Green, *Music, Gender and Education* (London: Cambridge University Press, 1997), 54, and Green's chapter 2, "Affirming Femininity: Women Singing, Women Enabling," and her chapter 3, "From Affirmation to Interpretation: Women Playing Instruments." See also Susan McClary, *Feminine Endings: Music, Gender, and Sexuality* (Minneapolis: University of Minnesota Press, 1991), 137–138.

27. For additional biographical material on Carreño, see Marta Milinowski, *Teresa Carreño: By the Grace of God* (New Haven: Yale University Press, 1940), and Anne E. Albuquerque, "Teresa Carreño, Pianist, Teacher and Composer," DMA thesis, University of Cincinnati, 1988. For a brief account of Urso's life, see Susan Kagan, "Camilla Urso: A Nineteenth-Century Violinist's View," *Signs: Journal of Women in Culture and Society* 2, no. 3 (Spring 1977), 727–734.

28. "Camilla Urso," *Dwight's Journal of Music* 2 (December 18, 1852): 86; "Lenora Jackson at Louisville Music Festival," *Musical Courier*, May 23, 1900, p. 9.

29. Olga Samaroff Stokowski, *An American Musician's Story* (New York: Norton, 1939), 33.

30. Untitled excerpt from Chicago newspaper, quoted in *Musical Courier*, December 1, 1909; "Carreño," clipping file, New York Public Library.

31. M. Leslie Petteys, "Julie Rivé-King: American Pianist" (DMA thesis, University of Missouri–Kansas City, 1987), 154.

32. "Fannie Bloomfield-Zeisler," *Musical Courier*, February 20, 1895, FBZ-AJA 3315.

33. Petteys, "Julie Rivé-King," 155.

34. Philip Hale, "Fannie Bloomfield-Zeisler," *Boston Journal*, March 13, 1893; in FBZ-AJA 3315.

35. Janet Coryell and Robert Myers, eds. *Adeline and Julia: Growing Up in Michigan and on the Kansas Frontier: Diaries from 19th Century America* (East Lansing: Michigan State University Press, 1999.)

36. Cited in Petteys, "Julie Rivé-King," 73–74.

37. Ibid., 196.

38. "Fannie Bloomfield-Zeisler," *Bridgeport Telegram*, December 10, 1903. This article includes a detail which illustrates either Bloomfield-Zeisler's vanity or the unfashionable nature of wearing eye glasses or both. "She was accompanied by her manager, who looks after the business. She is very near-sighted, and this gentleman had a unique way of indicating the stair which she would have to descend by placing on the edge a strip of white paper over the red carpet. She wears no glasses when she plays."

39. Alison Lurie, *The Language of Clothes* (London: Bloomsbury, 1992), 217–218.

40. "Should a Woman Singer Wear a Corset? A Symposium," *Musician* 19 (May-June 1914): 338–339, 410–411.

41. Ibid.

42. Lurie, *Language of Clothes*, 217–218.

43. Karen A. Shaffer and Neva Garner Greenwood, *Maud Powell: Pioneer American Violinist* (Arlington, Va.: Maud Powell Foundation; Ames, Iowa: Iowa State University Press, 1988), 24.

44. Ibid., 205–206.

45. See Chapter 6, pp. 100–102.

46. J. C. Fillmore, "The Occasional Correspondence of a Music Teacher," *Etude* 4 (June 1887): 84.

47. *New Harvard Dictionary of Music*, s.v. "Conducting."

48. Don Michael Randel, ed., *New Harvard Dictionary of Music* (Cambridge, Mass.: Harvard University Press, 1986), 178.

49. Lawrence Levine, *Highbrow, Lowbrow: The Emergence of Cultural Hierarchy in America* (Cambridge, Mass.: Harvard University Press, 1988), 136.

50. "Soloists and Concertos Make Their Re-Appearance," *Musical America* 53 (December 10, 1933): p. 16.

51. Cited in Horowitz, *Understanding Toscanini*, 96.

52. Oscar Thompson, "Otto Klemperer's Conducting Stirs Throng at First New York Concert," *Musical America* 43 (Jan. 30, 1926): 1, 4. Huneker quote cited in Horowitz, *Understanding Toscanini*, 41.

53. Dorothy Berliner Commins, *Making an Orchestra* (New York: Macmillan, 1931), 2; "Stokowski's Men Invade Baltimore," *Musical America* 31 (January 31, 1920): 41.

54. "Scarcity of American Conductors," *Musical America* 15 (April 20, 1912): 20.

55. "Leginska Conducts Last of Three Concerts of People's Symphony," *Musical Courier*, November 26, 1925, p. 24; "When Women Blow Horns," *Literary Digest* 113 (April 2, 1932): 19–20.

56. Amy Fay, *Music Study in Germany* (1880; reprint, New York: Dover, 1965).

57. Quaintance Eaton, "Ambitious to Conduct; But Says She Will Not," *Musical America* 47 (March 31, 1928): 32.

3. "Spoiled for Domesticity"

1. Olga Samaroff Stokowski, *An American Musician's Story* (New York: Norton, 1939), 14–16, 30.

2. Lucy Forsyth Townsend, "Jane Addams Abroad: Travel as Educational 'Finish.'" *Vitae Scholasticae* 6 (1987): 185–186.

3. Arthur Loesser, *Men, Women and Pianos: A Social History* (New York: Simon and Schuster, 1954), 538. By 1900 more than 5,000 American music students had gone to Europe to study, and the number of women increased dramatically between 1850 and 1900. At the Leipzig Conservatory, for example, more than 90 percent of the American students were men between 1851 and 1855; in the period 1871–1900, however, about half of the American students were women. Elam Douglas Bomberger, "The German Musical Training of American Students, 1850–1900" (Ph.D. diss., University of Maryland–College Park, 1991), 1–2, 60–61.

4. Bomberger, "German Musical Training," 9–10, 48.

5. Barbara Miller Solomon, *In the Company of Educated Women: A History of Women and Higher Education in America* (New Haven: Yale University Press, 1985), photos after page 114.

6. M. Leslie Petteys, "Julie Rivé-King: American Pianist" (DMA thesis, University of Missouri–Kansas City, 1987), 33–34. The American Jewish Archives in Cincinnati has a draft of a biography of Fannie Bloomfield-Zeisler by her husband Sigmund. This is in typescript with some pages unnumbered and others erratically numbered. Cited hereafter as SZ-AJA. Karen A. Shaffer and Neva Garner Greenwood, *Maud Powell: Pioneer American Violinist* (Arlington, Va.: Maud Powell Foundation; Ames, Iowa: Iowa State University Press, 1988), 28–29; Stokowski, *American Musician's Story,* 20.

7. Ibid., 67–68.

8. Donna Staley Kline, *Olga Samaroff Stokowski: An American Virtuoso on the World Stage* (College Station: Texas A & M Press, 1996), 11–12.

9. Stokowski, *American Musician's Story,* 18.

10. SZ-AJA.

11. Shaffer and Greenwood, *Maud Powell,* 11, 25.

12. Suzanne Gordon, *Off Balance: The Real World of Ballet* (New York: Pantheon, 1983), 66–67.

13. Piano playing was considered such a public nuisance in nineteenth-century Germany that there was a law forbidding playing a piano near an open window during certain hours. "In 1882 a case came to court in Bamberg involving a young woman who played the same three pieces by an open window from 8 PM to 10:30 PM. The neighbors called the police and she was taken to court, where the judge found in favor of the long-suffering neighbors. Testimony in the trial included earwitness accounts of her limited repertoire, her 'awful' [furchtbar] playing, and the acoustical properties of the street where she lived." Bomberger, "German Musical Training," 18–19.

14. Shaffer, *Maud Powell,* 28–29; Stokowski, *American Musician's Story,* 20; Elam Douglas Bomberger compares the cost of living in the United States and in Germany during the late nineteenth century, observing that many of the prices were comparable.

He also contrasts the cost of living in Berlin in 1858 and Munich in 1882–83 with a late twentieth-century consumer price index. See Bomberger, "German Musical Training," 33–36.

15. Shaffer, *Maud Powell*, 37–38.

16. Ibid., 39.

17. Ibid.

18. Letter from Fannie Bloomfield-Zeisler, *Philadelphia Musical Journal*, March, 1890, FBZ-AJA 3315.

19. Stokowski, *American Musician's Story*, 18; Shaffer, *Maud Powell*, 87–88.

20. Amy Fay, *Music Study in Germany* (1880; reprint, New York: Dover, 1965).

21. Margaret William McCarthy, *Amy Fay: America's Notable Woman of Music* (Warren, Mich.: Harmonie Park Press, 1995), 176–77; *More Letters of Amy Fay: The American Years, 1879–1916* (Detroit: Information Coordinators, 1986), xvi.

22. Fay, *Music Study*, 21.

23. Ibid., 40–41.

24. Ibid., 82.

25. Clara Clemens, *My Husband Gabrilowitsch* (New York: Harper Bros., 1938), 4.

26. "The Passing of the World's Most Famous Piano Teacher," *Musical America* 23 (November 27, 1915): 3–4.

27. "Noted Artists Pay Tribute to Leschetizky," *Musical America* 23 (December 4, 1915): 47.

28. Catherine Drinker Bowen, *"Free Artist": The Story of Anton and Nicholas Rubinstein* (New York: Random House, 1939), 169.

29. "Noted Artists Pay Tribute," 47.

30. *New Grove Dictionary of Music and Musicians*, s.v. "Leschetizky, Theodor."

31. Alice Miller, *For Your Own Good: Hidden Cruelty in Child-Rearing and the Roots of Violence* (New York: Noonday Press, 1990), 29–30.

32. Diana Ruth Hallman, "The Pianist Fannie Bloomfield-Zeisler in American Music and Society" (Master's thesis, University of Maryland, 1983), 20.

33. Cesar Saerchinger, *Artur Schnabel: A Biography* (Westport, Conn.: Greenwood, 1957), 13.

34. Samuel Lipman, "Piano Prodigy," *American Scholar* 62 (Winter, 1993): 31–50.

35. See discussion of Miller's theories in Gisela Moffit, *Bonds and Bondage: Daughter-Father Relationships in the Father Memoirs of German-Speaking Women Writers of the 1970s* (New York: Peter Lang, 1993), 48–51.

36. Hallman, 36.

37. Bird quoted in Eleanor Spencer, "Leschetizky's Stern Discipline Only an Armor to Shield a Deeply Warm Nature," *Musical America* 26 (May 26, 1917): 9.

38. Hallman, 66, 75.

39. SZ-AJA.

40. Fay, *Music Study*, 170; Stokowski, *American Musician's Story*, 20.

41. Spencer, "Leschetizky's Stern Discipline."

42. Fay, *Music Study*, 17. Amy Fay also described the language-related frustration she experienced in a music-theory class. When the professor asked her if she understood a particular concept, she was seized with uncertainty as to how to respond. "I

knew that if I said 'Ja' he might call on me for a proof, and that if I said 'nein,' he would undertake to enlighten me, and that I should not understand him." Cited in Bomberger, "German Musical Training," 20–21.

43. The Leipzig Conservatory enrolled more foreign students than any other German music school. "During the first fifty years of the conservatory's history there were 3,338 German and 2,828 foreign students, of whom 933 were from North America, 875 from Great Britain, and thirty-five from Australia. Given these proportions, English must have been nearly as common as German in the halls, if not in the classrooms." Bomberger, "German Musical Training," 62.

44. Ibid., 13.

45. Ibid., 336.

46. Edith Lynwood Wynn, "The Girl With a Bow," *Etude* 25 (September 1907): 612–613.

47. Henry T. Finck, *Success in Music and How It Is Won* (New York: C. Scribner's Sons, 1920), 437.

48. John Freund, "To a Young Girl Out West," *Musical America* 7 (February 29, 1908): 12.

49. John Freund, "One More Unfortunate," *Musical America* 19 (April 25, 1914): 9.

50. Constantin Von Sternberg, "Fallacies and Facts Regarding Study Abroad," *Musical America* 19 (January 31, 1914): 25; O. P. Jacob, "Berlin Aroused by Propaganda of *Musical America* " *Musical America* 19 (January 10, 1914):1–3; on concern over white slavery, see Ruth Rosen, *The Lost Sisterhood: Prostitution in America, 1900–1918* (Baltimore: Johns Hopkins University Press, 1982), 14–16, 112–135.

51. Franz Wilczek, "The Truth About Music Student Life in Vienna Revealed By a Viennese Virtuoso," *Musical America* 19 (February 21, 1914): 25–26.

52. Lenora Raines, "The Conditions, Moral and Spiritual, Under Which Our Students Abroad Work," *Musical America* 29 (November 23, 1918): 6.

53. Bert Leston Taylor, *The Charlatans* (Indianapolis: Bobbs-Merrill, 1906).

54. Unidentified clipping from Chicago newspaper, FBZ-AJA 3315.

55. Taylor, *Charlatans*.

56. Ibid.

57. Hallman, 58.

58. "'Don't,' Says Mrs. Zeisler," *Musical America* 15 (April 20, 1912): 36; Maud Powell, "'Let No Student Go Abroad Unchaperoned,' Warns Maud Powell, Celebrated Violinist," *Musical America* 19 (January 31, 1914): 4; Fay, *Music Study*, 347–48.

59. Shaffer, *Maud Powell*, 94–95.

60. SZ-AJA.

61. Stokowski, *American Musician's Story*, 31, 45–46.

62. Ibid., 33.

63. Shaffer, *Maud Powell*, 81.

64. Stokowski, *American Musician's Story*, 18.

4. *"An Able Musician and Delightful to Look At"*

1. S. Frederick Starr, *Bamboula! The Life and Times of Louis Moreau Gottschalk* (New York: Oxford, 1995), 118–120; *Academic American Encyclopedia*, s.v. "Railroads,"; Barbara L. Tischler, "Concert Music," in *Encyclopedia of American Social History* (New York: Scribner, 1993). See also Katherine Preston, *Opera on the Road: Traveling Opera Troupes in the United States, 1825–60* (Urbana: University of Illinois Press, 1993).

2. Starr, *Bamboula*, 118.

3. Ibid., 119. See also Lawrence Levine, *Highbrow, Lowbrow: The Emergence of Cultural Hierarchy in America* (Cambridge, Mass.: Harvard University Press, 1988),

4. R. Allen Lott, "The American Concert Tours of Leopold de Meyer, Henri Herz and Sigismund Thalberg" (Ph.D. diss., City University of New York, 1986), 35, 82.

5. Ibid., 447.

6. Lott, "American Concert Tours," 350; Starr, *Bamboula*, 330; Albertine Woodward Moore, "Rubinstein's Meteoric Tour of America," *Musical America* 29 (1911): 731–732; see also Lott, *American Concert Tours*, for list of dates, cities and a map of Thalberg's 1857 tour.

7. Philip Lewis, *Trouping: How the Show Came to Town* (New York: Harper and Row, 1973), 109.

8. Ibid., 109–111.

9. Louis Moreau Gottschalk, *Notes of a Pianist* (Philadelphia: J. B. Lippincott, 1881), 170.

10. Lewis, *Trouping*, 106–107.

11. Ibid., 106–110.

12. Ibid., 141–144.

13. Starr, *Bamboula*, 333.

14. Lott, "American Concert Tours," 301–302.

15. Ibid., 77.

16. Craig Roell, *The Piano in America, 1890–1940* (Chapel Hill: University of North Carolina Press, 1989), 144–145.

17. "Traveling Through America with the World's Greatest Artists," *Musical America* 13 (March 18, 1911): 17–18; Adam Zamoyski, *Paderewski* (New York: Atheneum, 1982), 116.

18. Ferruccio Busoni, *Letters to His Wife* (1938; reprint, New York: Dover, 1965), 167.

19. Patricia Cline Cohen, "Safety and Danger: Women on American Public Transport, 1750–1850," in Dorothy Helly and Susan Reverby, ed., *Gendered Domains: Rethinking Public and Private in Women's History* (Ithaca: Cornell University Press, 1992), 109–122.

20. Glenna Matthews, *The Rise of the Public Woman: Woman's Power and Woman's Place in the United States, 1630–1970* (New York: Oxford University Press, 1992), 102.

21. Cited in *Major Problems in the Gilded Age and the Progressive Era: Documents and Essays*, ed. Leon Fink (Lexington, Mass.: D. C. Heath, 1993), 378.

22. Charles Barnard, *Camilla: A Tale of a Violin, Being the Artist Life of Camilla Urso* (Boston: Loring, 1874), 106–110.

23. Eduardo Marzo, "Touring the United States with Strakosch's Stars in '73," *Musical America* 27 (February 2, 1918): 9, 11.

24. Ibid.

25. Clara Kathleen Barnett Rogers, *Memories of a Musical Career* (Boston: Little, Brown, 1919), 436–439.

26. "Carreño Objects to 'Circus' Advertising Given Musicians," *Duluth Herald*, November 16, 1916, "Carreño" clipping file, New York Public Library; Marta Milinowski, *Teresa Carreño: By The Grace of God* (New Haven: Yale University Press, 1940), 129, 134.

27. Marzo, "Touring the United States," 9; Milinowski, *Teresa Carreño*, 129.

28. Arthur Loesser, *Men, Women and Pianos: A Social History* (New York: Simon and Schuster, 1954), 539; John Philip Sousa once confessed to having grown a beard in order to appear "foreign," so that Americans would take his music more seriously. Margaret Hindle Hazen and Robert M. Hazen, *The Music Men: An Illustrated History of Bands in America, 1800–1920* (Washington: Smithsonian Institution Press, 1987), 17.

29. Karen Shaffer and Neva Garner Greenwood, *Maud Powell: Pioneer American Violinist* (Arlington, Va.: Maud Powell Foundation; Ames, Iowa: Iowa State University Press, 1988), 126; John Philip Sousa, *Marching Along: Recollections of Men, Women and Music* (Boston: Hale, Cushman and Flint, 1928), 244.

30. Sousa, *Marching Along*, 214, 244.

31. Paul Bierley, *John Philip Sousa, American Phenomenon* (New York: Appleton, Century, Crofts, 1973), 179; Shaffer and Greenwood, *Maud Powell*, 193; Kenneth Walter Berger, *The March King and His Band* (New York: Exposition Press, 1957), 52–53.

32. Joseph Horowitz, *Understanding Toscanini: How He Became an American Culture-God and Helped Create a New Audience for Old Music* (Minneapolis: University of Minnesota Press, 1987), 29; *New Grove Dictionary of American Music*, s.v. "Thomas, Theodore."

33. Frank Edwards, "Humor and Adventure: 'On the Road' with a Symphony Orchestra," *Musical America* 14 (August 26, 1911): 8.

34. Ezra Schabas, *Theodore Thomas: America's Conductor and Builder of Orchestras, 1835–1905* (Urbana: University of Illinois Press, 1989), 43.

35. M. Leslie Petteys, "Julie Rivé-King: American Pianist" (DMA thesis, University of Missouri — Kansas City, 1987), 277, 293.

36. Diana Ruth Hallman, "The Pianist Fannie Bloomfield-Zeisler in American Music and Society" (Master's thesis, University of Maryland, 1983), 147–48.

37. Ibid.

38. Ibid., 187.

39. Marzo, "Touring the United States," 9, 11.

40. "May Muckle With Thomas Orchestra," *Musical America* 7 (January 18, 1908): 7; "Ethel Leginska's Most Recent 'Stunt,'" *Musical Courier*, March 15, 1917, "Leginska," clipping file, New York Public Library (hereafter "Leginska," NYPL).

41. Lott, "American Concert Tours," 82.

42. Petteys, "Julie Rivé-King," 190.

43. Ibid.

44. Olga Samaroff Stokowski, *An American Musician's Story* (New York: Norton, 1939), 82.

45. Busoni, *Letters*, 154; Rose Fay Thomas, *Memoirs of Theodore Thomas* (1911; reprint, New York: Books for Libraries Press, 1971), 428.

46. "Extent of the Feminine Influence," *Musical America* 13 (April 15, 1911): 3.

47. Starr, *Bamboula*, 330; "Do Worries of Travel Hamper an Artist?" *Musical America* 19 (December 6, 1913): 19; "Traveling Through America," 17–18.

48. Edwards, "Humor and Adventure," 8.

49. The American Jewish Archives in Cincinnati has a draft of a biography of Fannie Bloomfield-Zeisler by her husband Sigmund. This is in typescript with some unnumbered and some erratically numbered pages. Hereafter cited as SZ-AJA; "Samaroff's Next American Tour," *Musical America* 10 (July 10, 1909): 6; Shaffer, *Maud Powell*, 87 .

50. Petteys, "Julie Rivé-King," 62.

51. Rogers, *Memories*, 442.

52. Milinowski, *Teresa Carreño*, 286–292.

53. "Mephisto's Musings," *Musical America* 8 (June 13, 1908): 13.

54. Petteys, "Julie Rivé-King," 99, 107–109.

55. Shaffer and Greenwood, *Maud Powell*, 198–206.

56. Joan Acocella, "Cather and the Academy," *New Yorker 71*, November 27, 1995, 66.

57. Jean Lyon, "New York's Feminine Orchestra Is Almost Ready to Make Music," *New York Sun,* February 10, 1932, p. 30.

58. Unidentified clipping, Leginska scrapbooks. (These are currently in the personal collection of one of her students.) See also Carolyn G. Heilbrun, *Writing a Woman's Life* (New York: W.W. Norton, 1988), for a brief discussion of the phenomenon of the unmarried artist whose friend sacrifices his or her own goals for those of the artist.

59. Untitled clipping, *Rockford Daily Gazette*, May 5, 1888, FBZ-AJA 3315.

60. "Mme. Samaroff's Pluck," *Musical America* 7 (December 28, 1907): 11.

61. "Maud Powell Champions the West's Taste for Music," *Musical America* 7 (December 14, 1907): 5.

62. Ibid.

63. It is difficult to compare the number of concerts played by men and women virtuosos, since most available information about schedules and itineraries consists of random bits inadvertently mentioned in discussions of other issues. In addition, some sources report the number of performances given per season and others per year.

64. Christine Ammer, *Unsung: A History of Women in American Music* (Westport, Conn.: Greenwood, 1980), 26–27; Petteys, "Julie Rivé-King," 200, 293; Milinowski, *Teresa Carreño*, 174; SZ-AJA; "Maud Powell Found Ready Response," *Musical America* 15 (December 23, 1911): 36; unidentified clipping, Leginska scrapbooks.

65. Stokowski, *American Musician's Story*, 74.

66. Petteys, "Julie Rivé-King,"198–199; Zamoyski, *Paderewski*, 75–76, 83.

67. Milinowski, *Teresa Carreño*, 253–254; "Zeisler: Lima Tenders an Ovation to a Great Artist," *Republican Gazette* (Lima, Ohio), January 14, 1898, FBZ-AJA 3315; letter from Fannie Bloomfield-Zeisler's manager to the director of music at Sweet Briar

College, Newberry Library, Chicago, Fannie Bloomfield-Zeisler Collection; Stokowski, *American Musician's Story*, 59–60, 74–75; Petteys, "Julie Rivé-King," 198–199.

68. John Henry Mueller, *The American Symphony Orchestra: A Social History of American Taste* (Bloomington: Indiana University Press, 1951), 30.

69. Horowitz, *Understanding Toscanini*, 30; Shaffer, *Maud Powell*, 152; SZ-AJA.

70. "Teresa Carreño In State of Collapse," *Musical America* 4 (June 23, 1906): 1; unidentified clipping, FBZ-AJA 3316; "Mme. Olga Samaroff a Victim of Amnesia," *Musical America* 25 (February 10, 1917): 2; "Leginska Ordered to Take Year's Rest," *New York Times*, January 31, 1926, p. 7.

71. John S. Haller and Robin M. Haller, *The Physician and Sexuality in Victorian America* (Urbana: University of Illinois Press, 1974), 5.

72. Ibid., 42.

73. Lorna Duffin, "The Conspicuous Consumptive: Woman as an Invalid," in *The Nineteenth-Century Woman: Her Cultural and Physical World*, Sara Delamont and Lorna Duffin, eds. (New York: Barnes and Noble, 1978), 26–56.

74. Peter Filene, *Him/Her/Self; Sex Roles in Modern America,* 2nd ed. (Baltimore: Johns Hopkins University Press, 1986), 15.

75. Starr, *Bamboula*, 346; Siegmund Levarie, "Hans von Bülow in America," *Institute for the Study of American Music Newsletter*, 11 (November, 1981): 10; Zamoyski, *Paderewski*, 135–136; David Joel Metzer, "The Ascendancy of Musical Modernism in New York City, 1915–1929" (Ph.D. diss., Yale University, 1993), 104–105. See also Peter Ostwald, "Psychodynamics of Musicians," *Medical Problems of Performing Artists* 7 (December 1992): 110–113.

76. "Teresa Carreño in State of Collapse," 1.

77. SZ-AJA.

78. Duffin, "Conspicuous Consumptive," 37; Carroll Smith-Rosenberg, "The Hysterical Woman: Sex Roles and Role Conflict in Nineteenth-Century America," in her *Disorderly Conduct: Visions of Gender in Victorian America* (New York: Knopf, 1985), 202.

79. SZ-AJA; "Samaroff Seeking Health in Europe," *Musical America* 12 (June 4, 1910): 2; Oliver Daniel, *Stokowski: A Counterpoint of View* (New York: Dodd, Mead, 1982), 179; "Leginska," *London Times*, February 9, 1909, sec. C, p. 8; "Leginska Not Found, Nerves Are Blamed," *New York Times*, January 28, 1925, p. 1.

80. "Pianist Returns," *Musical America* 22 (June 26, 1915): 8; "Mme. Olga Samaroff a Victim of Amnesia," *Musical America* 25 (February 10, 1917): 2 ; Oliver, *Stokowski: A Counterpoint of View* (New York: Dodd, Mead, 1982), 179; "Mephisto's Musings," *Musical America* 25 (February 17, 1917): 8; SZ-AJA.

81. Salman Akhtar and Ira Brenner, "Differential Diagnosis of Fugue-Like States," *Journal of Clinical Psychiatry* 40 (1979): 381–385.

82. "Roamed in a Daze, Leginska Asserts," *New York Times*, February 23, 1925, p. 2.

5. "A Paderewski in Petticoats"

1. The events described in this chapter, as well as any unfootnoted quotations, were taken from SZ-AJA. See Chapter 4, note 49.

2. "Pianist Tells of Her Work," *Daily Chronicle*, October 26, 1895. FBZ-AJA 3316.

3. *Baker's Biographical Dictionary of Music and Musicians*, s.v. "Prokofiev."

4. Peter G. Filene, *Him/Her/Self: Sex Roles in Modern America*, 2nd ed. (Baltimore: Johns Hopkins University Press, 1986), 15.

5. Nancy M. Theriot, *Mothers and Daughters in Nineteenth-Century America: The Biosocial Construction of Femininity* (Lexington: University of Kentucky Press, 1996), 103.

6. I .S. L. Loudon, "Chlorosis, Anemia and Anorexia Nervosa," *British Medical Journal* 281 (1980): 1669–1675; Joan Jacobs Brumberg, "Chlorotic Girls, 1870–1920: A Historical Perspective on Female Adolescence," *Child Development* 53 (1982): 1468–1477. Brumberg (1473–1474) notes a popular association between meat consumption and sexuality — a troubling connection for young adolescents.

7. Robert Lovett, *Lateral Curvature of the Spine and Round Shoulders* (Philadelphia: P. Blakiston's Son & Co., 1922), 114–115.

8. "Mephisto's Musings," *Musical America* 36 (July 8, 1922): 7–8.

9. See Craig Roell, *The Piano in America, 1890–1940* (Chapel Hill: University of North Carolina Press, 1989), for a detailed account of the business relationships between artists and piano manufacturers.

10. Ibid., 7–8. See also Diana Ruth Hallman, "The Pianist Fannie Bloomfield-Zeisler in American Music and Society." (Master's thesis, University of Maryland, 1983), 20.

11. Quoted in Arnold T. Schwab, *James Gibbons Huneker: Critic of the Seven Arts* (Stanford: Stanford University Press, 1963), 33.

12. *Dictionary of American Biography*, s.v. "Zeisler, Sigmund."

13. Karen Shaffer and Neva Garner Greenwood, *Maud Powell: Pioneer American Violinist* (Arlington, Va.: Maud Powell Foundation; Ames, Iowa: Iowa State University Press, 1988), 278.

14. Olga Samaroff Stokowski, *An American Musician's Story* (New York: Norton, 1939), 15.

15. "To the Young Wife," *Musical Courier*, September 7, 1898, p. 17.

16. "Why Artists Should Marry," *Musical Courier*, April 4, 1900, p. 20.

17. "Don't Give Up Music at the Altar," *Etude* 37 (July 1919): 407–408.

18. *San Francisco Chronicle*, August 11, 1936, quoted in Robert Magidoff, *Yehudi Menuhin: The Story of the Man and the Musician* (Westport, Conn.: Greenwood Press, 1973), 167.

19. Arthur L. Tubbs, "Olga Samaroff Preparing to Resume Career," *Musical America* 19 (December 6, 1913): 19.

20. The diaries and letters of Fannie and Sigmund Zeisler have not survived. The quote from her diary is from SZ-AJA.

21. Hallman, "Fannie Bloomfield-Zeisler," 23.

22. William L. Hubbard, "Letter," *Chicago Tribune*, November 26, 1893, cited in SZ-AJA.

23. Hallman, "Fannie Bloomfield Zeisler," 88.

24. SZ-AJA.

25. Again, these letters have not survived; Sigmund reports in SZ-AJA that they exchanged letters during this period.

26. SZ-AJA.

27. *Jewish Encyclopedia*, s.v. "Zeisler, Sigmund."

28. William Armstrong, "Fannie Bloomfield Zeisler," *The Banner of Gold*, April 17, 1897, FBZ-AJA 3315.

29. Peter Filene, *Him/Her/Self: Sex Roles in Modern America*, 2nd ed. (Baltimore: Johns Hopkins University Press, 1986), 40–41.

30. Shaffer and Greenwood, *Maud Powell*, 206.

31. Renee Fisher, *Musical Prodigies: Masters at an Early Age* (New York: Association Press, 1973), 177.

32. M. Leslie Petteys, "Julie Rivé-King: American Pianist" (DMA thesis, University of Missouri–Kansas City, 1987), 64.

33. "Children an Inspiration to Career of Woman Artist, Believes Samaroff," *Musical America* 35 (April 8, 1922): 3.

34. "Noted Pianiste Likes to Darn Hubby's Sox," undated clipping, *Detroit News*, FBZ-AJA 3315.

35. "Fannie Bloomfield-Zeisler's Silver Anniversary," *Musical Courier*, March 21, 1900, pp. 19–20.

36. Blanche Glassman Hersh, *The Slavery of Sex: Feminist-Abolitionists in America* (Urbana: University of Illinois Press, 1978), 234.

37. Bloomfield-Zeisler typically included a combination of light and more serious pieces on her programs, believing that a recital should be "a dinner with all the courses." She usually programmed a group of small character pieces or a larger work of Chopin, key works of Schumann and Mendelssohn, and sometimes a Beethoven sonata. She sometimes included pre-classical works by C. P. E. Bach, J. S. Bach, Rameau, Scarlatti and Couperin. Bloomfield-Zeisler's repertoire also consisted of about 15 concertos, among them those by Beethoven, Chopin, Grieg, Liszt, Mendelssohn, Mozart, Rubinstein, Saint-Saëns, Schumann, Tchaikovsky, Weber, and Litloff. Hallman, "Fannie Bloomfield Zeisler," 98. See also Hallman's Appendix A for a partial list of her career performances, Appendix B for a complete list of her programmed repertoire, and Appendix C for sample programs.

38. "Pianiste Is Now Well," *Chicago Record-Herald*, November 1, 1906, FBZ-AJA 3316.

39. S. Weir Mitchell, "The Educational Treatment of Neurasthenia and Certain Hysterical States," reprinted in *Psychotherapy and Multiple Personality: Selected Essays*, ed. Morton Prince (Cambridge, Mass.: Harvard University Press, 1975), 99–113.

40. Charlotte Perkins Gilman, *The Yellow Wallpaper* (Boston: Small and Maynard, 1892).

41. "Pianiste Is Now Well," FBZ-AJA 3316.

42. Philip Bregstone, *Chicago and Its Jews: A Cultural History* (Chicago: privately published, 1933), 45.

43. Jacob Marcus, *The American Jewish Woman, 1654–1980* (New York: KTAV Publishing House, 1981), 29.

44. Bregstone, *Chicago*, 45; see also Marcus, *American Jewish Woman*, 29–30.

45. "Fannie Bloomfield-Zeisler," *Grand Rapids Daily Democrat*, March 2, 1890, FBZ-AJA 3315.

46. Quoted in Harold Schonberg, *The Great Pianists* (New York: Simon and Schuster, 1963), 335. Diana Hallman has noted that "a large proportion of nineteenth century pianists — as well as singers and conductors — were Jewish, including Moscheles, Tausig, Rubinstein, Rosenthal, von Sauer and Gottschalk. Their success strengthened a nineteenth century belief in Jewish musical predilection attributed to sensitive, intellectual and emotional dispositions." Hallman, "Fannie Bloomfield Zeisler," 45.

47. FBZ-AJA 3315 and 3316.

48. Carnegie hall program, January 26, 1907, FBZ-AJA 3315.

49. Hallman, "Fannie Bloomfield Zeisler," 40.

50. "Bloomfield Zeisler Astounds New York," *Musical America* 31 (February 21, 1920): 17.

51. Untitled notice, *New York Evening Sun*, February 18, 1920, FBZ-AJA 3316.

52. Letters to Fannie Bloomfield-Zeisler from Steinway & Sons, December 22, 1903, and January 16, 1904; Fannie Bloomfield-Zeisler Collection, American Jewish Archives, Cincinnati.

53. Letter from Fannie Bloomfield-Zeisler to Rose Newberger, December 27, 1906, in "Bloomfield-Zeisler" clipping file, New York Public Library.

54. Fannie Bloomfield-Zeisler, "Woman in Music," in *Music Teachers National Association: Official Report of Annual Meeting*, 1890, pp. 38–44.

55. Harriette Brower, "Pianist's Mind Delicately Adjusted During Recital," *Musical America* 40 (December 18, 1915): 40.

56. William Armstrong, "Fannie Bloomfield-Zeisler," *Banner of Gold*, April 17, 1897, FBZ-AJA 3315.

57. Martin Bruhl, "Music and Musicians," *Burlington Gazette*, August 18, 1916, FBZ-AJA 3315.

58. "Fannie Bloomfield Zeisler," *Chicago Tribune*, December 25, 1901, FBZ-AJA 3316.

59. "Fannie Bloomfield-Zeisler," *Sacramento Daily Record-Union*, November 22, 1896, FBZ-AJA 3316.

60. *Jewish Encyclopedia*, s.v. "Zeisler, Sigmund."

61. Fannie Bloomfield-Zeisler, letters to her sons, Fannie Bloomfield-Zeisler Papers, Newberry Library, Chicago.

62. "A Week of Jubilation," *Chicago Musical Leader*, March 5, 1925, FBZ-AJA Box X186.

6. *"A Gypsy Demon Possessed the Little Woman"*

1. Carroll Smith-Rosenberg, "Bourgeois Discourse and the Progressive Era," in *Disorderly Conduct: Visions of Gender in Victorian America* (New York: Knopf, 1985), 176–178.

2. Carroll Smith-Rosenberg, "The New Woman as Androgyne," in *Disorderly Conduct: Visions of Gender in Victorian America* (New York: Knopf, 1985), 295–296.

3. "Ethel Leginska Avows She's a 'Topsy' Without a Single Musical Ancestor," *Musical America* 28 (October 13, 1917): 9.

4. Oscar Thompson, "Where Are the Prodigies of Yesteryear?" *Musical America* 31 (January 3, 1920): 5–6.

5. "Leginska, Ethel," in *Notable American Women, 1607–1950: A Biographical Dictionary* (Cambridge: Harvard, 1971); also "Ethel Leginska Describes the Joys of Study," *Musical America* 32 (July 31, 1920): 19.

6. "Whithorne, Emerson," in Nicholas Slonimsky, *Baker's Biographical Dictionary of Music and Musicians*, 8th ed. (New York: Schirmer, 1991).

7. "Music" *London Times,* June 16, 1906, p. 10a.

8. "Hippodrome," *Cleveland Plain Dealer*, January 22, 1908; "Leginska," clipping file, NYPL.

9. Lawrence Levine, *Highbrow, Lowbrow: The Emergence of Cultural Hierarchy in America.* (Cambridge, Mass.: Harvard University Press, 1988).

10. "Miss Leginska's Recital," *London Times*, November 20, 1908, p. 14b.

11. "Ethel Leginska's Peculiar Disappearance," *Musical America*, undated, in "Leginska," NYPL.

12. "Ethel Leginska's Concert," *Musical America* 13 (November 26, 1910): 17.

13. Arthur Strawn, "Women Let Trifles Ruin Their Careers," *St. Louis Post-Dispatch Daily Magazine*, March 25, 1932, from Ethel Leginska scrapbooks, privately owned by a former student (hereafter cited as Leginska scrapbooks); "Leginska," *Musical America,* November 6, 1915, in "Leginska," NYPL; Marguerite Marshall Moore, "Women's Love of Clothes a Barrier to Success," unidentified clipping, Leginska scrapbooks; "Leginska Has Very Modern Ideas of Women's Freedom, *Duluth Herald*, February 17, 1917, in "Leginska," NYPL; Ethel Leginska, "Leginska Bares Her Heart and Her Broken Romances," *Boston Sunday Post*, October 17, 1926, Leginska scrapbooks.

14. "Leginska," *Cleveland Press*, May 30, 1917, p. 2.

15. Leginska, "Leginska Bares Her Heart"; "Opera and Concert Programmes; Chat With Miss Leginska," *New York Herald*, January 3, 1915, Leginska scrapbooks.

16. "Leginska Recital," *Musical Courier*, March 10, 1913, in "Leginska," NYPL.

17. "Mlle. Leginska's Recital," *New York Times*, January 21, 1913, p. 13.

18. "Miss Leginska's Playing," *New York Times*, December 12, 1913, p. 11.

19. Ruth St. Denis, *An Unfinished Life: An Autobiography* (New York: Harper, 1937), 151.

20. "Ethel Leginska Creates Astounding Enthusiasm on Canadian and Western Tour," *Musical America* 27 (December 1, 1917): 14.

21. Leginska scrapbooks.

22. "Recital with Invisible Artist Suggested by Paula Pardee," *Musical America* 29 (February 8, 1919): 39; "Woman Pianist Plays Like Demon," *Chicago Herald*, in "Leginska," NYPL.

23. "Personalities," *Musical America*, January 9, 1909, in "Leginska," NYPL.

24. Undated clipping, "Leginska," NYPL.

25. Susan Gubar, "Blessings in Disguise: Cross-Dressing as Re-Dressing for Female Modernists," *Massachusetts Review* 22 (Autumn 1981): 477–508; Carolyn G. Heilbrun, *Writing a Woman's Life* (New York: W. W. Norton, 1988), 89–90; Ethel Leginska, "Clothes as a Hindrance to Woman's Greatness," *Musical America* 25 (March 24, 1917): 5.

26. "Energetic English Pianiste Tries Hard as She Can to Be Like a Man," *New York Press*, April 11, 1915, p. 6, Leginska scrapbook.

27. "Mme. Leginska Plays," *Boston Transcript*, February 25, 1916, in "Leginska," NYPL.

28. Carroll Smith-Rosenberg, "The New Woman as Androgyne," in *Disorderly Conduct*, 268.

29. Unidentified newspaper clipping fragment, in "Leginska," NYPL.

30. Dayton reviews quoted in "Leginska With New York Symphony," *Musical Courier*, January 27, 1915, "Leginska," NYPL; "Music Festival Auspiciously Opened," *Buffalo Enquirer*, May 12, 1916, in "Leginska," NYPL; *Detroit News*, January 31, 1923; clippings excerpted from ads in *Musical America* 25 (December 2, 1916): 10, and 37 (March 17, 1923): 24; "Leginska's Women's Orchestra Plays Extra Program," *Racine Times-Call*, November 20, 1929, "Leginska," NYPL.

31. "Leginska Grasps Emotion of Music," *Detroit Free Press*, n.d., "Leginska," NYPL.

32. James Huneker, "The Leginska Coiffure Now Prevalent Among Pianists," unidentified clipping, November 20, 1918, "Leginska," NYPL.

33. "Ethel Leginska Makes Converts to a Quaint Cause," *Musical America* 31 (December 27, 1919): 9; Huneker, "Leginska Coiffure."

34. "Pianiste Asks Divorce," *St. Louis Globe Democrat*, n.d., "Leginska," NYPL; Arthur Strawn, "Women Let Trifles Ruin Their Careers," *St. Louis Post-Dispatch Daily Magazine*, March 25, 1932, Leginska scrapbooks; "Leginska," *Musical America* 23 (November 6, 1915) in "Leginska," NYPL; Marguerite Marshall Moore, "Women's Love of Clothes a Barrier to Success," unidentified clipping, Leginska scrapbooks; "Leginska Has Very Modern Ideas of Women's Freedom," *Duluth Herald*, February 17, 1917, in "Leginska," NYPL; Ethel Leginska, "Leginska Bares Her Heart."

35. "Ethel Leginska's Protest," *Musical America* 39 (October 27, 1923): 10.

36. Smith-Rosenberg, "The New Woman of Androgyne," in *Disorderly Conduct*, 295–296.

37. Vivien Gardner and Susan Rutherford, eds., *The New Woman and Her Sisters: Feminism and the Theatre, 1850–1914* (Ann Arbor: University of Michigan Press, 1992), 4–5; "Mme. Leginska Plays," *Boston Transcript*, February 25, 1916, "Leginska," NYPL.

38. "True Artist Always Gets Stage Fright in Public," *Harrisburg Telegraph*, undated clipping, Leginska scrapbooks; "Energetic English Pianiste," *New York Press*, April 11, 1915, p. 6, Leginska scrapbooks.

39. "Famous Woman Pianist Seeks Son's Custody," *Cleveland Press*, May 30, 1917, p. 2; "Martha Hedman Raises the Ante; Sues for $50,000," *Chicago Sunday Tribune*, May 27, 1917, part I, p. 15; "Actress and Pianiste in Divorce Triangle," *Chicago Daily Journal*, May 25, 1917; "Wife Accuses Stage Beauty," *Chicago Daily Tribune*, May 25, 1917, both in Leginska scrapbooks.

40. "Demon Gypsy Announces Marriage in Divorce Court," unidentified clipping, Leginska scrapbooks.

41. "Pianiste Asks Divorce," unidentified clipping, "Leginska" NYPL; "Leginska Who Sues Hubby Isn't a Kid After All," *Detroit Journal*, May 25, 1917, "Leginska," NYPL.

42. *Notable American Women*, s.v. "Leginska."

43. "Torn Heartstrings Are Blamed for Illness of Pianist Who Fights Court Battle for Son," *Cleveland Press*, June 4, 1917, p. 7.

44. She once said that sometimes, when riding in an automobile on her way to a recital, she watched all the posts, hoping the car would crash into one and put her out of her agony. "Chat With Miss Leginska," *New York Herald*, January 3, 1915, Leginska scrapbooks.

45. "Dunsany Tale Inspires Leginska," *Musical America* 35 (February 11, 1922): 23; "Leginska Will Not Concertize during Season of 1920-21," *Musical Courier*, March 18, 1920, "Leginska," NYPL.

46. "From Execution to Composition," *Christian Science Monitor*, December 3, 1921, editorial page.

47. David Joel Metzer, "The Ascendance of Musical Modernism in New York City, 1915–1929" (Ph.D. diss., Yale, 1993), 342. For evocative descriptions of New York during this period, see Caroline Ware, *Greenwich Village, 1920–1930: A Comment on American Civilization in the Post-War Years* (Boston: Houghton-Mifflin, 1935); Allen Churchill, *The Improper Bohemians* (New York: Dutton, 1959); and June Sochen, *The New Woman: Feminism in Greenwich Village, 1910–1920* (New York: Quadrangle, 1972).

48. Metzer, "Ascendance," 229–230, 334; Richard Aldrich, "Music," *New York Times*, March 8, 1923, p. 12; "Personalities: Ethel Leginska Rests From Hard Season," *Musical America* 30 (October 18, 1919): 16.

49. "Introducing Ethel Leginska," *Musical Courier,* September 26, 1918, p. 42; "Ethel Leginska's 'Dance of a Puppet,'" *Musical America* 39 (January 26, 1924): 42; "Ethel Leginska Songs to Be Published by Schirmer," *Musical America* 29 (March 1, 1919): 43; "Sunday List Brings Prominent Visitors," *Musical America* 39 (December 22, 1923): 28.

50. Hal Crain, "Form: The Despair of the Iconoclast," *Musical America* 40 (August 16, 1924): 32.

51. "Ethel Leginska's 'Dance of a Puppet'"; "Sunday List," 28; "Scriabin's Divine Poem and Pieces by Leginska are Boston Novelties," *Musical America* 39 (March 8, 1924): 36.

52. "Mason, Daniel Gregory," in *Harvard Biographical Dictionary of Music* (Cambridge, Mass: Harvard, 1996; Daniel Gregory Mason, *Music in My Time* (1938; reprint, New York: Dover, 1966), 300.

53. Metzer, "Ascendance," 229–230, 334.

54. Letter from Ethel Leginska to David Mannes, May 26, 1919, Los Angeles Symphony Archives.

55. Metzer, "Ascendance," p. 85; "Leginska to Play in Chamber Music Programs on Coast," *Musical America* 39 (January 12, 1924): 21; also, programs in Leginska scrapbooks.

56. "Music Should Mirror Spirit of Age," *Musical America* 37 (April 14, 1923): 48.

57. "I'm So Glad I'm Not a Beauty," *Boston Sunday Post*, n.d., Leginska scrapbooks.

58. Harriett Bowen, "Are Women Men's Equals as Pianists?" *Musical America* 25 (December 16, 1916): 19.

59. Carole Rosen, *The Goossens: A Musical Century* (Boston: Northeastern University Press, 1994), 86.

60. *Notable American Women*, "Leginska."

61. "Ethel Leginska Conducts N.Y. Symphony," *Musical America* 41 (January 17, 1925): 6; Leonard Liebling, "Ethel Leginska, Pianist, Leads Orchestra." *New York American*, January 10, 1925.

62. Joseph Horowitz, *Understanding Toscanini: How He Became an American Culture-God and Helped Create a New Audience for Old Music* (Minneapolis: University of Minnesota Press, 1987), 94; Olin Downes, "The Philharmonic Concert," *New York Times*, January 9, 1925; "Conductors by the Score," *Musical America* 42 (October 17, 1925): 18.

63. *New York Sun*, January 10, 1925, quoted in an ad in *Musical America* 41(January 31, 1925): 21; Leonard Liebling, "Ethel Leginska, Pianist, Leads Orchestra," *New York American*, January 10, 1925; Deems Taylor, "Music," *The World*, January 10, 1925.

64. See Elliott W. Galkin, *A History of Orchestral Conducting* (New York: Pendragon, 1988), for references to the backgrounds of many orchestral conductors.

65. Ibid., 345–349.

66. Ibid., 619–621, 649.

67. Ibid., 669.

68. Olin Downes, "Ethel Leginska Conducts," *New York Times*, January 10, 1925; "Mme. Leginska Leads N.Y. Symphony," *New York Herald Tribune*, January 10, 1925; Frank Warren, "Realm of Music," *New York Evening World*, January 10, 1925; Leonard Liebling, "Ethel Leginska, Pianist, Leads Orchestra," *New York American*, January 10, 1925: all four from "Leginska scrapbooks. In an insightful essay on the nation's leading orchestras (the New York Philharmonic, the New York Symphony and the Boston, Philadelphia and Chicago ensembles), Daniel Gregory Mason analyzed the repertoire of each group and concluded that 69 percent of the programs were standard works by European composers. Cited in Metzer, "Ascendance," 37.

69. Henrietta Malkiel, "The Guest Conductor Faces the Music," *Musical America* 41 (January 24, 1925): 3, 38.

70. "Leginska Not Found, Nerves Are Blamed," *New York Times*, January 28, 1925, p. 1; Carroll Smith-Rosenberg, "The Hysterical Woman," in *Disorderly Conduct*, 197, 206.

71. "Must Artists Be Nervy?" undated article from *London Weekly Dispatch*, Leginska scrapbooks.

72. "Leginska Conducts People's," *Boston Post*, April 6, 1925.

73. "Leginska Conducts," *Musical Courier,* November 26, 1925, "Leginska," NYPL.

74. "People's Symphony," *Christian Science Monitor*, April 6, 1925; "Leginska Conducts," *Musical Courier*, November 26, 1925.

75. "People's Symphony," *Christian Science Monitor*, November 16, 1925, p. 4.

76. "Leginska Missing Again," *New York Times*, January 21, 1926, p. 7; "Leginska Again Fails to Appear for Concert," *New York Times*, October 24, 1925, p. 17; "Leginska Ordered to Take Year's Rest," *New York Times*, January 31, 1926, p. 7.

77. "Western Cities to Hear Leginska," *Musical America* 42 (May 30, 1925): 34.

78. Henrietta Malkiel, "Making Great Music Democratic in the Hollywood

Bowl," *Musical America* 42 (June 6, 1925): 3, 19, Leginska scrapbooks; Edwin Schalbert, "Leginska Has Great Triumph," *Los Angeles Times*, August 5, 1925, Leginska scrapbooks; "Leginska Greeted by Throng at Bowl," *Musical America* 42 (August 22, 1925): 24; Grace Koopal, *Miracle of Music: The History of the Hollywood Bowl* (Los Angeles: W. Ritchie, 1972), 93–95.

79. Leonard Liebling, "Ethel Leginska in Triple Musical Role," *New York American*, January 4, 1926.

80. Olga Samaroff, "Miss Leginska's Concert," *New York Evening Post*, January 4, 1926.

81. "Ethel Leginska Leaves Piano Recitals to Work in Other Music Fields," *Musical America* 44 (May 1, 1926): 41; "Leginska to Retire from Concert Stage," *New York Times*, April 22, 1926, p. 23.

82. "Larger Service to Music Sought by Ethel Leginska," *Christian Science Monitor*, June 3, 1926.

83. Norman Lebrecht, *The Maestro Myth: Great Conductors in Pursuit of Power* (Secaucus, N.J.: Carol Publishing Group, 1991), 170.

84. "Woman Triumphs in Role of Conductor," *Boston Globe*, October 25, 1926.

85. Ibid.

86. "Leginska," *Boston Post*, undated clipping, Leginska scrapbooks.

87. "Music — Real Music — For Everybody Dream of the Intense Leginska," *Boston Sunday Globe*, December 12, 1926.

88. "Music in Boston," *Christian Science Monitor*, April 11, 1927.

89. "Woman Triumphs," *Boston Globe*, October 25, 1926.

90. "Music — Real Music"; "Music in Boston."

91. "Orchestra Pools May End Deficits," *New York Times*, February 3, 1924, p. 20.

92. Alice Allen Drayton, "Federation Sponsors First American Women's Symphony Orchestra," *Federation Topics* 7 (March 1927), Leginska scrapbooks.

93. "Women are Successful," *Musical America* 45 (April 2, 1927): 35.

94. Ibid.

95. Tour of Boston Women's Symphony, October–December 1928: Amherst, MA — October 28; Millersville, PA — Afternoon, October 29; Coatesville, PA — Evening, October 29; Shippensburg, PA — Afternoon, October 30; Penn Hall, PA — Evening, October 30; Harrisburg, PA — October 31; Lynchburg, VA — November 1; Farmville, VA — Afternoon, November 2; Farmville, VA — Evening, November 2; Hampton, VA — November 3; Washington, D.C. — Afternoon, November 4; Washington, D.C. — November 5; Louisberg, PA — November 6; Bloomsburg, PA — November 7; Elmira, NY — November 8; Buffalo, NY — November 9; Cleveland, OH — November 10; Cleveland, OH — November 11; Ashtabula, OH — November 12; Mansfield, OH — November 13; Jackson, MI — Afternoon, November 14; Jackson, MI — Evening, November 14; Benton Harbor, MI — Afternoon, November 15; Benton Harbor, MI — Evening, November 15; Muskegon, MI — November 16; LaPorte, IN — Afternoon, November 19; LaPorte, IN — Evening, November 19; Milwaukee, WI — November 20; Kenosha, WI — Afternoon, November 21; Kenosha, WI — Evening, November 21; Aurora, IL — Afternoon, November 22; Aurora, IL — Evening, November 22; Beloit, WI — Afternoon, November 23; Beloit, WI —

Evening, November 23; LaSalle, IL — November 24; LaSalle, IL — November 25; Quincy, IL — Afternoon, November 26; Quincy, IL — Evening, November 26; St. Louis, MO — November 27; LaFayette, IN — Afternoon, November 28; LaFayette, IN — Evening, November 28; Danville, IL — Afternoon, November 29; Danville, IL — Evening, November 29; Richmond, IN — November 30; Dayton, OH — December 2; Portsmouth, OH — December 3; Charleston, WV — Afternoon, December 4; Charleston, WV — Evening, December 4; Parkersburg, WV — December 5; Steubenville, OH — December 6; Warren, OH — December 7; Canton, OH — December 8.

96. New York Symphony Box, Walter Damrosch Papers, New York Public Library.

97. *Evening Star*, Washington, D.C., November 5, 1928; *Evening Star*, Washington, D.C., November 6, 1928 — cited in advertisement in *Musical Courier*, January 3, 1929.

98. "Boston Women Players to Increase Activities," *Musical America* 45 (June 25, 1927): 23.

99. Rae Linda Brown, "The Woman's Symphony Orchestra of Chicago and Florence B. Price's Piano Concerto in One Movement," *American Music* 11 (Summer 1993): 190.

100. "Sundstrom New Conductor of Woman's Symphony of Chicago," *Musical Courier*, October 5, 1929, p. 23.

101. "Concerts in Havana," *Musical America* 53 (January 25, 1933): 13; "Music and Art: The Personality to Launch a Ninth Symphony," *Dallas Morning News*, January 14, 1934, Leginska scrapbooks; "Leginska Conducts Players in Dallas," *Musical America* 53 (March 19, 1933): 30.

102. *Musical Courier,* November 28, 1931, p. 5; "Notable Revival of 'Boccaccio' in English," *Musical America* 51 (November 25, 1931): 30; "Boccaccio Receives Ovation in New York," *Musical Courier*, November 28, 1931, p. 5.

103. Ammer, *Unsung*, 174.

104. W. J. Henderson, "Women's Symphony Concert," *New York Sun*, March 14, 1932, Leginska scrapbooks.

105. Smith-Rosenberg, "The New Woman as Androgyne," 295–296.

106. Horowitz, *Understanding Toscanini*, 199–200; "The Native Conductor," *New York Times*, January 29, 1933, sec. 9, p. 6.

107. "Teaching Viewed as Fascinating Recreation by Ethel Leginska," *Musical America* 30 (May 3, 1919): 29.

108. James Lynch interviewed by author, Long Beach, California, May 23, 1994.

109. Marilyn Neely, interviewed by author, tape recording, Washington, D.C., February 15, 1995.

110. Lisa Sitjar, interviewed by author, tape recording, New York City, February 16, 1995.

111. Alfred Price Quinn, "Music," *B'nai Brith Messenger*, May 18, 1945, Leginska scrapbooks.

112. "Young Pianists at Town Hall," unidentified clipping, January 5, 1944, "Leginska," NYPL.

113. Letters to conductors, Leginska scrapbooks.

114. "Obituaries," *Los Angeles Times*, February 28, 1970, part I, p. 26; "Obituaries," March 1, 1970, sec. D, p. 17.

115. Heilbrun, *Writing a Woman's Life*, 26.

116. Helen De Motte, "Statue and Musician Stir One Who Admires Courage," *Richmond News Leader*, October 26, 1929.

7. *"Why Not Dr. Brico?"*

1. Carroll Smith-Rosenberg, "The New Woman as Androgyne," in *Disorderly Conduct: Visions of Gender in Victorian America* (New York: Knopf, 1985); 294–296.

2. "Antonia Brico's Triumph," *Newsweek*, August 1, 1938, p. 21.

3. "Renowned Conductor Brico Dies in Rest Home at Age 87," *Denver Post*, August 4, 1989, sec. B, p. 1.

4. Judy Collins and Jill Godmilow, *Antonia: A Portrait of the Woman*. Produced by Rocky Mountain Productions, Phoenix/BFA Films and Video, 1974.

5. Biographical details about Brico's early life which are not separately footnoted may be found in an autobiographical account she dictated to an interviewer during 1970-71. This is in typescript at the Colorado Historical Society, MSS. 1457. Hereafter cited as MSS. 1457, CHS.

6. See Patricia Stanley, "Dr. Antonia Brico and Dr. Albert Schweitzer: A Chronicle of Their Friendship," in Geoffrey C. Orth, ed., *Literary and Musical Notes: A Festschrift for Wm. A. Little* (Bern: Peter Lang, 1995), 185–203. See also Charles E. Samson, "Antonia Brico and Jean Sibelius," Master's thesis, University of Northern Colorado, 1991.

7. "Report on Candidate," Box 7, MSS. 1457, CHS. Translated by Carolin Blueml.

8. Tenesa Rasmussen, "Antonia Brico and the New York Women's Symphony Orchestra, 1934–1939," (Master's thesis, Southern Methodist University, 1997), 39.

9. Quoted in "Antonia Brico, 87, a Conductor," *New York Times*, August 5, 1989, sec. 1, p. 10; "Miss Brico Triumphs as Berlin Conductor," *New York Times*, February 15, 1930, p. 14.

10. Redfern Mason, "U. of C. Co-ed Wins Triumph in San Francisco Concert," *San Francisco Examiner*, August 27, 1930, Box 51, MSS. 1457, CHS.

11. Rasmussen, "Antonia Brico," 42.

12. Ibid., 44.

13. "200 Idle Musicians Forming Orchestra," *New York Times*, March 15, 1932, p. 17; "The Mother of Invention," *New York Times*, April 3, 1932, sec. 8, p. 7.

14. "Woman to Conduct Musicians' Symphony," *New York Times*, December 28, 1932, p. 15.

15. Jean Lyon, "Antonia Brico, First Woman to Conduct in Metropolitan," *New York Sun*, January 10, 1933, p. 28. Brico was apparently engaged to conduct 20 Metropolitan concerts, but faced opposition before her third concert, when noted baritone John Charles Thomas refused to sing with a woman conductor. The conflict

resulted in Brico having to step down and not complete the series, which, not surprisingly, she found disillusioning. In a 1975 lecture she recalled, "I was so optimistic [I thought] that if I did a good job at everything, that's all that would be necessary. Of course, I found out differently. It wasn't all that was necessary. You see, I was born in the wrong body." Rasmussen, "Antonia Brico," 48.

16. "Orchestra Commences Series in Westchester," *Musical America* 53 (July 1933): 4.

17. "White Plains 'Pops' Opens Brilliantly," *New York Times*, June 29, 1933, p. 22.

18. Biography folder, MSS. 1457, CHS.

19. Carl Lindstrom, "Wants Orchestras Subsidized by Cities," unidentified newspaper clipping, Box 51, MSS. 1457, CHS.

20. "The Woman's Orchestra," *Commonweal*, March 1, 1935, p. 512.

21. Eleanor Roosevelt, "My Day," *Washington Daily News*, May 9, 1939, p. 18.

22. "Women's Symphony Orchestra of 80 Will Make Its Debut Here Monday," *New York Times*, January 24, 1935, p. 21.

23. "Women's Symphony Orchestra Holds First Public Rehearsal," *New York Herald Tribune*, January 30, 1935, Box 51, MS. 1457, CHS; "Women Rehearse Orchestral Debut," *New York Times*, February 1, 1935, p. 19.

24. "Miss Brico and Her Woman's Symphony," *New Yorker*, February 1935, in Box 51ff, MSS. 1457, CHS.

25. "Sandwich Girls Balk at Parade," *New York Times*, March 15, 1935, p. 23.

26. W. J. Henderson, "Women as Conductors," *New York Sun*, March 16, 1935.

27. Mrs. R. C. Bolling to Nikolai Sokoloff, Division of Music, WPA, August 12, 1936, in August 7–30, 1935, Box 8, MSS. 1457, CHS.

28. Jeanette Scherer to Antonia Brico, March 3, 1936, Box 8, MSS. 1457, CHS.

29. "Women Musicians Plan Six Concerts," *New York Times*, October 10, 1935, p. 31.

30. "Brico Heads Women's Symphony," *Musical America* 55 (November 25, 1935): 12.

31. "Women's Orchestra to Include Ten Men," *New York Times*, November 29, 1936, sec. 2, p. 1.

32. "Women's Orchestra in Concert," *New York Times*, December 2, 1936, p. 33.

33. Joseph Kaye, "Maestra Disbands her Amazons and Gives the Boys a Chance to Play," *Cincinnati Enquirer*, January 9, 1939.

34. "250 in Chorus Sing 'Hora Novissima,'" *New York Times*, March 31, 1937, p. 28.

35. Rasmussen, "Antonia Brico," 85.

36. John Kendel, "Antonia Brico Given Ovation at Denver Symphony's Concert," *Denver Post*, December 11, 1940; Anne Stein Roth, "Antonia Brico Provides Feast of Fine Music," *Rocky Mountain News,* December 11, 1940.

37. Box 7, MSS. 1457, CHS.

38. Letter to "Joanne," November 3, 1960, Box 2, MSS. 1457, CHS.

39. "Denver Businessman's Orchestra," undated folder, Box 8, MSS. 1457, CHS.

40. Wayne Johnson, "Businessmen's Orchestra Gets Standing Ovation," unidentified clipping, Box 52, MSS. 1457, CHS.

41. *New Grove Dictionary of American Music*, s.v. "Denver."

42. Wayne Johnson, "Dr. Brico Logical Symphony Guest," *Denver Post*, May 26, 1963, p. 4.

43. Wayne Johnson, "Symphony City's Top Music Group," *Denver Post*, June 2, 1963; Marjorie Barrett, "Why Not Dr. Brico to Head Denver Symphony?" *Rocky Mountain News*, June 3, 1963, p. 83.

44. Michael J. Bandler, "The Return of Antonia Brico: 'Everything is Different,'" U.S. Information Service News Release, U.S. Embassy Press Office, Manila, Philippines, September 23, 1975, in Antonia Brico Collection, MSS. 1452, Box 1, #13, Colorado Historical Society; Burt A. Folkart, "Antonia Brico, 87: Pushed from Podium by Sexism," *Los Angeles Times*, August 5, 1989, p. 34.

45. Pamphlet (c. 1975), Box 7, folder 213, MSS. 1457, CHS.

46. Bandler, "The Return of Antonia Brico."

47. Ibid.

48. "Renowned Conductor Brico Dies in Rest Home at Age 87," *Denver Post*, August 4, 1989, sec. B, p. 1.

8. *"Playing with Style"*

1. Allan Kozinn, "Women in the Theater and in Music Pause to Assess Their Status," *New York Times*, October 22, 1988, sec 1, p. 11; John Henken, "What Do Women Musicians Want?" *Los Angeles Times*, May 25, 1997, Calendar, p. 50.

2. Richard Dyer, "Triumphant Oppens Dodges Impediments," *Boston Globe*, December 9, 1997, sec. D, p. 3; Gordon Sparber, "Paula Robison and Ruth Laredo" *Washington Post*, October 5, 1989, sec. D, p. 13.

3. Ann Gilbert, "Women in the Big 5 Orchestras" (Ph.D. diss., University of Akron, 1994), 49.

4. *New Grove Dictionary of American Music*, s.v. "Dwyer, Doriot Anthony."

5. Gilbert, "Women in the Big 5 Orchestras," 47.

6. Carol Kleiman, "Screening Process Has Clear Potential to Defeat Job Bias," *Chicago Tribune*, April 22, 1977, Business, p. 3.

7. I derived these figures by obtaining membership rosters from American symphony orchestras from each decade, counting the number of men and women who played each instrument, and calculating the percentages. I did not count unisex names or unusual names where it was not possible to determine the sex of the player. The number of women in large, prestigious symphony orchestras is generally far smaller than in the semiprofessional orchestras found in somewhat smaller cities. This study combines both types of orchestra.

8. Leonard Feather, "Female Musicians Still Struggle for Acceptance," *Los Angeles Times*, August 26, 1990, Calendar, p. 63.

9. Gilbert, "Women in the Big 5 Orchestras," 251–256.

10. Richard Dyer, "Of Gender, Bravado and Brass," *Boston Globe*, April 21, 1991, sec. B, p. 1.

11. "Music," *New Yorker* 66 (April 16, 1990): 19.

12. Dyer, "Of Gender, Bravado and Brass," sec. B, p. 1.

13. Christine Ammer, *Unsung: A History of Women in American Music* (Westport, Conn.: Greenwood, 1980), 67.

14. "Classically Modern," *Maclean's*, December 5, 1988, p. 31.

15. "Vienna Lady Orchestra," *Dwight's Journal of Music* 31 (September 23, 1871): 104.

16. "Frederique Petrides," *New York Times*, April 11, 1937, sec. 6, p. 6.

17. Paula Deitz, "Playing with Style," *New Yorker*, November 4, 1996, p. 91.

18. Derrick Henry, "Women and Music," *Atlanta Journal and Constitution*, April 4, 1991, sec. E, p. 1.

19. Herman Trotter and Kevin Collison, "Falletta Parlays Guest Spot into Job of Leading Philharmonic," *Buffalo News*, May 3, 1998, sec. A, p. 1.

20. Wynne Delacoma, "Taking It from the Top: Falletta Traces Her Route to Conducting," *Chicago Sun-Times*, March 9, 1997, SHOW, p. 3.

21. Allan Kozinn, "An American Woman Conductor on the Way Up," *New York Times*, March 24, 1985, sec. 2, p. 23.

22. Ibid.

23. Ibid.

24. Herman Trotter, "BPO's Next Conductor Took up Baton Early," *Buffalo News*, December 16, 1997, sec. C, p. 1. Although it might seem logistically impossible to lead so many groups all over the country, it is common practice for the concertmaster or first violinist to rehearse the orchestra during the early, learning stages and for the conductor to shape and polish the works for a period of days immediately before the performance.

25. Greta Beigel, "Music, Maestra," *Los Angeles Times*, September 9, 1990, Calendar, p. 3.

26. "Leginska at Academy," *Brooklyn Eagle*, undated, "Leginska," NYPL.

27. Richard Dyer, "Tanglewood Music Center's Star Student Conductor," *Boston Globe*, September 3, 1988, Living/Arts, p. 9.

28. Ibid.

29. Fred Crafts, "Her Path to the Podium," *Los Angeles Times*, November 14, 1991, Calendar, Part F, p. 1.

30. K. Robert Schwarz, "A Maestra in the Wings," *New York Times*, April 10, 1994, sec. 2, p. 33; Scott Duncan, "Familiar Becomes Fresh Under a Guest Baton," *Orange County Register*, January 12, 1996, SHOW, p. 7; Charles Staff, "Tandem Gives Gershwin Performance Not to Miss," *Indianapolis Star*, June 6, 1998, sec. B. p. 5.

31. Diane Wittry, "Roll Over, Beethoven," *Newsweek*, September 12, 1994, p. 10.

32. A March 5, 1996, *New York Times* review of a concert by Marin Alsop and her chamber orchestra Concordia referred to the conductor (who was pictured in a photograph in a tuxedo and short hair) as "Mr. Alsop." The paper issued a correction the next day, which read, "Marin Alsop is a woman."

33. Greta Beigel, "A Concerted Effort: For Women Conductors, the Dress Code Combines Freedom of Movement with an Emphasis on Glamour," *Los Angeles Times*, April 13, 1990, sec. E, p. 2.

34. Peter Spencer, "A Sexy Note to Classical Music Selling," *Cleveland Plain Dealer*, May 24, 1996, Arts and Living, p. 1E.

35. David Patrick Stearns, "Fiddlers on the Move: Orchestrated Careers of Young Violin Stars," *USA Today*, September 1, 1994, sec. D, p. 1.

36. Ethel Leginska, "I'm So Glad I'm Not a Beauty," *Boston Sunday Post*, n.d., Leginska's scrapbooks.

37. James Chute, "Mutter Mixes Beauty, Brains, a Violinist's Bow," *Orange County Register*, August 26, 1990, SHOW, p. L06.

38. James Chute, "Female Musicians Place a New Accent on Image," *Orange County Register*, August 26, 1990, SHOW, p. L06.

39. Jamie James, "Sex and the 'Singles' Symphony," *New York Times*, May 2, 1993, sec. 2, p. 1.

Conclusion

1. D. B. Clark and W. S. Agras, "The Assessment and Treatment of Performance Anxiety in Musicians," *American Journal of Psychiatry* 148 (May, 1991): 598–605; P. M. Lehrer, et al, "Treating Stage Fright in Musicians: The Use of Beta Blockers," *New Jersey Medicine* 84 (January, 1984): 27–33.

2. Heidi Waleson, "Music, Maestra, Please," *New York Times*, April 16, 1989, sec. 2, p. 1.

3. Ibid.; Wynne Delacoma, "Taking It from the Top," *Chicago Sun-Times*, March 9, 1997, SHOW, p. 3.

Bibliography

A.K.C. "Woman's Symphony of Chicago Completes Successful Season." *Musical Courier*, May 24, 1930, p. 16.

Acocella, Joan. "Cather and the Academy." *New Yorker* 71 (November 27, 1995): 66.

"Actress and Pianiste in Divorce Triangle." *Chicago Daily Journal*, May 25, 1917.

Akhtar, Salman, and Ira Brenner. "Differential Diagnosis of Fugue-Like States." *Journal of Clinical Psychiatry* 40 (1979): 381–385.

Albuquerque, Anne E. "Teresa Carreño: Pianist, Teacher and Composer." DMA thesis, University of Cincinnati, 1988.

Aldrich, Richard. "Music." *New York Times*, March 8, 1923, p. 12.

Ammer, Christine. *Unsung: A History of Women in American Music.* Westport, Conn.: Greenwood, 1980.

"Antonia Brico, 87, a Conductor." *New York Times*, August 5, 1989, Sec. 1, p. 10.

"Antonia Brico's Triumph." *Newsweek*, August 1, 1938, p. 21.

Armstrong, William. "Fannie Bloomfield-Zeisler." *The Banner of Gold*, April 17, 1897.

Banner, Lois. *American Beauty.* New York: Knopf, 1983.

Barnard, Charles. *Camilla: A Tale of a Violin, Being the Artist Life of Camilla Urso.* Boston: Loring, 1874.

Barnes, Edwin. *Music As an Educational Asset.* Philadelphia: Theodore Presser, 1927.

Barrett, Marjorie. "Why Not Dr. Brico to Head Denver Symphony?" *Rocky Mountain News*, June 3, 1963, p. 83.

Barron, James. "A Sax Craze Inspired by the Simpsons." *New York Times*, January 14, 1996, Sec. 4, p. 2.

"Beauty Plus." *School Musician* 6 (January 1935): 27.

Beigel, Greta. "A Concerted Effort: For Women Conductors, the Dress Code Combines Freedom of Movement with an Emphasis on Glamour." *Los Angeles Times*, April 13, 1990, Sec. E, p. 2.

_____. "Music, Maestra." *Los Angeles Times*, September 9, 1990, Calendar, p. 3.

Berger, Kenneth Walter. *The March King and His Band.* New York: Exposition Press, 1957.

Berryman, Joe. "The Bugle-Lyra in the Girls' Drum Corps." *School Musician* 8 (March 1937): 18.

Bierley, Paul. *John Philip Sousa, American Phenomenon.* New York: Appleton, Century, Crofts, 1973.

"Black Swan." *Dwight's Journal of Music* 3 (April 9, 1853): 2.

Block, Adrienne Fried. *Amy Beach: Passionate Victorian*. New York: Oxford University Press, 1998.

_____. "Two Virtuoso Performers in Boston: Jenny Lind and Camilla Urso." In *New Perspectives in Music: Essays in Honor of Eileen Southern*. Warren, Mich.: Harmonie Park Press, 1992.

_____, and Carol Neuls-Bates. *Women in American Music: A Bibliography of Music and Literature*. Westport, Conn.: Greenwood, 1979.

Bloomfield-Zeisler, Fannie. "Woman in Music." *Music Teachers National Association: Official Report of Annual Meeting*, 1890, pp. 38–44.

"Bloomfield-Zeisler Astounds New York." *Musical America* 31 (February 21, 1920): 17.

"Boccaccio Receives Ovation in New York." *Musical Courier*, November 28, 1931.

Bomberger, Elam Douglas. "The German Musical Training of American Students, 1850–1900" Ph.D. diss., University of Maryland–College Park, 1991.

"Boston Women Players to Increase Activities." *Musical America* 45 (June 25, 1927): 23.

Bowen, Catherine Drinker. *"Free Artist": The Story of Anton and Nicholas Rubinstein*. New York: Random House, 1939.

Bowen, Harriett. "Are Women Men's Equals as Pianists?" *Musical America* 25 (December 16, 1916): 19.

Bregstone, Philip. *Chicago and Its Jews: A Cultural History*. Chicago: privately published, 1933.

"Brico Heads Women's Symphony." *Musical America* 55 (November 25, 1935): 12.

Brower, Harriette. "Pianist's Mind Delicately Adjusted During Recital." *Musical America* 40 (December 18, 1915): 40.

Brown, Rae Linda. "The Woman's Symphony Orchestra of Chicago and Florence B. Price's Piano Concerto in One Movement." *American Music* 11 (Summer, 1993): 190.

Brumberg, Joan Jacobs. "Chlorotic Girls, 1870–1920: A Historical Perspective on Female Adolescence." *Child Development* 53 (1982): 1468–1477.

Busoni, Ferruccio. *Letters to His Wife*. 1938. Reprint, New York: Dover, 1966.

"Camilla Urso." *Dwight's Journal of Music* 2 (December 18, 1852): 86.

"Carreño Objects to 'Circus' Advertising Given Musicians." *Duluth Herald*, November 16, 1916.

"Chat With Miss Leginska." *New York Herald*, January 3, 1915.

"Chicago Holds Her Solo Contest." *School Musician* 1 (January 1930): 18.

"Children an Inspiration to Career of Woman Artist, Believes Samaroff." *Musical America* 35 (April 8, 1922): 3.

Churchill, Allen. *The Improper Bohemians*. New York: Dutton, 1959.

Chute, James. "Mutter Mixes Beauty, Brains, a Violinist's Bow." *Orange County Register*, August 26, 1990, SHOW.

Citron, Marcia J. *Gender and the Musical Canon*. New York: Cambridge, 1993.

Clark, D. B. and W. S. Agras. "The Assessment and Treatment of Performance Anxiety in Musicians." *American Journal of Psychiatry* 148 (May 1991): 598–605.

"Classically Modern." *Maclean's*, December 5, 1988, p. 31.

Clemens, Clara. *My Husband Gabrilowitsch*. New York: Harper Bros., 1938.

Coates, Roy R. "Put the Girls to Work in a Drum Corps." *School Musician* 8 (September 1937): 8.

Cohen, Patricia Cline. "Safety and Danger: Women on American Public Transport, 1750–1850." In *Gendered Domains: Rethinking Public and Private in Women's History*, edited by Dorothy Helly and Susan Reverby, 109–122. Ithaca: Cornell University Press, 1992.

Collins, Judy, and Jill Godmilow. *Antonia: A Portrait of the Woman*. Produced by Rocky Mountain Productions. 58 minutes. Phoenix/BFA Films and Video, Inc., 1974. Videocassette.

Commins, Dorothy Berliner. *Making an Orchestra*. New York: Macmillan, 1931.

"Concerts in Havana." *Musical America* 53 (January 25, 1933): 13.

"Conductors by the Score." *Musical America* 42 (October 17, 1925): 18.

Coryell, Janet, and Robert Myers, eds. *Adeline and Julia: Growing Up in Michigan and on the Kansas Frontier: Diaries from 19th Century America*. East Lansing: Michigan State University Press, 1999.

Cowling, Elizabeth. *The Cello*. New York: Charles Scribner's Sons, 1983.

Crafts, Fred. "Her Path to the Podium." *Los Angeles Times*, November 14, 1991.

Crain, Hal. "Form: The Despair of the Iconoclast." *Musical America* 40 (August 16, 1924): 32.

Daniel, Oliver. *Stokowski: A Counterpoint of View*. New York: Dodd, Mead, 1982.

Deitz, Paula. "Playing with Style." *New Yorker*, November 4, 1996, p. 91.

Delacoma, Wynne. "Taking It from the Top: Falletta Traces Her Route to Conducting." *Chicago Sun-Times*, March 9, 1997, SHOW.

De Motte, Helen. "Statue and Musician Stir One Who Admires Courage," *Richmond News Leader*, October 26, 1929.

"Do Worries of Travel Hamper an Artist?" *Musical America* 19 (December 6, 1913): 19.

"Don't Give Up Music at the Altar." *Etude* 37 (July 1919): 407–408.

"'Don't,' Says Mrs. Zeisler." *Musical America* 15 (April 20, 1912): 36.

Downes, Olin. "Ethel Leginska Conducts." *New York Times*, January 10, 1925.

_____. "The Philharmonic Concert." *New York Times*, January 9, 1925.

Drayton, Alice Allen. "Federation Sponsors First American Women's Symphony Orchestra." *Federation Topics* 7 (March 1927): n.p.

Duffin, Lorna. "The Conspicuous Consumptive: Woman as an Invalid." In *The Nineteenth-Century Woman: Her Cultural and Physical World*, edited by Sara Delamont and Lorna Duffin. New York: Barnes and Noble, 1978.

Duncan, Scott. "Familiar Becomes Fresh Under a Guest Baton." *Orange County Register*, January 12, 1996, SHOW.

"Dunsany Tale Inspires Leginska." *Musical America* 35 (February 11, 1922): 23.

Dutcher, Ray W. "Eastside High School Augments its Band with Flag Twirlers." *School Musician* 12 (February 1941): 17.

Dyer, Richard. "Of Gender, Bravado and Brass." *Boston Globe*, April 21, 1991, Sec. B, p. 1.

_____. "Tanglewood Music Center's Star Student Conductor." *Boston Globe*, September 3, 1988, Living/Arts.

_____. "Triumphant Oppens Dodges Impediments." *Boston Globe*, December 9, 1997, Sec. D, p. 3.

Eaton, Quaintance. "Ambitious to Conduct, But Says She Will Not." *Musical America* 47 (March 31, 1928): 32.

Edwards, Frank. "Humor and Adventure: 'On the Road' with a Symphony Orchestra." *Musical America* 14 (August 26, 1911): 8.

"Elsa Reugger." *Musical Courier*, November 12, 1902, p. 27.

"Energetic English Pianiste Tries Hard as She Can to Be Like a Man." *New York Press*, April 11, 1915.

"Ethel Leginska Avows She's a 'Topsy' Without a Single Musical Ancestor." *Musical America* 28 (October 13, 1917): 9.

"Ethel Leginska Conducts N.Y. Symphony." *Musical America* 41 (January 17, 1925): 6.

"Ethel Leginska Creates Astounding Enthusiasm on Canadian and Western Tour." *Musical America* 27 (December 1, 1917): 14.

"Ethel Leginska Describes the Joys of Study." *Musical America* 32 (July 31, 1920): 19.

"Ethel Leginska Leaves Piano Recitals to Work in Other Music Fields." *Musical America* 44 (May 1, 1926): 41.

"Ethel Leginska Makes Converts to a Quaint Cause." *Musical America* 31 (December 27, 1919): 9.

"Ethel Leginska Songs to Be Published by Schirmer."*Musical America* 29 (March 1, 1919): 43.

"Ethel Leginska's Concert." *Musical America* 13 (November 26, 1910): 17.

"Ethel Leginska's 'Dance of a Puppet.'" *Musical America* 39 (January 26, 1924): 42.

"Ethel Leginska's Most Recent 'Stunt.'" *Musical Courier*, March 15, 1917.

"Ethel Leginska's Protest." *Musical America* 39 (October 27, 1923): 10.

"Extent of the Feminine Influence." *Musical America* 13 (April 15, 1911): 3.

"Famous Woman Pianist Seeks Son's Custody." *Cleveland Press*, May 30, 1917.

"Fannie Bloomfield-Zeisler." *Musical Courier*, December 28, 1898, p 40.

"Fannie Bloomfield-Zeisler." *Musical Courier*, January 3, 1900, p. 18.

"Fannie Bloomfield-Zeisler's Silver Anniversary." *Musical Courier*, March 21, 1900, pp. 19–20.

Fay, Amy. *Music Study in Germany.* 1880. Reprint, New York: Dover, 1965.

Feather, Leonard. "Female Musicians Still Struggle for Acceptance." *Los Angeles Times*, August 26, 1990, Calendar, p. 63.

Feldman, Mary Ann. "George Upton: Journalist, Music Critic and Mentor to Early Chicago." Ph.D. diss., University of Minnesota, 1983.

Filene, Peter G. *Him/Her/Self: Sex Roles in Modern America.* 2nd edition. Baltimore: Johns Hopkins University Press, 1986.

Fillmore, J. C. "The Occasional Correspondence of a Music Teacher." *Etude* 4 (June 1887): 84.

Finck, Henry T. *Success in Music and How It Is Won.* New York: C. Scribner's Sons, 1920.

Fink, Leon, ed. *Major Problems in the Gilded Age and the Progressive Era: Documents and Essays.* Lexington, Mass.: D.C. Health, 1993.

Fisher, Renee. *Musical Prodigies: Masters at an Early Age.* New York: Association Press, 1973.

"Florence Austin, A Violin Virtuosa," *Musical Courier*, November 1910, p. 19.

Folkart, Burt A. "Antonia Brico, 87: Pushed from Podium by Sexism." *Los Angeles Times*, August 5, 1989, p. 34.

"Frederique Petrides." *New York Times*, April 11, 1937, Sec. 6, p. 6.

Freund, John. "One More Unfortunate." *Musical America* 19 (April 25, 1914): 9
_____."To a Young Girl Out West." *Musical America* 7 (February 29, 1908): 12.
"From Execution to Composition," *Christian Science Monitor*, December 3, 1921.
Galkin, Elliott W. *A History of Orchestral Conducting*. New York: Pendragon, 1988.
Gardner, Vivien, and Susan Rutherford, eds. *The New Woman and Her Sisters: Feminism and the Theatre, 1850–1914*. Ann Arbor: University of Michigan Press, 1992.
Garrison, Dee. *Apostles of Culture: The Public Librarian and American Society*. New York: Free Press, 1979.
Gilbert, Ann. "Women in the Big 5 Orchestras." Ph.D. diss., University of Akron, 1994.
Gilbert, Douglas. *American Vaudeville: Its Life and Times*. New York: Dover, 1963.
Gilman, Charlotte Perkins. *The Yellow Wallpaper*. Boston: Small and Maynard, 1892.
Goldman, Edwin Franko. *Band Betterment: Suggestions and Advice to Bands, Bandmasters and Band-players*. New York: Carl Fischer, 1934.
Gordon, Suzanne. *Off Balance: The Real World of Ballet*. New York: Pantheon, 1983.
Gottschalk, Louis Moreau. *Notes of a Pianist*. Philadelphia: J. B. Lippincott, 1881.
Grau, Robert. "A Strange Public Aversion to Contraltos as Compared with the Sopranos of Great Fame." *Musician* 21 (November 1916): 694.
Green, Lucy. *Music, Gender and Education*. London: Cambridge University Press, 1997.
Groh, Jan Bell. *Evening the Score: Women in Music and the Legacy of Frederique Petrides*. Fayetteville: University of Arkansas Press, 1991.
Gubar, Susan. "Blessings in Disguise: Cross-Dressing as Re-Dressing for Female Modernists." *Massachusetts Review* 22 (Autumn 1981): 477–508.
Hale, Phillip. *Musical Record*, June 1, 1900.
Haller, John S., and Robin M. Haller. *The Physician and Sexuality in Victorian America*. Urbana: University of Illinois Press, 1974.
Hallman, Diana Ruth. "The Pianist Fannie Bloomfield-Zeisler in American Music and Society." Master's thesis, University of Maryland, 1983.
Handy, D. Antoinette. "Black Women and American Orchestras: An Update." In *New Perspectives on Music: Essays in Honor of Eileen Southern*, edited by Josephine Wright, 451–462. Warren, Mich.: Harmonie Park Press, 1992.
_____. *Black Women in American Bands and Orchestras*. Metuchen, N.J.: Scarecrow Press, 1981.
Hazen, Margaret Hindle, and Robert M. Hazen. *The Music Men: An Illustrated History of Bands in America, 1800–1920*. Washington: Smithsonian Institution Press, 1987.
Heilbrun, Carolyn G. *Writing a Woman's Life*. New York: W.W. Norton, 1988.
Henderson, W. J. "Music and Musicians." *New York Sun*, November 16, 1935.
_____. "Women as Conductors." *New York Sun*, March 16, 1935.
_____. "Women's Symphony Concert." *New York Sun*, March 14, 1932.
Henken, John. "What Do Women Musicians Want?" *Los Angeles Times*, May 25, 1997, Calendar, p. 50.
Henry, Derrick. "Women and Music." *Atlanta Journal and Constitution*, April 4, 1991, Sec. E, p. 1.
Hersh, Blanche Glassman. *The Slavery of Sex: Feminist-Abolitionists in America*. Urbana: University of Illinois Press, 1978.
Horowitz, Joseph. *Understanding Toscanini: How He Became an American Culture-God*

and Helped Create a New Audience for Old Music. Minneapolis: University of Minnesota Press, 1987.

Huneker, James. "The Leginska Coiffure Now Prevalent Among Pianists." Unidentified clipping, November 20, 1918.

"Introducing Ethel Leginska." *Musical Courier*, September 26, 1918, p. 42.

Jacob, O. P. "Berlin Aroused by Propaganda of *Musical America*." *Musical America* 19 (January 10, 1914): 1–3.

James, Jamie. "Sex and the 'Singles' Symphony." *New York Times*, May 2, 1993, Sec. 2, p. 1.

Johnson, Wayne. "Dr. Brico Logical Symphony Guest." *Denver Post*, May 26, 1963, p. 4.
_____. "Symphony City's Top Music Group." *Denver Post*, June 2, 1963.

Kagan, Susan. "Camilla Urso: A Nineteenth-Century Violinist's View." *Signs: Journal of Women in Culture and Society* 2, no. 3 (Spring 1977): 727–734.

Kaye, Joseph. "Maestra Disbands her Amazons and Gives the Boys a Chance to Play." *Cincinnati Enquirer*, January 9, 1939.

Kendel, John. "Antonia Brico Given Ovation at Denver Symphony's Concert." *Denver Post*, December 11, 1940.

Kessler-Harris, Alice. *Out to Work: A History of Wage-Earning Women in the United States.* New York: Oxford University Press, 1982.

Kleiman, Carol. "Screening Process Has Clear Potential to Defeat Job Bias." *Chicago Tribune*, April 22, 1977, Business, p. 3.

Kline, Donna Staley. *Olga Samaroff Stokowski: An American Virtuoso on the World Stage.* College Station, Texas: Texas A & M Press, 1996.

Koopal, Grace. *Miracle of Music: The History of the Hollywood Bowl.* Los Angeles: W. Ritchie, 1972.

Korn, Ralph. *How to Organize the Amateur Band and Orchestra.* New York: Greenberg, 1928.

Koza, Julia Eklund. "Music and the Feminine Sphere: Images of Women as Musicians in *Godey's Lady's Book*, 1830–1877." *Musical Quarterly* 75 (Summer 1991): 103–129.
_____ "The 'Missing Males' and Other Gender Issues in Music Education: Evidence from the *Music Supervisors' Journal*, 1914–1924." *Journal of Research in Music Education* 41 (Fall 1993): 212–32.

Kozinn, Allan. "An American Woman Conductor on the Way Up." *New York Times*, March 24, 1985, Sec. 2, p. 23.
_____. "Women in the Theater and in Music Pause to Assess Their Status." *New York Times*, October 22, 1988, Sec. 1, p. 11.

Krebs, T. L. "Women as Musicians." *Sewanee Review* 2 (November 1893): 76.

"Lads of the Third Division." *School Musician* 6 (February 1935): 23.

Landau, Rom. *Ignace Paderewski, Musician and Statesman.* New York: Thomas Y. Crowell, 1934.

Lanier, Sidney. *Music and Poetry: Essays Upon Some Aspects and Interrelations of the Two Arts.* New York: C. Scribner's Sons, 1898.

"Larger Service to Music Sought by Ethel Leginska." *Christian Science Monitor*, June 3, 1926.

Laubach, P. E. "Girls." *School Musician* 11 (January 1940): 8.

Lebrecht, Norman. *The Maestro Myth: Great Conductors in Pursuit of Power.* Secaucus, N.J.: Carol Publishing Group, 1991.

Leginska, Ethel. "Clothes as a Hindrance to Woman's Greatness." *Musical America* 25 (March 24, 1917): 5.

_____. "Leginska Bares Her Heart and Her Broken Romances." *Boston Sunday Post* October 17, 1926.

"Leginska." *Cleveland Press,* May 30, 1917.

"Leginska." *London Times* February 9, 1909, Sec. C, p. 8.

"Leginska Again Fails to Appear for Concert." *New York Times,* October 24, 1925, p. 17.

"Leginska Conducts." *Musical Courier,* November 26, 1925.

"Leginska Conducts Last of Three Concerts of People's Symphony." *Musical Courier,* November 26, 1925, p. 24.

"Leginska Conducts Peoples." *Boston Post,* April 6, 1925.

"Leginska Conducts Players in Dallas." *Musical America* 53 (March 19, 1933): 30.

"Leginska Greeted by Throng at Bowl." *Musical America* 42 (August 22, 1925): 24.

"Leginska, Guest Conductor of Chicago Woman's Symphony, to Play Solo." *Musical Courier,* April 28, 1927, p. 32–33.

"Leginska Has Very Modern Ideas of Women's Freedom." *Duluth Herald,* February 17, 1917.

"Leginska Missing Again." *New York Times,* January 21, 1926, p. 7.

"Leginska Not Found, Nerves Are Blamed." *New York Times,* January 28, 1925, p. 1.

"Leginska Ordered to Take Year's Rest." *New York Times,* January 31, 1926, p. 7.

"Leginska Recital." *Musical Courier,* March 10, 1913.

"Leginska to Retire from Concert Stage." *New York Times,* April 22, 1926, p. 23.

"Leginska Who Sues Hubby Isn't a Kid After All." *Detroit Journal,* May 25, 1917.

"Leginska Will Not Concertize During Season of 1920-21." *Musical Courier,* March 18, 1920.

Lehrer, P. M., et al. "Treating Stage Fright in Musicians: The Use of Beta Blockers." *New Jersey Medicine* 84 (January 1984): 27–33.

"Lenora Jackson at Louisville Music Festival." *Musical Courier,* May 23, 1900, p. 9.

Lerner, Gerda. *The Majority Finds Its Past: Placing Women in History.* New York: Oxford University Press, 1979.

Lesinsky, Adam. "Give the Girls a Chance." *School Musician* 1 (February 1930) 7.

Levarie, Siegmund. "Hans von Bülow in America." *Institute for the Study of American Music Newsletter* 11 (November 1981): 10.

Levine, Lawrence. *Highbrow, Lowbrow: The Emergence of Cultural Hierarchy in America.* Cambridge, Mass.: Harvard University Press, 1988.

Lewis, Philip. *Trouping: How the Show Came to Town.* New York: Harper and Row, 1973.

Liebling, Leonard. "Ethel Leginska in Triple Musical Role." *New York American,* January 4, 1926.

_____. "Ethel Leginska, Pianist, Leads Orchestra." *New York American,* January 10, 1925.

Lipman, Samuel. "Piano Prodigy." *American Scholar* 62 (Winter 1993): 31–50.

Loesser, Arthur. *Men, Women and Pianos: A Social History.* New York: Simon and Schuster, 1954.

Lott, R. Allen. "The American Concert Tours of Leopold de Meyer, Henri Herz and Sigismund Thalberg." Ph.D. diss., City University of New York, 1986.

Loudon, I. S. L. "Chlorosis, Anemia and Anorexia Nervosa." *British Medical Journal* 281 (1980): 1669–1675.

Lovett, Robert. *Lateral Curvature of the Spine and Round Shoulders*. Philadelphia: P. Blakiston's Son & Co., 1922.

Lurie, Alison. *The Language of Clothes*. London: Bloomsbury, 1992.

Lynch, James. Interview by author. Long Beach, Calif. May 23, 1994.

Lyon, Jean. "Antonia Brico, First Woman to Conduct in Metropolitan." *New York Sun*, January 10, 1933, p. 28.

———."New York's Feminine Orchestra Is Almost Ready to Make Music," *New York Sun*, February 10, 1932.

McCarthy, Margaret William. *Amy Fay: America's Notable Woman of Music*. Warren, Mich.: Harmonie Park Press, 1995.

McClary, Susan. *Feminine Endings: Music, Gender, and Sexuality*. Minneapolis: University of Minnesota Press, 1991.

Macleod, David. *Building Character in the American Boy: The Boy Scouts, YMCA, and Their Forerunners, 1870–1920*. Madison: University of Wisconsin Press, 1983.

"Mme. Leginska Leads N.Y. Symphony." *New York Herald Tribune*, January 10, 1925.

"Mme. Leginska Plays." *Boston Transcript*, February 25, 1916.

"Mme. Olga Samaroff a Victim of Amnesia." *Musical America* 25 (February 10, 1917): 2.

"Mme. Samaroff's Pluck." *Musical America* 7 (December 28, 1907): 11.

Maddy, Joseph E., and T. P. Giddings. *Instrumental Techniques for Orchestra and Band*. Cincinnati: Willis Music Co., 1926.

"Mlle. Leginska's Recital." *New York Times*, January 21, 1913, p. 13.

Magidoff, Robert. *Yehudi Menuhin: The Story of the Man and the Musician*. Westport, Conn.: Greenwood Press, 1973.

Malkiel, Henrietta. "The Guest Conductor Faces the Music." *Musical America* 41 (January 24, 1925): 3, 38.

———. "Making Great Music Democratic in the Hollywood Bowl." *Musical America* 42 (June 6, 1925): 3, 19.

Marcus, Jacob. *The American Jewish Woman, 1654–1980*. New York: KTAV Publishing House, 1981.

"Martha Hedman Raises the Ante; Sues for $50,000." *Chicago Sunday Tribune*, May 27, 1917, Part I, p. 15.

Marzo, Eduardo. "Touring the United States with Strakosch's Stars in '73." *Musical America* 27 (February 2, 1918): 9, 11.

Mason, Daniel Gregory. *Music in My Time*. 1938. Reprint, New York: Dover, 1966.

Mason, Redfern. "U. of C. Co-ed Wins Triumph in San Francisco Concert." *San Francisco Examiner*, August 27, 1930.

Matthews, Glenna. *The Rise of Public Woman: Woman's Power and Woman's Place in the United States, 1630–1970*. New York: Oxford University Press, 1992.

"Maud Powell Champions the West's Taste for Music." *Musical America* 7 (December 14, 1907): 5.

"Maud Powell Found Ready Response." *Musical America* 15 (December 23, 1911): 36.

"May Muckle with Thomas Orchestra." *Musical America* 7 (January 18, 1908): 7.

"Mephisto's Musings." *Musical America* 25 (February 17, 1917): 8.

"Mephisto's Musings." *Musical America* 36 (July 8, 1922): 7–8.

Metzer, David Joel. "The Ascendance of Musical Modernism in New York City, 1915–1929." Ph.D. diss., Yale University, 1993.

Milinowski, Marta. *Teresa Carreño: By the Grace of God.* New Haven: Yale University Press, 1940.

Miller, Alice. *For Your Own Good: Hidden Cruelty in Child-Rearing and the Roots of Violence.* New York: Noonday Press, 1990.

"Minnie Coons." *Musical Courier,* January 31, 1906, p. 24.

"Miss Brico and Her Woman's Symphony." *New Yorker,* MSS 1457, Box 51, Colorado Historical Society.

"Miss Brico Triumphs as Berlin Conductor." *New York Times,* February 15, 1930, p. 14.

"Miss Leginska's Playing." *New York Times,* December 12, 1913, p. 11.

"Miss Leginska's Recital." *London Times,* November 20, 1980, p. 14b.

"Mr. Eichberg's Violin Classes." *Dwight's Journal of Music* 39 (January 4, 1879): 7.

Mitchell, S. Weir. "The Educational Treatment of Neurasthenia and Certain Hysterical States." In *Psychotherapy and Multiple Personality: Selected Essays,* edited by Morton Prince. Cambridge, Mass.: Harvard University Press, 1975.

Moffit, Gisela. *Bonds and Bondage: Daughter-Father Relationships in the Father Memoirs of German-Speaking Women Writers of the 1970s.* New York: Peter Lang, 1993.

"A Monster Concert by Young Ladies." *Dwight's Journal of Music* 3 (August 6, 1853): 142.

Moore, Albertine Woodward. "Rubinstein's Meteoric Tour of America." *Musical America* 29 (1911): 731–732.

Morin, Raymond. *The Worcester Music Festival, Its Background and History, 1855–1945.* Worcester, Mass.: Worcester County Music Association, 1946.

"The Mother of Invention." *New York Times,* April 3, 1932, Sec. 8, p. 7.

Mueller, John Henry. *The American Symphony Orchestra: A Social History of American Taste.* Bloomington: Indiana University Press, 1951.

"Music and Art: The Personality to Launch a Ninth Symphony." *Dallas Morning News,* January 14, 1934.

"Music in Boston." *Christian Science Monitor,* April 11, 1927.

"Music — Real Music — For Everybody Dream of the Intense Leginska." *Boston Sunday Globe,* December 12, 1926.

"Music Should Mirror Spirit of Age." *Musical America* 37 (April 14, 1923): 48.

"The Native Conductor." *New York Times,* January 29, 1933, Sec. 9, p. 6.

Naylor, Blanche. *The Anthology of the Fadettes.* Boston: The Author, 1941, p. 18.

Neely, Marilyn. Interview by author. Washington, D.C., February 15, 1995.

Neuls-Bates, Carol. "Women's Orchestras in the United States, 1925–45." In *Women Making Music: The Western Art Tradition, 1150–1950,* edited by Jane Bowers and Judith Tick, 349–369. Urbana: University of Illinois Press, 1986.

"The New Woman in Music." *Musical America* 9 (April 28, 1906): 8.

"Notable Revival of 'Bocaccio' in English." *Musical America* 51 (November 25, 1931): 30.

"Noted Artists Pay Tribute to Leschetizky." *Musical America* 23 (December 4, 1915): 47.

Oliver, Daniel. *Stokowski: A Counterpoint of View.* New York: Dodd, Meed, 1982.

"Opera and Concert Programmes: Chat with Miss Leginska." *New York Herald*, January 3, 1915.

"Orchestra Commences Series in Westchester." *Musical America* 53 (July 1933): 4.

"Orchestra Pools May End Deficits." *New York Times*, February 3, 1924, p. 20.

"Orchestral Women." *Scientific American* 73 (November 23, 1895): 327.

Ostwald, Peter. "Psychodynamics of Musicians." *Medical Problems of Performing Artists* 7 (December 1992): 110–113.

Paige, Raymond. "Why Not Women in Orchestras?" *Etude* 70 (January 1952): 14–15.

"The Passing of the World's Most Famous Piano Teacher." *Musical America* 23 (November 27, 1915): 3–4.

"People's Symphony." *Christian Science Monitor*, April 6, 1925.

Perenyi, Eleanor. *Liszt: The Artist as Romantic Hero*. Boston: Little, Brown, 1974.

"Personalities: Ethel Leginska Rests From Hard Season." *Musical America* 30 (October 18, 1919): 16.

Petrides, Frederique Joanne. "Women in Orchestras." *Etude* 56 (July 1938): 429–430.

Petteys, M. Leslie. "Julie Rivé-King: American Pianist." DMA thesis, University of Missouri–Kansas City, 1987.

"Pianist Returns." *Musical America* 22 (June 26, 1915): 8.

Powell, Maud. "'Let No Student Go Abroad Unchaperoned' Warns Maud Powell, Celebrated Violinist." *Musical America* 19 (January 31, 1914): 4.

Preston, Katherine. *Opera on the Road: Traveling Opera Troupes in the United States, 1825–60*. Urbana: University of Illinois Press, 1993.

"Pretty Girls with Flashing Batons." *School Musician* 12 (February 1941): 28.

Quinn, Alfred Price. "Music." *B'nai Brith Messenger*, May 18, 1945.

Raines, Lenora. "The Conditions, Moral and Spiritual, Under Which Our Students Abroad Work." *Musical America* 29 (November 23, 1918): 6.

Randel, Don Michael, ed. *New Harvard Dictionary of Music*. Cambridge, Mass.: Harvard University Press, 1986.

Randolph, Harold. "The Feminization of Music." In *Music Teachers National Association: Papers and Proceedings of the 44th Annual Meeting*. New York, 1922.

Rasmussen, Tenesa. "Antonia Brico and the New York Women's Symphony Orchestra, 1934–1939." Master's thesis, Southern Methodist University, 1997.

"Recital with Invisible Artist Suggested by Paula Pardee." *Musical America* 29 (February 8, 1919): 39.

"Renowned Conductor Brico Dies in Rest Home at Age 87." *Denver Post*, August 4, 1989, Sec B., p. 1.

"Roamed in a Daze, Leginska Asserts." *New York Times*, February 23, 1925, p. 2.

Roell, Craig. *The Piano in America, 1890–1940*. Chapel Hill: University of North Carolina Press, 1989.

Rogers, Clara Kathleen Barnett. *Memories of a Musical Career*. Boston: Little, Brown, 1919.

Roosevelt, Eleanor. "My Day." *Washington Daily News*, May 9, 1939, p. 18.

Rosen, Carole. *The Goossens: A Musical Century*. Boston: Northeastern University Press, 1994.

Rosen, Ruth. *The Lost Sisterhood: Prostitution in America, 1900–1918*. Baltimore: Johns Hopkins University Press, 1982.

Rosenberg, Charles E. *No Other Gods: On Science and American Social Thought.* Baltimore: Johns Hopkins University Press, 1976.

Roth, Anne Stein. "Antonia Brico Provides Feast of Fine Music." *Rocky Mountain News,* December 11, 1940.

Russett, Cynthia Eagle. *Sexual Science: The Victorian Construction of Womanhood.* Cambridge, Mass.: Harvard University Press, 1989.

Ryan, Mary P. *Womanhood in America: From Colonial Times to the Present.* New York: Franklin Watts, 1983.

Saerchinger, Cesar. *Artur Schnabel: A Biography.* Wesport, Conn.: Greenwood, 1957.

St. Denis, Ruth. *An Unfinished Life: An Autobiography.* New York: Harper, 1937.

Samaroff, Olga. "Miss Leginska's Concert." *New York Evening Post,* January 4, 1926.

"Samaroff Seeking Health in Europe." *Musical America* 12 (June 4, 1910): 2.

"Samaroff's Next American Tour." *Musical America* 10 (July 10, 1909): 6.

Samson, Charles E. "Antonia Brico and Jean Sibelius." Master's thesis, University of Northern Colorado, 1991.

"Sandwich Girls Balk at Parade." *New York Times,* March 15, 1935, p. 23.

"Scarcity of American Conductors." *Musical America* 15 (April 20, 1912): 20.

Schabas, Ezra. *Theodore Thomas: America's Conductor and Builder of Orchestras, 1835–1905.* Urbana: University of Illinois Press, 1989.

Schaffer, Karen and Neva Garner Greenwood. *Maud Powell: Pioneer American Violinist.* Arlington, Va.: Maud Powell Foundation; Ames, Iowa: Iowa State University Press, 1988.

Schalbert, Edwin. "Leginska Has Great Triumph." *Los Angeles Times,* August 5, 1925.

Schiebinger, Londa. *The Mind Has No Sex?* Cambridge, Mass.: Harvard University Press, 1989.

Schonberg, Harold. *The Great Pianists.* New York: Simon and Schuster, 1963.

Schultz, Gladys Denny. *Jenny Lind, the Swedish Nightingale.* Philadelphia: Lippincott, 1962.

Schwab, Arnold T. *James Gibbons Huneker: Critic of the Seven Arts.* Stanford: Stanford University Press, 1963.

Schwarz, K. Robert. "A Maestra in the Wings." *New York Times,* April 10, 1994, Sec. 2, p. 33.

"Scriabin's Divine Poem and Pieces by Leginska Are Boston Novelties." *Musical America* 39 (March 8, 1924): 36.

"Should a Woman Singer Wear a Corset? A Symposium." *Musician* 19 (May-June 1914): 338–339.

Sicherman, Barbara. "Working It Out: Gender, Profession and Reform in the Career of Alice Hamilton." In *Gender, Class, Race and Reform in the Progressive Era,* edited by Noralee Frankel and Nancy S. Dye. Lexington: University Press of Kentucky, 1991.

Siebels, Fanny Marks. *Wishes Are Horses: Montgomery, Alabama's First Lady of the Violin.* New York: Exposition Press, 1958.

Sitjar, Lisa. Interview by author. New York City, February 16, 1995.

Smith-Rosenberg, Carroll. "Bourgeois Discourse and the Progressive Era." In her *Disorderly Conduct: Visions of Gender in Victorian America,* 167–181. New York: Knopf, 1985.

Smith-Rosenberg, Carroll. "The Hysterical Woman: Sex Roles and Role Conflict in Nineteenth-Century America." In her *Disorderly Conduct: Visions of Gender in Victorian America*. New York: Knopf, 1985. 197–216.

————. "The New Woman as Androgyne." In her *Disorderly Conduct: Visions of Gender in Victorian America*. New York: Knopf, 1985. 245–296.

Sochen, June. *The New Woman: Feminism in Greenwich Village, 1910–1920*. New York: Quadrangle, 1972.

"Soloists and Concertos Make Their Reappearance." *Musical America* 53 (December 10, 1933): 16.

Solomon, Barbara Miller. *In the Company of Educated Women: A History of Women and Higher Education in America*. New Haven: Yale University Press, 1985.

Sousa, John Philip. *Marching Along: Recollections of Men, Women and Music*. Boston: Hale, Cushman and Flint, 1928.

Sparber, Gordon. "Paula Robison and Ruth Laredo." *Washington Post*, October 5, 1989, Sec. D, p. 13.

Spencer, Eleanor. "Leschetizky's Stern Discipline Only an Armor to Shield a Deeply Warm Nature." *Musical America* 26 (May 26, 1917): 9.

Spencer, Peter. "A Sexy Note to Classical Music Selling." *Cleveland Plain Dealer*, May 24, 1996, Arts and Living, p. 1E.

Staff, Charles. "Tandem Gives Gershwin Performance Not to Miss." *Indianapolis Star*, June 6, 1998, Sec. B, p. 5.

Stanley, Patricia. "Dr. Antonia Brico and Dr. Albert Schweitzer: A Chronicle of Their Friendship." In *Literary and Musical Notes: A Festschrift for Wm. A. Little*, edited by Geoffrey C. Orth, 185–203. Bern: Peter Lang, 1995.

Starr, S. Frederick. *Bamboula! The Life and Times of Louis Moreau Gottschalk*. New York: Oxford University Press, 1995.

Stearns, David Patrick. "Fiddlers on the Move: Orchestrated Careers of Young Violin Stars." *USA Today*, September 1, 1994, Sec. D, p. 1.

Stearns, Peter N. *Be a Man: Males in Modern Society*. New York: Holmes and Meier, 1979.

Stokowski, Olga Samaroff. *An American Musician's Story*. New York: Norton, 1939.

————. "Women in Music." *Music Clubs Magazine* 17 (September-October 1937): 7–9, 12.

"Stokowski's Men Invade Baltimore." *Musical America* 31 (January 31, 1920): 41.

Stoltzfus, Mary L. "Eve in the Ensemble." *Musical Courier*, December 1, 1947, p. 9.

Strawn, Arthur. "Women Let Trifles Ruin Their Careers." *St. Louis Post-Dispatch Daily Magazine*, March 25, 1932.

"Sunday List Brings Prominent Visitors." *Musical America* 39 (December 22, 1923): 28.

"Sundstrom New Conductor of Woman's Symphony of Chicago." *Musical Courier* October 5, 1929.

"The Symphony Society." *New York Times*, January 20, 1889, p. 3.

Taylor, Bert Leston. *The Charlatans*. Indianapolis: Bobbs-Merrill, 1906.

Taylor, Deems. "Music." *The World*, January 10, 1925.

"Teresa Carreño In State of Collapse." *Musical America* 4 (June 23, 1906): 1.

Theriot, Nancy M. *Mothers and Daughters in Nineteenth-Century America: The Biosocial Construction of Femininity*. Lexington: University of Kentucky Press, 1996.

Thomas, Rose Fay. *Memoirs of Theodore Thomas*. 1911. Reprint, New York: Books for Libraries Press, 1971.

Thompson, Oscar. "Otto Klemperer's Conducting Stirs Throng at First New York Concert." *Musical America* 43 (January 30, 1926): 1, 4.

_____. "Where Are the Prodigies of Yesteryear?" *Musical America* 31 (January 3, 1920): 5–6.

Tick, Judith. *American Women Composers Before 1870*. Ann Arbor: UMI Research, 1983.

_____. "Passed Away Is the Piano Girl: Changes in American Musical Life, 1870–1900." In *Women Making Music: The Western Art Tradition, 1150–1950*, edited by Jane Bowers and Judith Tick, 325–48. Urbana: University of Illinois Press, 1986.

Tischler, Barbara L. "Concert Music." In *Encyclopedia of American Social History*. New York: Scribner, 1993.

"To the Young Wife." *Musical Courier*, September 7, 1898, p. 17.

"Torn Heartstrings Are Blamed for Illness of Pianist Who Fights Court Battle for Son." *Cleveland Press*, June 4, 1917.

Townsend, Lucy Forsyth. "Jane Addams Abroad: Travel as Educational 'Finish.'" *Vitae Scholasticae* 6 (1987): 185–186.

"Traveling Through America with the World's Greatest Artists." *Musical America* 13 (March 18, 1911): 17–18.

Trotter, Herman. "BPO's Next Conductor Took Up Baton Early." *Buffalo News*, December 16, 1997, Sec. C, p. 1.

Trotter, Herman, and Kevin Collison. "Falletta Parlays Guest Spot into Job of Leading Philharmonic." *Buffalo News*, May 3, 1998, Sec. A, p. 1.

Tubbs, Arthur L. "Olga Samaroff Preparing to Resume Career." *Musical America* 19 (December 6, 1913): 19.

"200 Idle Musicians Forming Orchestra." *New York Times*, March 15, 1932, p. 17.

"250 in Chorus Sing 'Hora Novissima.'" *New York Times*, March 31, 1937, p. 28.

Upton, George P. *Musical Memories: My Recollections of Celebrities of the Half-Century 1850– 1900*. Chicago: A. C. McClurg, 1908.

_____. *Woman in Music: An Essay*. Boston: James R. Osgood and Co., 1880.

Vallas, Leon. *Claude Debussy: His Life and Works*. New York: Dover, 1973.

Van der Straeten, E. *The Techniques of Violoncello Playing*. London: The Strad, 1915.

"Vienna Lady Orchestra." *New York Times*, September 13, 1871, p. 5

"Vienna Lady Orchestra." *Dwight's Journal of Music* 31 (September 23, 1871): 104.

"Virtuosos and Virtuosity." *Dwight's Journal of Music* 25 (September 22, 1855): 193.

Von Sternberg, Constantin. "Fallacies and Facts Regarding Study Abroad." *Musical America* 19 (January 31, 1914): 25.

Waleson, Heidi. "Music, Maestra, Please." *New York Times*, April 16, 1989, Sec. 2, p. 1.

Ware, Carolin. *Greenwich Village, 1920–1930: A Comment on American Civilization in the Post-War Years*. Boston: Houghton-Miflin, 1935.

Warren, Frank. "Realm of Music." *New York Evening World*, January 10, 1925.

"Western Cities to Hear Leginska." *Musical America* 42 (May 30, 1925): 34.

"When Women Blow Horns." *Literary Digest* 113 (April 2, 1932): 19–20.

"White Plains 'Pops' Opens Brilliantly." *New York Times*, June 29, 1933, p. 22.

"Whithorne, Emerson." In *Baker's Biographical Dictionary of Music and Musicians*. 8th edition. Edited by Nicholas Slonimsky. New York: Schirmer, 1991.

"Why Artists Should Marry." *Musical Courier*, April 4, 1900, p. 20.

"Wife Accuses Stage Beauty." *Chicago Daily Tribune*, May 25, 1917.

Wilczek, Franz. "The Truth About Music Student Life in Vienna Revealed By a Viennese Virtuoso." *Musical America* 19 (February 21, 1914): 25–26.

Wiltse, Franklyn. "Girls!" *School Musician* 4 (April 1933): 8.

Wittry, Diane. "Roll Over, Beethoven." *Newsweek*, September 12, 1994, p. 10.

"Woman to Conduct Musicians' Symphony." *New York Times*, December 28, 1932, p. 15.

"Woman Triumphs in Role of Conductor." *Boston Globe*, October 25, 1926.

"The Woman's Orchestra." *Commonweal*, March 1, 1935, p. 512.

"Women are Successful." *Musical America* 45 (April 2, 1927): 35.

"Women Musicians Plan Six Concerts." *New York Times*, October 10, 1935, p. 31.

"Women Rehearse Orchestral Debut." *New York Times*, February 1, 1935, p. 19.

"Women's Orchestra in Concert." *New York Times*, December 2, 1936, p. 33.

"Women's Orchestra to Include Ten Men." *New York Times*, November 29, 1936, Sec. 2, p. 1.

"Women's Symphony Orchestra Holds First Public Rehearsal." *New York Herald Tribune*, January 30, 1935.

"Women's Symphony Orchestra of 80 Will Make Its Debut Here Monday." *New York Times*, January 24, 1935, p. 21.

"World of Music." *Etude* 34 (April 1916): 320

Wright, Josephine. "Black Women in Classical Music in Boston During the Late Nineteenth Century: Profiles of Leadership." In *New Perspectives on Music: Essays in Honor of Eileen Southern*, edited by Josephine Wright, 373–408. Warren, Mich.: Harmonie Park Press, 1992.

Wynn, Edith Lynwood. "The Girl With a Bow." *Etude* 25 (September, 1907): 612–613.

Zamoyski, Adam. *Paderewski*. New York: Atheneum, 1982.

Z.A.S. "Salt Lake Women Give Worthy Orchestral Concert." *Musical America* 22 (May 22, 1915): 27.

Archival Sources

American Jewish Archives, Cincinnati, Ohio: Fannie Bloomfield-Zeisler materials; includes an unpublished draft of a biography by her husband, and two scrapbooks containing clippings and some programs. Scrapbooks are Microfilm #3315 and #3316.

Colorado Historical Society, Denver, Colorado: Antonia Brico collection, consisting of 56 boxes of programs, clippings, interviews, and other materials.

New York Public Library: Clipping files on Teresa Carreño and Ethel Leginska.

Newberry Library, Chicago: some papers and letters of Fannie Bloomfield-Zeisler.

Two of Ethel Leginska's personal scrapbooks, currently in the personal collection of one of her students.

Index